INTERTEXTUALITY

AND THE READING OF ROMAN POETRY

INTERTEXTUALITY

AND THE READING OF ROMAN POETRY

LOWELL EDMUNDS

THE JOHNS HOPKINS UNIVERSITY PRESS | BALTIMORE AND LONDON

© 2001 The Johns Hopkins University Press
All rights reserved. Published 2001
Printed in the United States of America on acid-free paper
2   4   6   8   9   7   5   3   1

The Johns Hopkins University Press
2715 North Charles Street
Baltimore, Maryland 21218-4363
www.press.jhu.edu

Library of Congress Cataloging-in-Publication Data
Edmunds, Lowell.
Intertextuality and the reading of Roman poetry /
Lowell Edmunds.
p.   cm.
Includes bibliographical references (p.   ) and index.
ISBN 0-8018-6511-5 (acid-free paper)
1. Latin poetry — History and criticism. 2. Authors and
readers — Rome. 3. Books and reading — Rome. 4. Rome —
Intellectual life. 5. Intertextuality. 6. Allusions. I. Title.
PA6047 .E36 2001
871' 0109 — dc21   00-026865

A catalog record for this book is available
from the British Library.

Contents

Preface

This book approaches intertextuality in Roman poetry not from examples or case studies but from fundamental, and presumably determining, concepts like author, text, and reader. As for the terminology of intertextuality, I wait until the final chapter to make a proposal. Until then, I use the more or less standard "allusion" or some periphrasis. Each of the concepts just named is now unstable in the field of classics.

Several of the younger (and sometimes not so young) classicists cited in these pages refer without awkwardness to different kinds of readers, and Stanley Fish's notion of "interpretive communities" has been cited approvingly in a work of classical scholarship (cited further on) that many, including those who might disdain the work of Stanley Fish, would consider authoritative. The existence of such communities even within the subfield of Roman literature is obvious. Within the sub-subfield of intertextual studies, too, one senses the emergence of opposing camps. Consider the position papers of Don Fowler (1997b) and Stephen Hinds (1997) in the issue of *Materiali e discussioni* dedicated to intertextuality. The ancient reader, for his or her part, is no longer a touchstone but is now just a member, perhaps not a very interesting one, of another community. One lives with "the apparent paradox that it is precisely the contemporary generation who are often worst placed to respond to original works in ways which later generations will find at all helpful" (Feeney 1995: 310).

Readers occupy new positions in classical research. What of authors? It is now, I think, fashionable to repudiate the intention of the author as a critical principle. Here especially, the existence of different communities causes difficulty for my exposition. If I start to argue against the intention of the author, some will doze, thinking that I am repeating what they already know and believe. But I have something for both sides. For the converted, I am putting some new nails in the coffin's lid. For the unconverted, I am preserving a certain role for the author, which does not contradict, I hasten to add, my laying to rest of intention. I am not making the fashionable gesture and then also retaining intention under some guise.

As for the text, it might seem to be the only thing that is still sacred, and, probably as I write these words, someone somewhere is appealing to "the text itself" as authority for something or other. The reader ought to remain "bound" to the text, to use a metaphor repeated four times in a short space by Gian Biaggio Conte and Alessandro Barchiesi in their summa on intertextuality in *Lo spazio letterario* (1989: 90 n. 12). But, on its own, completely apart from any influence of literary theory, the field of classics has already long since relativized the notion of "the text itself." It has discovered that there was poetry before books of any kind and even before writing — poetry before texts. And once books, of whatever kind, come into existence, they bear particular, historically conditioned relations to literature, as classicists are well positioned to know, not least because of their experience with electronic publication. Book or text and literature are not the same thing. So the text is no longer the hardened emplacement of meaning that it once was.

AS OFTEN, I owe thanks to Charles Segal: this time, however, for something that he did *not* do, namely, make opening remarks at a conference on intertextuality in Cagliari, November 1994. The opportunity to stand in for him caused me to articulate various thoughts on the subject. With the invitation to teach a seminar on a Latin subject at Princeton the following spring, I was then emboldened to choose intertextuality in Horace's *Odes* as the theme. Two members of the seminar, Ingo Gildenhard and Andrew Zissos, organized a panel on intertextuality in Ovid's *Metamorphoses* for the 1996 American Philological Association and invited me to participate. So began a reading, which has continued off and on, up to the present, of Ovid's "Aeneid" (13.623–14.608), of which some reflexes appear in this book.

An invitation to give the keynote talk at a graduate student conference on intertextuality, April 10, 1998, at Yale University marks the point at which this book reached its final stage. My talk was based on, and led to a thorough revision of, my chapter on the theory and terminology of intertextuality. My preparation for the talk included reading Stephen Hinds's book, *Allusion and Intertext* (1998), which had appeared only a few weeks earlier, and, on the train to New Haven, Alessandro Barchiesi's "Otto punti di una mappa dei naufragi," which had arrived in the mail the day before. (The thematic issue of *Materiali e discussioni* on intertextuality in which it was to appear was not yet available in the United States.) The sense of participating in an ongoing discussion continues to be strong, and, with it, the fear that one has failed to cite something or other, or, worse, to know something that would have materially affected one's arguments. Even at the last minute — which lasted about a month, the month of July 1998 — I was reading the manuscript of chapters of Andrew Laird's book on speech presentation (1999) and realizing that much of what I had said could be rethought from his point of view. In sum, my failure to cite such-and-such does not always mean (though it often means) that I have not read it, nor does it mean, if I have read it, that I think it is valueless.

During the summer of 1998, Michèle Lowrie read Chapter 8, Shirley Werner and also Laird read Chapter 2, and Nelly Oliensis read the whole manuscript, as did Susan Edmunds. I am deeply grateful to them for their comments, which, they will see, were taken seriously. I also thank Alessandro Barchiesi, John Bodel, Ingo Gildenhard, Frank D. Gilliard, John Irwin, William Johnson, Aaron Meskin (who read Chapter 1 in the summer of 1997), Christine Perkell (who read the whole manuscript as it stood in the summer of 1997), William Santamaria, Penny Small, Alden Smith, Andrew Zissos, and *convegnisti* at Yale and Cagliari.

The last minute was not, of course, the last minute. The Press's reader, Ralph Hexter, submitted an extraordinarily detailed and trenchant report, which caused me to rethink and rewrite large parts of this book and also to reorder the chapters. His influence on this second last minute, which occupied most of the fall semester of 1999, has been so great that I would almost like to invert the usual acknowledgment formula and to say that any remaining faults are his.

Introduction

One of the chief excitements in the study of Roman literature in the 1980s and
1990s was intertextuality. The various ways in which one text can signal its
relation to another (or others) came to be seen not in static terms of imitation
and influence but as artistic devices that have the same status as figures of
speech or anything else in the poet's stylistic repertory. The history of Roman
literature, it now seems, was being written emblematically in each new poem,
not to mention the history of Roman literature's relation to Greek. Awareness
of the possibilities led, in those two decades, to a gold rush of scholarly investigation, but, unlike the California gold rush of 1848, this one produced a very
high percentage of finders, and the findings were rich, luring a second generation, including me, in the same direction.

But the belated prospector encounters a disturbed landscape. The study of
intertextuality in Roman poetry has prompted debates: Is this an allusion or is
it just a chance resemblance between one text and another? The answer to
such a question often depends on the answer to some larger question. For
example, is intertextuality to be understood with reference to the intention of
the poet? If I want to argue that this phrase in this poet's work is an allusion to
a particular phrase in another poet's work, I might want to be able to refer the
allusion I have found to the alluding poet's intention, which would be an
anchor for my finding. The second chapter of this book addresses the subject
of intention. If, as I shall argue, intertextuality is not to be referred to the
poet's intention, then to what is it to be referred? The answer to this question
emerges in the third chapter.

But in passing, a comment on the still vexed question of authorial intention.
Though lately repudiated in the field of classics, intention has not disappeared.
Barred at the front door, it manages to enter through the postern gate in some

disguise or other, for example, the "reader-addressee" (see Chapter 3). The fact of the matter for anyone studying Roman poems is that clues to intentions are almost always lacking and have to be inferred from poems. An appeal to the intention of the poet is therefore either *petitio principii* or the scholar's rhetorical add-on at the conclusion of an interpretation. For the poetry of more recent times, sources for intention external to poems are often abundant, and it is easy to see why even those who understand the theoretical arguments against intentionalism want to keep it in play.[1] And it is natural to proceed from the perfectly sound notion that everybody has intentions to the less sound notion that the intentions of poets are what one must be looking for in poems. As I have already suggested, classicists are in a happy position: The conditions of their research have already decided the issue for them.

Another fundamental question that lurks behind many scholarly discussions of intertextuality is the status of intertextuality as a poetic device. Is it an occasional, delimitable one, confined, as it were, by the poem in which it appears, or should intertextuality be considered as *in principle* the mode of Roman poetry, so that observable instances of intertextuality in the course of a poem are only the most conspicuous signs of its relation to an antecedent and contemporary corpus? The answer to this question about the status of intertextuality presupposes a still more fundamental question: What is a text? If, for example, a text is fundamentally intertextual, then is it not ultimately imponderable—a tissue of reminiscences so complex and subtle that it defies understanding? Then how could it become a text-object, a work of literature, the thing that classicists are perhaps referring to when they speak of "the text itself"? The first chapter addresses these questions. In the course of the first two chapters, various aporias point to the importance of the reader for the understanding of intertextuality. In arguing, in Chapter 3, for the role of the reader, I take my cue from Giorgio Pasquali. In his foundational essay on intertextuality in Roman poetry, he said: "Allusions do not produce their intended effect except on a reader who clearly recalls the text to which reference is made."[2] I also follow him in taking intertextuality as primarily—that is, in the perspective of the reader—an artistic or aesthetic device. The title of his essay was "Arte allusiva."

Hans Robert Jauss speaks of the aesthetic character of poetry as a "herme-

1. E.g., Raval 1993; Patterson 1995.

2. Pasquali 1968: 275: "Le allusioni non producono l'effetto voluto se non su un lettore che si ricordi chiaramente del testo cui si riferiscono."

neutic bridge" between past and present—"that which makes possible the historical understanding of art across the distance in time in the first place, and which therefore must be integrated into the execution of the interpretation as a hermeneutic premise."[3] For a method, then, the need that presents itself in this book is a way of understanding intertextuality in the dimension of the aesthetic, and, in Chapter 3, I have followed, as in *From a Sabine Jar* (1991) but with greater methodological elaboration, Jauss's method of a sequence of readings. By the "aesthetic" character of poetry, I mean pleasing or intriguing, often unordinary, uses of language that convey or portend some meaning valuable to the reader. My appeal to the aesthetic, of course, invites the shibboleth *ideology* from a hostile tribe. At various points in this book, I address this tribe's claim to a master discourse of historical-ideological disclosure.

For the aesthetic orientation, I take an example from a contiguous field. Adam Parry, in his introduction to his father's collected works, speaks of influences that Milman Parry experienced in Paris at the time he was writing his master of arts thesis: Mathias Murko (collector and student of Yugoslav poetry) and Marcel Jousse (psycholinguist), among others.

> These influences helped to show Parry the implications of his perceptions of the nature of Homeric verse. . . . But the perception itself seems simply to have been Parry's direct reaction to the text of Homer. . . . It is from an aesthetic perception of the quality of Homeric verse that the whole thesis develops. What Parry later speaks of as the *historical method*, i.e. the attempt to explain the specific product of an age by the unique conditions of life in that age, is necessary to the development. But the first thing is the reader's experience of the style of the poem.[4]

Although Parry establishes statistical investigation as the basis for proof of the formulaic quality of Homer, both in the master's thesis and throughout his work, "the appeal to the experience of the reader is over and again the strongest argument which he can adduce."

With Chapter 3, on the reader, the framework for an approach to intertextuality in Roman poetry is established. The next two chapters return, from different angles, to the fundamental question of intertextuality and readership. Chapter 4 is on the persona, the internal speaker of the poem, sometimes the implied (not the real) poet, sometimes a narrator. Chapter 5 takes up,

3. Jauss 1982a: 146.
4. Parry 1971: xxiv.

apropos of a recent book by Mario Citroni, the question of the addressee as an approach to Roman poems. Citroni, in a profoundly historicizing spirit, argues that the communicative moment of individual poems, the presence of a particular historical addressee, conditions the overall articulation of the poem, its language, and everything else. This historical reality limits the significance of the poem. Once it is identified, the significance of the poem is exhausted. But, I argue, clearly it is not exhausted. The poem has ever new significance in a process that begins even within the poet's own lifetime.

Again, I take an example from scholarship on the poems of Homer, which would seem to require to be read, to the extent possible, as oral (in delivery and, depending on one's views, also in composition) and performed, not read (i.e., to be read now in a strictly historical spirit). James P. Holoka, who is unlikely to be considered a rebel against the historical approach to Homer as oral poetry, has said that

> from the point of view of our own inescapably literate apprehension of them, the *Iliad* and the *Odyssey* must be treated as independent entities, proper sources in themselves of verification for literary-critical assertions. They may legitimately be viewed as poetic texts rather than exclusively as oral performances, for the former they patently are, the latter they can never be again (if indeed they ever were). We have to do with two distinct perspectives, the one literary-critical, the other historical. . . . Neither stance disallows the other, because each addresses itself to a discrete object.[5]

Holoka sees a cleavage between the original status of the text (it was not a text but a performance) and the present one (object of literary-critical study). In the case of Roman poetry, one would like to believe that there is some continuity in the status and meaning of a text from Roman times to the present. I have posed the question in terms of reading.

But the fact of difference remains. A reading of the *Aeneid* at the end of the twentieth century will inevitably find meanings that Vergil's first readers would not have found. Lee T. Pearcy provided a good example in a review of Catharine Edwards's *Writing Rome: Textual Approaches to the City*:

> At his village on what will become the site of Rome, the Arcadian chief Evander names for Aeneas places that do not yet exist, in a city not yet founded (*Aen.* 8.347–48):

5. Holoka 1991: 481.

hinc ad Tarpeiam sedem et Capitolia ducit,
aurea nunc, olim silvestribus horrida dumis.

Augustan present and imagined Augustan past coincide; furthermore, as James Zetzel suggested in his 1993 Jackson Knight Memorial Lecture, *olim* may look ahead to an imagined Augustan future, when the center of Rome will once again be overgrown with wild vegetation, like the monuments of Janus and Saturn which Evander also points out. Rome is eternal, and eternally in ruins. Yet it is nearly impossible for us to read the past, present, and future of Rome and its ruins simply through Augustan eyes, even when we encounter them in Augustan literature. A dozen lines later, Evander takes Aeneas onto the Palatine, and they gaze over the pastoral scene: *passimque armenta videbant / Romanoque foro et lautis mugire Carinis* (*Aen.* 8.360–361). For anyone who has seen or read early modern depictions of the Campo Vaccino, these lines have a penumbra of transhistorical reference that they could not have had for Vergil or his Augustan readers and hearers. There is nothing we can do to silence this additional resonance. Time has added it to our Vergil, transforming him in the process — and is it possible that a Piranesi print or a remark in Gibbon predisposed Zetzel to call our attention to the multiple valences of *olim,* and predisposes us to accept his suggestion?[6]

Pearcy's testimony to the resonances of reading appears here not in some argument for a reader-response approach to literature but as a commonsense observation, elegantly stated, on the experience of the sophisticated reader. What is literature but this accumulation of readings, starting from some common point in the past, but always moving into an unforeseen future?[7]

Chapter 6 explores the relevance of possible worlds theory to poetry, and to Roman poems in particular, and proposes that the reader's "intertextual encyclopedia," to use Umberto Eco's phrase, is one of the main things that enables him to participate in possible worlds. Chapter 7 considers evidence for the existence, in the first century B.C.E., of private reading in *something like* the sense of reading that I have developed in earlier chapters. This undertaking proceeds in full awareness of the "bibliographic" dimension of reading (Jerome

6. Pearcy 1998. Zetzel's Jackson Lecture is cited at Edwards 1996: 31.

7. Cf. Manguel 1997: 9, col. 4: "As every reader knows, the point, the essential quality of the act of reading, now and always, is that it tends to no foreseeable end, to no conclusion. Every reading prolongs another, begun in some afternoon thousands of years ago and of which we know nothing; every reading projects its shadow onto the following page, lending it content and context. In this way, the story grows, layer after layer, like the skin of the society whose history the act preserves."

McGann), of "the order of books" (Roger Chartier). No simple equivalence between ancient Roman reading and twentieth-century hermeneutics is or can be imagined, but I am convinced that private reading for private pleasure and edification was going on. In this chapter, I therefore have to oppose the view of Florence Dupont in *L'invention de la littérature* (1994) that a fundamental orality continues to prevail among the Romans, and I offer a critique of her interpretation of Catullus 50 (*hesterno, Licini, die*).

The first seven chapters lay the groundwork for the theory of intertextuality presented in Chapter 8. Before I introduce this chapter, I will say what I think literary theory is and does. First, while "critical theory" and "literary theory" are now used as synonyms, and while it is impossible to return to the original, Frankfurt School sense of the former, a distinction between the two could be preserved. Literary theory is concerned with specifically literary phenomena. Critical theory takes literature as an example of something or other — for example, ideology, sexism, the unconscious — with the implicit or explicit claim of intervening, through its revelations, in the social order and thus making the world better. Although the wielder of critical theory has the advantage of clearly articulated principles, the results of his interpretation are often predictable from his principles, and offer little or nothing that is new except insight into the "theoretical naiveté" of his predecessors or opponents. In this book, I am dealing with specifically literary phenomena, and I am presenting a method that makes it possible for interpretation to "accept the responsibility of confronting the politics of interpretation."[8] I do not believe that a political *parti pris*, no matter how self-conscious, is an acceptance of responsibility if it leaves the literary object untouched in its literariness. (What its literariness is, what the specificity of the literary object is, is another question.)

Second, literary theory is not philosophy. It takes models or metaphors from philosophy or some more formalized body of theory (especially linguistics and speech act theory) and applies them to literary problems. The fit will always be inexact.[9] In practice, literary theory is usually tied very closely to textual examples, and the relation between theory and examples is not always honest. Further, the great bulk of it, unfortunately for one who hopes to borrow and steal, tends to be based on prose fiction. Almost all of my examples come from Roman poetry. In general and in the case of this book, all that

8. To quote a phrase from Fowler 1995.
9. See the aperçu of this problem in Henkel 1996: ch. 1.

literary theory does is provide a framework and sometimes a method for interpretation by establishing general conceptions or models of literature. Theory sometimes guides interpretation in such a way that texts come to mean something new, often something contradictory to the prevailing norms of understanding in a discipline. (So the study of literature as literature can ultimately have the result that critical theory aims at directly.) Ancient theory is of little use for a theory of intertextuality. In particular, it is unaware of systemic intertextuality and is thus untroubled by the now troubling distinction between artistic allusion to and unmarked reuse of poetic tradition.[10]

Chapter 8 is the longest chapter but it is organized around a single idea, which has to do with the mode in which intertextuality functions. An allusion creates a relation between one text and another — but how? Let me say, indulging myself in a crude expression for the sake of convenience, that one text "refers" to another. The "reference" creates the intertextual relation. The words in one text somehow resemble the words in another text, and so a "reference" has occurred. But the reference is a result or an effect. Everything I have said up to now is a matter of result or effect. The question remains: What did the business of referring, what caused the words in one text to be brought into relation with the words in another text? The answer is that there is nothing *in addition to* the alluding words that causes the allusion or the reference to be made (these, to repeat, are results). Reference, or allusion, has no linguistic or semiotic basis. This idea might seem paradoxical, but it corresponds exactly to common sense. As Richard Thomas once said to me in an e-mail message, "Your artistic allusion is someone else's chance resemblance."

The common sense of the matter is that it is extremely difficult to say what is an intertextual allusion and what is not. And, even when there is agreement, it is still extremely difficult to define the boundaries of an allusion. So one has to accept the test proposed by Earl Miner: "The test for allusion is that it is a phenomenon that some reader or readers may fail to observe."[11] I am not sure if Miner meant that allusions are really there and some readers just fail to observe them or if he meant, as I do, that the allusions are really *not* there

---

10. Systemic intertextuality has been formulated by Hinds 1998: 26 as follows: "There is no discursive element in a Roman poem, no matter how unremarkable in itself, and no matter how frequently repeated in the tradition, that cannot in some imaginable circumstances mobilize a specific allusion." On the relation of ancient to modern theory of intertextuality, see Conte and Most 1996; Innes 1989.

11. Miner 1994.

materially or linguistically. Again, common sense is a witness. Everyone would agree that there are dozens of possible allusions in Vergil that are unknown because the texts to which they allude are lost. If from the Villa dei Papiri emerge rolls of Ennius, new allusions in Vergil will also emerge. Until then, they do not exist, and, further, their nonexistence has never troubled anyone, never made Vergil a lesser poet.

Chapter 8 thus comes back to the reader, offering a model to a larger scholarly discourse in which the reader has become more important than ever before but has still remained undertheorized. The discourse to which I refer is the *New Latin*. In his manifesto of the New Latin in *Arachnion* in 1995, Don Fowler said "the reader is figured as operating on the text to produce meaning, rather than attempting to recover authorial intention."[12] Fowler went on to suggest that intertextuality be located in the reader.[13] Large questions remain. Who is the reader? What is reading? For now, only a preliminary indication of the difficulties. Intertextuality is, in fact, the acid test for reading. When the reader activates allusion, reading becomes a struggle between a "linear," forward-moving impulse and the retrograde or distracting pull of other texts. Intertextuality demands the interpretation of at least two texts.[14] So it is a challenge to reading and also to a theory of a reading like Jauss's, which begins with the aesthetic, with the performance of the meaning of the text, with hope of artistic wholeness. And yet Jauss's hermeneutics provides for a series of readings, so that what might have been neglected or overlooked at first can be integrated into a later reading.

The model that I am proposing is, I believe, a way out of the conflict that seems to arise when a New Latin–minded scholar both affirms the reader and tries to remain true to historicizing philology. Stephen Hinds's recent book serves well as an example of this impasse.[15] This book has, in the first place, served as an inspiration to my book, my debts are acknowledged along the way, and Hinds's readings of individual cases dazzle the mind. My hope is simply, by a stronger affirmation of the reader, linked to a particular model, usefully to extend the theory of intertextuality for Latin studies. At this point, then, I link up my discussion with that of Hinds.

When he states that "no two readers will ever construct a set of [intertex-

---

12. More strongly: Fowler 1997b: 24.
13. Fowler 1997b: 27.
14. This is one of the guiding ideas of Barchiesi 1997.
15. Hinds 1998. Page references are given in the text.

tual] cues in quite the same way; no one reader, even the author, will ever construct a set of cues in quite the same way twice" (47), he affirms New Latin principles. He intends to move decisively beyond what he calls "philological fundamentalism." But now consider Hinds in his chapter on literary history. In a series of brilliant readings of incipits in Vergil, Ennius, and Livius Andronicus, he shows how the later poet reduces the earlier poet to the status of antique or archaic. Hinds then proceeds to show how this process, which is internal to Roman poetry, is played out at another level in the reception of that poetry in Cicero, Horace, and Aulus Gellius. His approach is resolutely historicizing: "Let us attempt to resist the later history of . . . reception" (56). In his conclusion, he says that "if we as modern literary critics privilege one of these viewpoints to the exclusion of the other, we had better be aware of what we are doing" (63). The implication seems to be that we (note the monitory first-person plural) are somehow chastened and restrained when we become aware of the conflicting perspectives on literary history that we find already in antiquity.

The question remains: What was the purpose of relativizing that history, as Hinds did so masterfully? If there is no such thing as historical accuracy but only "partiality" and "provisionality," to use Hinds's terms (74, 81), then what, besides a negative result for standard literary histories, have "we" gained? Is there any positive result? Hinds himself seems to have been troubled by this question, because he asks: "With what vantage-point in the history of Ennius-reception should we align ourselves, and why?" (73). He does not give an answer and he may have intended the question as a rhetorical one, meaning that we cannot align ourselves with any vantage point and there is no reason to try to do so. But there is still the question why undertake the historicizing reading in the first place? For me, the answer to the question is Hinds himself. He is aligned, I assume, with his own vantage point, which is the one that sees that within the ancient history of reception there is no vantage point. He is outside that reception or rather beyond it, in a new era of reception. Obviously, self-consciousness about one's place in a history of reception is a characteristic of this new era. In fact, at one point Hinds refers to his generation of critics as one "whose readings owe something to the late twentieth century aesthetic which privileges meta-literary self-consciousness as its master-term" (89–90).

Although Hinds offers one or two fleeting observations on himself as reader, for the most part he allows himself to be eclipsed by his own discourse.[16] It, the discourse of classical philology, operates under professional and disciplinary constraints that are still severe and still override the proclamations of the New Latin. Neither Hinds nor any other classicist can easily present himself as a reader. Rather, Hinds and everyone else will have to say, I am going to tell you what this poem means to some other reader, a historical one or an imaginary one (cf. Fowler's "reader figured as . . ."). So Hinds, at least in his own mind, is not entirely a reader on the new model proposed by the New Latin, but he is hardly a reader on the old philological model. I believe that the force of his readings is the liberating effect of the new model.

Many of those who rushed to northern California in 1848 and to the Yukon in 1886 never became prospectors at all but drifted into other occupations for which new populations had created a need. So I have here opened an assayer's office, have worked on geological surveys, have mapped and registered claims. I have been only a weekend prospector. The few flakes of gold that I think I have found are for others to assay.

16. At one point, he says: "Being a reader of the *Metamorphoses* in the mid-1990s, . . . I myself am naturally inclined to envisage a stronger Ovidian reading of the *Aeneid* than . . . ," etc. (1998: 106).

INTERTEXTUALITY

AND THE READING OF ROMAN POETRY

ONE

Text

It seems to be impossible for literary scholars to discuss intertextuality without referring to or assuming a thing called a text, indeed two or more such things and the relations between them. Paradoxically, however, Julia Kristeva coined the term *intertextuality* to designate not those intriguing relations but the inevitable process by which any single text comes into existence. The main purpose of this chapter is to confront some of classicists' most common notions concerning the text with Kristeva's radical alternative and to ask if anything in the latter contributes to, or could contribute to, the activities of those studying intertextuality in Roman poetry. Kristeva, as will be seen, relied on Ferdinand de Saussure. But the story of Saussure's influence on theories of the text does not end with Kristeva. In the same years in which she was introducing her theory of intertextuality, Jacques Derrida subjected Saussure to a critique that, in Kristeva's neat formulation of the matter, replaced the linguistic sign with *différance*.[1] Derrida extended différance to texts, a move that is discussed briefly at the end of this chapter.

The Classical Text: Two Models

On the philological model, *text* means "the wording adopted by an editor as (in his opinion) most nearly representing the author's original work; a book or edition containing this; also, with qualification, any form in which a writing exists or is current, as a *good, bad, corrupt, critical, received text*."[2] To establish a text representing an ancient author's original words was for centuries,

---

1. Kristeva 1969b: 205 n. 21: Derrida "substitue . . . le terme de *différance* à la notion chargée d'idéalismes de *signe*."
2. *OED*[3], s.v. "text" (1.d).

and in some quarters is still, held to be the primary and most honorable function of the classical scholar. The critical edition was, and for some still is, the chef d'oeuvre of classical studies. The intertextual future of a text is already included, at least in its most overt aspects, in the critical edition, if, in the register just below the text and above the critical apparatus, the editor gives the sources of all quotations of the text. Allusions or imitations may be distinguished from direct quotations by *cf., respicit,* or *imit.*[3] Next in importance after the critical edition is, according to the traditional view, the commentary. Along with discussion of the meanings of words, grammatical phenomena, metrics, realia, and so forth, commentators identify the intertextual elements of texts, often referring to the author's "sources" or the "influence" that he has undergone or his desire to "imitate" a forebear. This approach to intertextuality in the philologically conceived text, one that observes the phenomenon but leaves it without interpretation, is not confined to the commentary but also takes the form of the article or the book.[4]

On the interpretive model, the text is something that has meaning that is to be understood. The text has boundaries that are not only material (the blank spaces that set off the printed lines) but aesthetic (structural, formal) and intellectually intelligible (significant, meaningful). The text thus constitutes a work of literature.[5] The study of intertextuality in the text so conceived focuses on its meaning and/or its aesthetic value. A new phase of intertextual study in classics in fact began with an affirmation of the aesthetic value of allusion. In 1942, on the front page of the November–December issue of the literary periodical *L'Italia che scrive: Rassegna per il mondo che legge,* Giorgio Pasquali began by conjuring up an objection against classicists' fondness for parallel passages: "They say: 'You, when you explain the ancient classics, . . . suffocate them with comparisons.' "[6] Pasquali defended himself by saying that he did not study "reminiscences" and "imitations" but "allusions," and the significant title of his article was "Arte allusiva." Intertextuality as allusion had a parallel development in the United States. Although it cannot point to a "first finder" like Pasquali, it was clearly defined as a subfield of literary studies

3. West 1973: 83.
4. Perhaps the best-known example in recent decades is Knauer 1979.
5. The critique and defense of Hirsch 1967 by Iseminger 1992b entails an ontological distinction between work (poem) and text (91–93).
6. Pasquali 1968: 275.

by 1965, as the article "Allusion" in the first edition of the *Princeton Encyclopedia of Poetry and Poetics* shows.[7]

Textual Criticism

These two models, often distinguishable in practice, are easily conflated. The product of the labor of editing a text is a real physical object, a book, which enshrines an ideal object, a classic work.[8] It is, furthermore, the editor's copyrighted "publication" and the property of the press that published it. This triply or quadruply sanctioned object is a powerful combination of the material, the ideal, and the legal.[9] Its ultimate authority is, of course, the author. The modern editor attempts "to establish what the author originally wrote," which is the same as "what the author intended to say."[10] The intention of the author as a principle in interpreting poems as works of literature, and thus in interpreting allusions in poems, returns in Chapter 2. Here, the separate question of authorial intention as a principle of textual criticism is addressed. Because the question has exercised editors of medieval and modern texts in recent decades, their discussion provides a useful starting point.

In 1983, Jerome McGann, in *A Critique of Modern Textual Criticism,* stepped into an ongoing controversy over, among other things, the choice of copy-text. Should it be the first printed edition or (when it is preserved) the author's manuscript? Both sides came to believe that the choice was to be determined by the author's final intentions. Despite the apparent clarity and usefulness of this principle for modern texts, McGann was able to show that in many cases it could not be applied. His critique was not, however, a radical one. He did not repudiate authorial intention altogether, but showed its limitations as a critical tool. He did so by describing the literary work as in fact a series of texts that are the products of social institutions and, in particular, of the interactions between the author and various other persons that these institutions enable. In the case of W. H. Auden's famous "September 1, 1939,"

7. Preminger 1965. The bibliography cites some works by classicists. There is a new version of the article in Preminger and Brogan 1994. Cf. also the bibliography in Perri 1978.

8. Cf. Selden 1987: 38 on the conflation of the two models.

9. The reader must accordingly remain in "bondage" to the text, to use a metaphor repeated four times in a short space by Conte and Barchiesi in their summa on intertextuality (1989: 90 n. 12). Conte (1986: 27) asserts the "centrality of the text as a unified, complete, interlocking system."

10. West 1973: 48.

he showed that no single text, except perhaps the suppressed, ghost text in the final *Collected Poems,* reflects the author's intentions — or all of them do.[11] McGann held that

> the concept of the critical edition . . . induces the illusion among scholars that the chief obstacles standing in the way of the reconstitution of an original text lie in the past, with its accumulated corruptions and interfering processes. The critical editor enters to remove these obstacles and recover the authoritative original. . . . Such a scholarly project must be prepared to accept an initial (and insurmountable) limit: that a definitive text, like the author's final intentions, may not exist, may never have existed, and may never exist at any future time.[12]

The preoccupation with the original, the "tendency to idealize the lost original," has been seen as characteristic of the editors of Greek and Latin texts.[13] It has two, roughly contemporary sources. One is romanticism, with its notion of original genius, and the other is Protestant editing of the New Testament, aiming to restore the word of God and render it directly accessible. Karl Lachmann edited the New Testament, and the stemmatic method that bears his name and is fundamental for the field of classics was derived from earlier Protestant editors.[14]

Some editors of classical texts would be scandalized by McGann's position and by any skepticism toward the notion of the original. Others would not. Study of the practices of ancient editors and of copyists has led to conclusions not unlike McGann's. James Zetzel has emphasized, against Lachmann's assumption of faithful copying, the self-interested aspect of each new copy of a manuscript. Each had its own purpose, and the nature of the text changed accordingly. "In a certain sense," Zetzel says, "every ancient text is a palimpsest: it embodies within itself, in ways which we can scarcely now discern, the history of the changes of taste and purpose through which it passed, and the preoccupations of the readers who used it."[15] And he regards this process as continuing to the time of the modern edition, though he is not fundamentally

---

11. McGann 1983: 88–89.

12. McGann 1983: 89–90.

13. Tarrant 1995b: 98.

14. On romanticism and editing, cf. Greetham 1999: 36, 404–5 (in the context of critique of McGann). On the New Testament and Lachmann, cf. Pasquali 1962: 8–12; Zetzel 1993: 102–4.

15. Zetzel 1993: 103, 112–13.

skeptical about the possibility of reconstructing ancient texts (as McGann is not about modern texts).

The social pressures that affect the text go back to the beginnings of textual criticism in Alexandria in the third century B.C.E. Zetzel suggests, following Rudolf Pfeiffer, that the editions of the poet-scholars of the Museum arose from their desire for standard texts in relation to which they could define their own imitations and adaptations.[16] So a self-consciously intertextual literature guided by the principle "nothing unattested" (Call. fr. 612 Pfeiffer) had to establish, and, following Zetzel's implication, in a sense to create an antecedent literature. Not only, however, did the editing of texts begin in intertextuality; the very fixation of texts in writing, when it first appears in Western literature, is already intertextual. Before I turn to Julia Kristeva, I digress on two of the earliest examples of written texts in Western literature and, in so doing, begin a skeleton history of writing and reading in ancient Greece that will be continued, again more or less digressively, in Chapters 2 and 4 and brought down to Roman times in Chapter 7. This history, sporadic and nonsequential, stands in a hypertextual relation to my main argument concerning intertextuality and reading.[17] The immediate purpose of the present digression is to provide a historical perspective on Kristeva's theory of intertextuality.

The Dipylon Oinochoe (or Jug) and the Cup of Nestor

The earliest Greek inscription of more than a few letters is the hexameter on the so-called Dipylon jug (ca. 740–730 B.C.E.).

hος νυν ορχεστον παντον αταλοτατα παιζει   (*IG* I² 919)

Whoever of all the dancers now dances most friskily[18]

A second line begins with letters that can be interpreted to mean "of him this" and then trails off into what seem to be letters (*kappa, mu,* and *nu*) inscribed for practice. (Are they the equivalent of κτλ or "etc."?) "This" would be the jug itself, a prize for the best dancer. The language of the first line is Homeric, as is the versification.[19] Even if one holds that writing was not used

16. Zetzel 1993: 112 and n. 38.
17. For the term *hypertextual*, see Chapter 8, note 19.
18. The translation is that of Powell 1991: 159. The inscription does not appear in *IG* I³.
19. Watkins 1976: 437–38; Powell 1991: 160.

for composition in archaic inscriptions but only for the recording of the utterance and that, read aloud, not silently, these inscriptions are tantamount to
performances, the fact remains that the line quoted here is a text in writing and
this writing presupposes and depends on an antecedent composition, which I
have referred to as "Homeric." If, however, Homeric epic was known to the
composer of the inscription on the Dipylon jug only from performances, if the
first written text of Homer postdates the inscription, what is the basis in
"Homer" of the composer's imitation?

Gregory Nagy has described "text" in this early period as the process of
text fixation or textualization "whereby each composition-in-performance becomes progressively less changeable in the course of diffusion — with the pro-
viso that we understand text here in a metaphorical sense."[20] Writing is unnecessary to textualization in this sense. Already at the time of the Dipylon jug,
the oral performance tradition of Homeric epic has attained stylistic fixity
sufficient to permit the kind of imitation displayed in the inscribed hexameter. This inscription has taken the decisive step to literal textualization, and
will remain the same text during the long (as many believe) period in which
Homeric epic will continue to be composed orally, and thus variously, in
performance.

The intertextual basis of the formation of a written text appears again in
the inscription on the so-called cup of Nestor (720–712 B.C.E.), found on the
island of Pithecusae, modern Ischia.[21]

Νεστορος : ε[μι] : ευποτ[ον] : ποτεριον
ηος δ αν τοδε πιεσι : ποτερι[ ] : αυτικα κενον
ηιμερος ηαιρεσει : καλλιστε[φα]νο : Αφροδιτες

I am the cup of Nestor, pleasant to drink.
And whoever drinks from this cup, straightway that one
desire will take for fair-crowned Aphrodite.[22]

In the first line, which may or may not be in verse, the cup uses a proprietary
formula ("I am" + name of owner + word for cup) found on other cups of the

20. Nagy 1996: 40.
21. For the date, cf. Pavese 1996: 2–3.
22. Or take the genitive as possessive ("Aphrodite's desire"): Pavese 1996: 17, comparing *Il.*
14.198.

same period.[23] Here ownership is referred to the old Homeric hero from Pylos, and the cup thus asserts its identity as that other famous cup, Nestor's, which one has heard of but never seen. The cup's "performance," as in the case of the Dipylon jug, but more pointedly, looks to the performance tradition of Homeric epic and, in particular, to lines 632–37 of what is now called book 11 of the *Iliad,* and thus presupposes some degree of fixity of that tradition.

But, already in the first line, with "pleasant to drink," the cup slyly begins to distinguish itself from the cup that it is claiming to be. This light object (ten by fifteen centimeters), from its very look and heft, cannot be the one that only Nestor could lift. That one, massive, heavy, with elaborate ornamentation, was likely to be not a cup but a mixing bowl.[24] Nestor and the wounded Machaon are drinking a posset of wine, barley, and grated cheese. The Pithecusan cup is for drinking wine at a symposium, as the second and third lines of the inscription show. These lines parody another kind of formula seen in inscriptions on archaic cups, which curses anyone who steals the object.[25] Here the curse proves to be playful. Erotic desire will be the drinker's "punishment." At the same time, the use of the epic hexameter in these two lines keeps the contrast with Nestor's cup in play. This contrast, in the broadest terms, is between love and war. It is the one dramatized in the juxtaposition of battlefield and bedroom in book 3 of the *Iliad,* and becomes a theme in Western literature.

The inscription as a whole is thoroughly and multiply intertextual. Both poetic and nonpoetic texts serve as models and are synthesized, through parody and imitation, in a new text. As for the oral performative antecedent, as I have already said, it must, to serve the epigrapher's purpose, have attained some degree of fixity, but a performance is a repeatable, variable event, and the series of performances continues past the time of the inscription. The cup is also, in a sense, a repeatable event: The potter who made it can make many others, almost identical. But the desire to secure an identity, even if only a humorous one, for this particular cup led the composer of the inscription to a particular act of intertextuality. As in the case of the Dipylon jug, the act of writing down something as long as a sentence required an intertextual foundation: no written text without an antecedent text, whether or not itself written.

23. For an argument that it is a trimeter, see Pavese 1996: 9–10.
24. Pavese 1996: 11.
25. Powell 1991: 166–67.

Julia Kristeva and Intertextuality

Kristeva's work on intertextuality, which entails a revolutionary concept of text, dates from 1966, when she presented a paper on M. M. Bakhtin to Roland Barthes's seminar.[26] It was at this time that she coined the word *intertextuality*.[27] Her theory of intertextuality was complete, published, and ready to be summarized by Oswald Ducrot and Tzvetan Todorov in 1972 in their *Dictionnaire encyclopédique des sciences du langage*.[28] Text, as conceived intertextually by Kristeva, was a critical concept and was opposed to the traditional notion of work as in *work of literature*. Her concept was popularized in the English-speaking world by writers whose French was easier than hers to understand and to translate, notably by Barthes himself. The title of Barthes's essay "From Work to Text" epitomizes the new development.[29]

The inspiration for Kristeva's revolutionary model was Marxist, and it was built on the linguistics of Ferdinand de Saussure. Kristeva absolutized Saussure's notion of language as a process, as distinguished from a substance, with the result that the text, too, became not a product but a process. It could thus be viewed in Marxist terms as another form of social practice. "To the aestheticizing ideology of the art object . . . the text would oppose the reinsertion of its signifying practice . . . within the *articulated whole of the social process* . . . in which it participates."[30] The text as social practice stood in a merely "redistributive" relation to language, not an artistic one. At this point, intertextuality enters the picture.[31] The transition from Bakhtin's notion of the dialogized word in the novel to intertextuality can be seen in this formulation by Kristeva: "each word (text) is an intersection of words (texts) where at least one other word (text) can be read. . . . Any text is constructed as a mosaic of quotations; any text is the transformation and absorption of another."[32] In

---

26. Kristeva 1985: 189. The work was published in 1967 (cf. Kristeva 1969a).

27. "Le mot, le dialogue et le roman" (written 1966), *Critique* 23 (1967): 438–65; repr. with slight changes in Kristeva 1969a: 143–73. English trans.: Kristeva 1980. For histories of the concept of intertextuality: Angenot 1983; Lachmann 1989; Pfister 1985: 1–11; Mai 1991: 38–41; Rose 1993: 177–86. For Kristeva's reminiscence of the origin of the concept, see Kristeva 1985: 189.

28. Ducrot and Todorov 1979: 356–61.

29. Barthes 1977c.

30. Ducrot and Todorov 1979: 357 (their emphasis).

31. Kristeva 1968: 299.

32. Eng. trans.: Kristeva 1980: 66. I return to the dialogized word in Chapter 8.

this way, intertextuality assumes the function of a critical concept. In place of the author, the controlling subject who is the source of the work, Kristeva presents the continual redistribution and reutilization of linguistic material.[33] In place of the work, she presents the text.

Bakhtin's notion of the dialogized word obviously fitted her case, but she went beyond him both in abandoning his distinction between dialogic and monologic texts and also in other ways that lie outside the present discussion.[34] For the understanding of Kristeva's model of intertextuality, her critical, Marxist orientation is of the greatest importance. Intertextuality is not a way of referring to particular texts or particular kinds of text, and its usefulness for most kinds of literary studies is thus limited.[35] At the same time, Kristeva's theory presents literary studies with the challenge of understanding the nonliterary or nonpoetic, synchronic intertextual dimension of texts. Her view can be contrasted with that of Gian Biaggio Conte, for whom intertextuality operates within a specifically literary history.[36] He speaks of the "cardinal and privileged role of memory within poetry," a notion that seems to exclude or override any contemporary literary strands of the textual network. He sees an autonomous poetic tradition as the locus of intertextuality, of a "chain of poetic discourse" in which individual poems find their place.[37] In short, for Conte, intertextuality is a matter of a poem's relation to the past, to its particular literary past, whereas, for Kristeva, intertextuality will be a matter of a poem's relation to its present.

An example of nonliterary synchronic intertextuality can be found in one

33. On the subject, cf. Kristeva 1985: 190 (in an interview): "Analysis should not limit itself simply to identifying texts that participate in the final texts, or to identifying their sources, but should understand that what is being dealt with is a specific dynamics of the subject of the utterance, who consequently, precisely because of this intertextuality, is not an individual in the etymological sense of the term, not an identity." A nice summary of the critical function of Kristevan intertextuality is Angenot 1983: 130–31.

34. For a critique of Kristeva's appropriation of Bakhtin, see Pfister 1985: 1–11.

35. Angenot (1983: 124–25) observes that in Kristeva intertextuality has no particular application. "L'intertextualité se présente . . . dans une grande indétermination anhistorique, dans des passages quasi-allégoriques où Texte, Société, et Histoire entretiennent des rapports courtois mais imprécis. L'idée d'intertextualité comme engendrement du texte sert au telquelien à proclamer la bonne nouvelle de la mort du Sujet." Kristeva's own practice as a scholar of literature can be seen in her analyses of Lautréamont and Mallarmé in Kristeva 1974, which are based on a distinction between the *semiotic* and the *symbolic*. The former is the domain of primary, indeed prelinguistic, psychological processes.

36. Conte 1986: 49.

37. Conte 1986: 42–44; cf. 56–57.

of the best-known Augustan poems, Horace *Odes* 1.9 (*Vides ut alta stet nive candidum / Soracte*). This ode begins by establishing what Pasquali called a "motto," with a citation of Alcaeus. Indeed, the sympotic scene at the beginning of the ode is modeled on a poem of Alcaeus (338 Lobel and Page) and employs the same stanza, called "Alcaic," as that poem. Now within this scene, the speaker proposes to a certain Thaliarchus that he pour out wine from a Sabine jar. The word for jar is *diota*, emphatic in its climactic position at the end of the second stanza. This Greek word is not Greek in the same sense as the Alcaic motto. *Diota* is very probably an "unpoetic word" that comes from the vocabulary of the household and/or of the wine trade.[38] Horace's contemporary audience read or heard and experienced this word in its incongruence with the Alcaic model, as a Greek loanword in contemporary Latin. The effect of the word would have been to introduce a contrast, perhaps an opposition, between two kinds of Greekness, the old and the contemporary. In this way, among others, Horace prepares the reader for the rejection of the Greek model in favor of specifically Roman opportunities. *Diota* is thus an illustration of how, in Kristeva's sense, intertextuality marks the point at which the text enters history.

Kristeva's theory of poetic language was, like her theory of intertextuality, based on Saussure, but not on his general linguistic theory. This had taken the form of lectures and then the *Cours de linguistique générale,* published in 1916, three years after his death. Its influence was profound long before Kristeva was born. Saussure's approach to poetry was guided by his general linguistics but was pursued as a separate research project from 1906 to the early months of 1909.[39] This research remained unknown until Jean Starobinski published some extracts from Saussure's notebooks in *Mercure de France* in 1964.[40] Starobinski continued to publish extracts in the form of articles in the 1960s, and then a collection, with extensive commentary, in a book in 1971.[41] One of the central notions in Saussure's research on poetry, which focused on Greek (Homer), Vedic, and Latin (a range of poets from Naevius to Politian), was what he called the "anagram." He believed that the poet must distribute

---

38. Cf. Edmunds 1992: 31–32. By *unpoetic word* I mean a colloquial or prosaic word that falls outside the canon of diction of lyric poetry. Axelson 1945: ch. 4 gives a list of such words in the *Odes* of Horace.

39. Starobinski 1979: vii.

40. Starobinski 1964.

41. Starobinski 1971. This publication remains the principal source and discussion. I cite the translation: Starobinski 1979.

phonemes in his verse in such a way as to constitute a "theme," which was a word or words, usually a proper name, "chosen by the poet," or in the case of an epigraphic text, "by the person who is paying for the inscription."[42] For example, in

Taurasia(m) Cisaunia(m) | Samnio cepit

(10 Courtney = 7 *CLE*)

he captured Taurasia, Cisaunia, Samnium

Saussure could read the name "Scipio," and indeed this line is from the epitaph of Lucius Cornelius Scipio.[43] Despite the implication of authorial intention in the definition of "theme," Saussure denied intention in the early poets, and did not recognize it until the time of the "personal" poetry of Ovid and Vergil.[44]

The notion of the chance, thus arbitrary, distribution of significant phonic materials in poetry was obviously congenial to Kristeva. In 1966, she adapted Saussure's anagram to a theory of poetic language, using the term *paragram*.[45]

> The literary text presents itself as a system of multiple *connections* that one could describe as a structure of paragrammatic networks (*réseaux*). We use the term paragrammatic network for the *tabular* (non-linear) *model* of the elaboration of the literary image, in other words, the dynamic, spatial graphism designating the pluridetermination of sense (different from the semantic and grammatical norms of ordinary language) in poetic language. The term network replaces univocity (linearity) while including it, and suggests that each ensemble (sequence) is the end and the beginning of a plurivalent relation. In this network, the elements present themselves as the *highpoints* of a graph . . . , which will help us to formalize the symbolic function of language as dynamic mark, as moving "gram" (thus as *paragram*) that makes rather than expresses a meaning.[46]

42. Starobinski 1979: 12–13.
43. Starobinski 1979: 16.
44. Starobinski 1979: 95–96.
45. A term that Saussure had also used, as well as *hypogram*: Starobinski 1979: 18. The reason for Kristeva's choice of *paragram* is not clear, though for her the prefix *para-* seems to have something to do with motion.
46. 1969b: 184. Some phrases from this passage, in an intertextual gesture, are quoted by Ducrot and Todorov 1979: 359 without attribution. Neither *anagram* nor *paragram* appears in Engler 1968; but, for a sketch of the history of these terms, see, besides Starobinski 1971, de Man 1981: 24–26.

There are lessons to be drawn from this remarkable, not to say almost incomprehensible, passage. One is the extreme difficulty, on materialist premises like those seen in Kristeva's general formulation of intertextuality, of describing the nonordinary language that Kristeva must concede that poetry is. Another is the complete irrelevance of Kristeva's theory of poetic language to any of the activities of scholars studying intertextuality in Roman poetry. Kristeva's views, as I shall suggest, can still, in some ways, be useful to a theory of intertextuality; but she is hardly the model of a reader.[47] But, against the background of the archaic inscriptions just discussed, one wants to ask why a theory of poetic intertextuality goes immediately to the level of language ("language as dynamic mark, as moving 'gram' "). In those inscriptions, at the dawn of Western writing, an explicit and indeed ironic intertextuality is immediately encountered at the level of diction and meter. What is the orientation that defies the common sense of the reader, ancient or modern, vis-à-vis those texts and wishes to perceive the "spatial graphisms" of "paragrammatic networks"?

The relation between the paragram and intertextuality lies in the author's reading of the anterior or synchronic literary corpus.

> The literary text inserts itself in the ensemble of texts: it is a writing-reply (function or negation) of another (other) text(s). By his manner of writing as he reads the anterior or synchronic literary corpus, the author lives in history, and society is inscribed in the text. Paragrammatic science must therefore take account of an ambivalence: poetic language is a dialogue of two discourses. A foreign text enters into the network of the writing: the latter absorbs it according to laws that remain to be discovered. Thus there function in the paragram of a text all the texts of the space read by the writer. In an alienated society, beginning with his alienation itself, the writer participates by means of a paragrammatic writing.[48]

One does not have to accept the Marxism of this formulation in order to retain three notions still useful to a theory of intertextuality. One is the synchronic literary corpus, which, as I have already suggested, on the basis of Kristeva's essay on Bakhtin, can be extended even further, into nonliterary dimensions of the synchronic. The second, following from the first, is the synchronic orientation of all intertextuality, no matter whether the "foreign" texts are synchronic

47. For an example of Kristeva at work as a reader of a text, see her discovery of the phallus in a passage of Lautréamont: Kristeva 1969b:186.

48. Kristeva 1969b: 181.

or anterior. The writer's "reply" is determined by some contemporary concern (I choose a vague word) that is either unknown to readers in later ages or, at best, only partly known. Therefore these later readers, like Conte, inevitably tend to conceive of the "reply," of the intertextuality, in terms of a poetic tradition.

Only when, or especially when, the poetic tradition is silent does the synchronic dimension of an allusion thrust itself forward. In *Odes* 3.3.9–12, Horace says that Augustus, reclining with Pollux and Heracles among the gods, "will drink nectar with rosy lips" (*purpureo bibet ore nectar*). The allusion is to Simonides (fr. 80 Page), and Catullus had earlier made the same allusion (45.12). The Catullan allusion — it refers to a girl, as it did in Simonides — only sharpens the apparent incongruity of the reference to Augustus in Horace. I doubt that a fuller context in Simonides would solve the problem. It would still be a girl with rosy lips. What one needs is more information about the synchronic context of reception. Augustus was a reader of Simonides, and is reported to have used a line of the Greek poet in a reply, with ominous illocutionary force, to the philosopher Athenodorus (582 Page).[49] Horace alludes to the line in *Odes* 3.2.25–26 — "loyal silence, too, has its sure reward" (*est et fideli tuta silentio / merces*) — but with a new application, to the Eleusinian mysteries.[50]

The third notion that can be retained from Kristeva's theory of intertextuality is more fundamental: Any poetic text is in principle, not secondarily and occasionally, intertextual. At this general level, the impression that comes immediately from the archaic Greek inscriptions confirms Kristeva: She said "any text is the transformation and absorption of another" and the inscriptions, standing at the very beginning of Western writing, say, in effect, the same. Once again, the contrast between Kristeva and Conte is illuminating. As pointed out, Conte understands allusion in terms of a specifically rhetorical function, as analogous to the trope. "When a past text is summoned up allusively and its latent vitality spreads throughout a new poem, allusion works as an extension of the other weapons in the poet's armory. Allusion, in fact, exploits a device well known to classical rhetoric, 'figurae elocutionis' (tropes)."[51] Although, recalling a favorite New Critical idea, Conte refers to

49. Dio 52.36.4 (speech of Maecenas in 29 B.C.E.) provides a terminus ante quem for Athenodorus in Rome. *Odes* 1–3 were published in 23 B.C.E.
50. This line is discussed in Chapter 8.
51. Conte 1986: 38.

the "tension" between the two terms of the intertextual trope, he clearly regards allusion as a device under the control of the poet (note "armory" and "exploits"). The tension is ultimately reducible to a reality at least "known to the poet," whether or not the reader ever grasps it. In Kristeva's view, the tension is irreducible because it is a condition of the writing of poetry in the first place: The poet is not a controlling subject who determines if and when a foreign text will be admitted into his text. His text will always be a "mosaic of quotations."

The comparison of Conte and Kristeva ends here. Conte's theory of intertextuality is for the most part implicit and, when explicit, not argued for at length. It is not clear how he would counter or adapt the arguments of Kristeva. What a specifically literary theory of intertextuality needs is a concept of the text as text-object or work (to this extent in Conte's spirit) that, at the same time, admits the three notions from Kristeva discussed here. This concept would combine the process character of the text — its synchronic orientation and its primary condition of intertextuality — with its identity as a text-object or (at least relatively) fixed work. Although Kristeva's paragram seems to be an attempt to explain how a literary text can present itself in its evident individuality within the flux of the continual redistribution of linguistic material, and although she retains something like the traditional notion of text as work (a text is a semiotic practice "faite à travers la langue et irréductible à ses catégories"),[52] it remains difficult, on her view, to distinguish text from historical context or to regard a text as anything but the product of its historical circumstances. Writing as a Marxist in the 1960s, in a triumphant mood that has become less and less available, she had her own dogmatism, namely, the transparency to Marxism of the real social and economic conditions that drive history. For this reason, she could assume, in relations to texts, the detached gaze of a "sujet connaissant."[53] She knew, as in the foregoing quotations, that the truth of a text lay in the conditions of production at the time of its own production through the agency of an alienated writer.

One does not have to look outside Marxism for a concept of the text that

52. Kristeva 1969c: 113 and cf. 378 (index: C.I.2) for further indications.

53. Kristeva 1968: 311: "Pour le sujet connaissant, l'intertextualité est une notion qui sera l'indice de la façon dont un texte lit l'histoire et s'insère en elle. Le mode concret de réalisation de l'intertextualité dans un texte précis donnera la caractéristique majeure ('sociale,' 'esthétique') d'une structure textuelle." With this autonomous subject, compare the death of the subject elsewhere proclaimed by Kristeva. Cf. note 35.

would satisfy the desideratum just stated (i.e., for a concept of the text-object that would still admit the three Kristevan notions). Developments in Marxism that were beginning at about the same time as Kristeva proposed her theory of intertextuality led to various nonreductive ways of thinking about literature. In the mid-1960s, Louis Althusser was problematizing the relation between the production of material goods, on the one hand, and literary or artistic production, on the other, and both from him and from others under his influence literary texts received sophisticated analysis that acknowledged them as products in their own right, irreducible to production in the classical Marxist sense.[54] Then came poststructuralism, demanding that Marxism give up its claim to the status of metalanguage and acknowledge its own discursivity. An essay that cheerfully agrees to do so and that wants simply to put Marxist readings of texts into political struggle with other readings is Tony Bennett's "Texts in History: The Determinations of Readings and Their Texts." Bennett repudiates the referral of a text's meaning to the conditions of production obtaining at the time of its origin and, in terms very suggestive of reception theory, speaks of the modifications that these conditions, as they enter texts, undergo in the course of a text's history. Some may disappear; others may be heightened; others may undergo other changes of emphasis. Under these circumstances, it is more pressing to know how a text is functioning in the present than it is to know what its original conditions of production were. Marxist literary theory should, then, concentrate on what Bennett calls "reading formations."

> By a reading formation I mean a set of discursive and inter-textual determinations which organize and animate the practice of reading, connecting texts and readers in specific relations to one another in constituting readers as reading subjects of particular types and texts as objects-to-be-read in particular ways. This entails arguing that texts have and can have no existence independent of, anterior to, or above the varying reading formations through which their historical life is variantly modulated.[55]

Bennett stresses — and here is the crux of his concept of reading — that neither text nor context is determining for the other. A reading formation mediates between the two. The context is not an extradiscursive force but a "set of inter-

---

54. Guides to a massive literature: Dopp 1993; Kellner 1993; Habib and Wihl 1994.
55. Bennett 1984: 7.

textual and discursive relations which produce readers for texts and texts for readers." The Marxist literary critic will attempt to intervene in pregiven, ideologically determined reader formations, to upset them, and thus to create new ones. Although Bennett thus brings revolutionary struggle in the domain of literary criticism, his proposal is strangely similar to the hermeneutics that I propose later in this book.

What Bennett adds to Kristeva is the notion of reading. Whereas, for her, intertextuality was a function of the writer's alienation, for Bennett it is a way of creating a reading formation, that is, the relation of a text and a reader. Bennett adds force to the synchronic thrust of Kristeva's intertextuality, relocating synchronicity to the time of the reader.

Jacques Derrida

A more radical challenge than Kristeva's to the evident individuality of the text appeared in the thought of Jacques Derrida. In his writings in the 1970s, he extended his concept of the linguistic sign as différance to the text as a whole and raised in particular the question of the borderlines or margins of the text.[56] He referred to "a 'text' that is . . . no longer a finished corpus of writing, some content enclosed in a book or its margins, but a differential network, a fabric of traces referring endlessly to something other than itself, to other differential traces."[57] A reflection on Derrida's removal of the margin can begin with the word *fabric* in the quotation just given. A fabric is something woven. Something woven is a *textum*, a text. Not even Derrida can cast the individuality of the text into doubt without simultaneously reasserting it. Indeed, the concept of différance may be an organicist one, a metaphysics of totality, if Richard Shusterman is right to argue that the differential production of meaning would be impossible without a totality (even if an ever expanding one) within which all of the traces of signs are interrelated.[58]

Putting aside these general considerations, one can give reasons, contrary to Derrida, for the evident and functional individuality of texts. First, texts, especially poetic ones, have the capacity to represent their own margins or borders. This capacity is not vitiated by their pregiven intertextual status. On the contrary, intertextuality is one of the ways of representing a margin, most

56. Derrida 1982, especially the preface, "Tympan"; Derrida 1978.
57. Derrida 1979: 84.
58. Shusterman 1989.

notably in the case of the "motto," by which the opening of an earlier text marks the opening of a new text and also, in inevitable differences between the two, the individuality of the new text. Paradoxically, the absence of the "cited" text contributes to the establishment of a starting place, a margin for the new text. Texts also have ways of inscribing the reader's desire for an ending and even an ending beyond the ending.[59]

I am not certain that Derrida's discussion of the frame in *The Truth in Painting* has the relevance to literature that is often claimed for it; a fortiori I doubt that the frame bears on the question of the text. Derrida concentrated on three examples in Kant's *Critique of Judgment*: the frames of pictures, the draperies on statues, and the colonnades of palaces. Kant called these three things *parerga*. In other words, Derrida took visual examples, and he distinguished at the outset between visual and temporal art objects.[60] (Poetry would belong to the latter category.) Derrida did not, in this book, apply his concept of the parergon to fiction or poetry.

Conclusion

But an even stronger and, at the same time, a more silent (indeed absolutely silent) contributor to the top margin of the text is the implicit, topmost sentence with which, Samuel Levin proposes, poems begin: "I imagine (myself in) and invite you to conceive of a world in which (I say to you) . . ." This sentence is never written, never spoken, never heard by the inner ear. It remains in pure implicitude, thus before or beyond différance, and yet it has a world-creating power. The sentence stands for a convention, the workings of which are difficult to explain and belong to some field other than literary theory. But from an early age, the readers of poetry have understood how to anticipate its fictive worlds, just as a child instinctively grasps the mimetic premise of drama. In his *Defence of Poesy*, Sir Philip Sidney asked, "What child is there, that, coming to a play, and seeing *Thebes* written in great letters upon an old door, doth believe that it is Thebes?"[61]

Derrida's work on margins, like Kristeva's on intertextuality, proceeds directly from language to literature. Whatever is true of language will, in their

---

59. Cf. Roberts 1997; Fowler 1997a. It seems to be impossible to discuss endings without reference to the reader, though I have tried in this chapter to concentrate on the text.

60. Derrida 1978: 58 = Derrida 1987: 50.

61. Sidney [1595] 1970: 36.

procedure, also be true of literature. A literary-critical approach to intertextuality will, for its part, want to establish an autonomy of author, or of text, or of reader and to maintain that the literary text is in principle greater than the sum of its linguistic parts. This opposition between the linguistic and the literary appeared in many versions in twentieth-century literary theory and will reappear in this book. As the preceding paragraph has already indicated, I argue for a literary or aesthetic approach to intertextuality. What reader is there, coming to a book of poems, who believes that he or she will encounter only the phenomena of language?

TWO

Poet

Can intertextuality be understood in relation to the poet, that is, to the empirical, historical person who was the source of the psychophysiological activity necessary to the production of the poem? The answer to this question might seem to be self-evident: That the poet, as the source of the poem, is the source of intertextuality in the poem is a matter of common sense. An explanation of some particular example of intertextuality ought to be referable to the poet, and it ought to be possible to make a statement, for example, to the effect that Vergil "seems, after the *Eclogues,* to have avoided polemical or other reference to contemporary poets."[1] I believe, and shall later give reasons for believing, that a general statement of this kind does in fact have some value. But the problem remains of the particular observations on which this statement is based. What links poetic reference, or the avoidance of it, to the poet? Presumably it is the poet's intention to which such phenomena are to be assigned.

And Roman poets had intentions for their poems. A most obvious one is to please a patron. Another is Roman poets' often evident intention to say something about Rome. Further, Roman poets were understood to be intending to say something, as Augustus's reaction to Ovid's *Ars amatoria* shows. Ovid reported: "I am accused of being a teacher of shameful adultery" (*arguor obsceni doctor adulterii; Tristia* 2.212). And nothing prevents a scholar from speculating on other intentions of the poet. Indeed, Giorgio Pasquali sometimes explained intertextuality in biographical terms. Vergil, he said, quoted a line of Varius (preserved in Macrobius) at *Eclogues* 8.88 in order to pay his friend a compliment,[2] and the same impulse may lie behind Vergil's near-

---

1. Thomas 1986: 187. I am here concerned with this *kind* of statement, not with whether or not this particular statement is correct. For qualifications, see Thomas 1988: 8–9.
2. Pasquali 1968: 278.

quotation of a line of Parthenius.[3] Perhaps Pasquali was right. The presumption of an intertextuality operating within a literary coterie can be attractive, as in the case of Catullus's allusion (96.5–6) to Calvus's elegy on the death of his wife Quintilia (16 Morel = 15–16 Courtney).[4]

Intentions of this kind can be thought of as prior to and distinct from the poems in which they are embodied. They are the intentions defended by E. D. Hirsch Jr. in *Validity in Interpretation* because they are, according to him, the only basis for determining meaning. As the index to this book shows (s.v. "intention"), Hirsch thought of intention as will. He held that "the determinant power of authorial will . . . is required in order to make the [linguistic] signs [of a text] represent *something*" to which an interpretation can refer.[5] Responses to Hirsch in the field of philosophy tend to focus on questions of meaning, validity, and the truth conditions of interpretive statements. Here, however, I am discussing the question of authorial intention, and, to begin with, the external authorial intention that is epitomized in Hirsch's act of authorial will, namely, an intention distinguishable from and independent of the work in which it is embodied.[6]

One of the New Critical objections to this externally conceived intention was epistemological: The interpreter does not have access to the mind of the poet. He must be a poem reader; he cannot be a mind reader.[7] In the case of Roman poems, this epistemological argument is reinforced by historical circumstances. For Roman poets, the only kinds of intention now available to interpreters and scholars are those mentioned previously. If one asks what a Roman poet's intentions were for any particular poem, one draws a blank. Records of these intentions do not survive, if they ever existed.

Another New Critical objection to intentionalist interpretation was that, even if records of authorial intentions existed, the task of comparing them with achieved intentions would remain.[8] Did the poet achieve what he in-

---

3. G. 1.437. The line of Parthenius is preserved by Aulus Gellius (*NA* 13.27) and in a slightly different form by Macrobius (*Sat.* 1.17.8). See Thomas 1988: 140–41.

4. Conte 1994a: 135–36. Another interesting case is the allusion to Hor. *C.* 3.1 at Verg. *Aen.* 9.774–77, on which see Mörland 1968a and 1968b. I return to this biographical approach apropos of Citroni 1995 in Chapter 5. For now, I only observe that Quintilia goes in the same group with Lesbia, Lycoris, and Cynthia at Prop. 2.34.87–94.

5. Hirsch 1967: 6.

6. Cf. the characterization of this kind of intention by Wimsatt and Beardsley 1946: 469: "Intention is design or plan in the author's mind. Intention has obvious affinities for the author's attitude toward his work, the way he felt, what made him write."

7. Brooks 1963.

8. See Wimsatt and Beardsley 1946; Stallman 1994. This objection is inherited from Russian formalism; see Tynianov [1927] 1965: 132.

tended? This question can only be answered by interpretation of the poem in
question, and thus the intention of the poet, if known, is only a starting point,
not a conclusion. As for intertextuality, in their essay, "The Intentional Fallacy" (1946), W. K. Wimsatt Jr. and M. C. Beardsley discussed allusion as
especially prone to (mis)interpretation as intentional: "It may be for today the
most important illustration" of the issue of intentionalism.[9] They refer to their
contemporary situation, "today," with T. S. Eliot in mind, whose footnotes to
The Waste Land (1922) posed an obvious challenge to their views. These
footnotes seemed to record Eliot's intentions separately from the poem and
thus to provide a key to the poem's meaning. Wimsatt and Beardsley argued
that the footnotes were themselves intertextual, as one would now say, with
the poem, demanding to be integrated into its interpretation.

> Ultimately, the inquiry must focus on the integrity of such notes as parts of the
> poem, for where they constitute special information about the meaning of the
> phrases in the poem, they ought to be subject to the same scrutiny as any of
> the other words in which it is written. . . . Whereas notes tend to seem to justify
> themselves as external indexes to the author's *intention,* yet they ought to be
> judged like any other parts of the composition.[10]

But Wimsatt and Beardsley could have made a simpler and more telling point:
Because some of Eliot's notes are misleading, these notes become not the key to
Eliot's intentions but a new locus of interpretative uncertainty. Did Eliot intend to mislead his readers concerning his intertextual intentions or did
he not?[11]

The example of Eliot, a highly allusive twentieth-century poet, has been
useful to students of highly allusive Roman poets.[12] An instance of intertex-

9. Wimsatt and Beardsley 1946: 485. Allusion was, however, uncongenial to New Criticism,
and it is amusing to read the defensive pages of Wellek and Warren on the matter (1956: 257–59).
   I have not pursued Paul de Man's critique of the New Critical position on intentionality and his
shifting of intention to the structure of the poem (de Man 1983; the article is from the 1960s). Cf.
Mao 1996: 244: "It is hard to see what de Man's insistence on intention as a cause of structure does
for criticism that Wimsatt's attention to structure as effect does not do, except to remove to an even
greater distance the potentially threatening question of reader response."
   10. Wimsatt and Beardsley 1946: 484. Their view is borne out by the selectiveness (now well
known) of Eliot's notes. Scott (1995) has called attention to Madison Cawein's "Waste Land"
(1913), which might have served as a model for Eliot's poem of the same name but was un-
acknowledged by Eliot in his notes. Cf. the following note.
   11. Cf. Broich 1985: 45 n. 31: "Etliche dieser *notes* sind . . . ein Beweis dafür, daß es auch
irreführende Markierungen von Intertextualität gibt. Allerdings läßt sich heute wohl nicht mehr
mit Sicherheit entscheiden, ob Eliot den Leser bewußt oder unbewußt in die Irre geführt hat."
   12. Cf. the use of Eliot's *Prufrock* by Pucci 1998: 27–28, 32, 33, 35, 39, 40–42.

tuality in the *The Waste Land* that has emerged in recent years bears on the question of intentionality. John Newton identified the source of the phrase "a handful of dust" in *The Waste Land* as a poem by Charlotte Mew (1916).[13] Within a matter of weeks, five challengers to Newton appeared. They found the source of the phrase variously in Alfred, Lord Tennyson (twice), John Donne, Joseph Conrad, and Walter de la Mare. They also compared *pulveris exigui iactu* (Verg. G. 4.87) and *pulveris exigui . . . parva munera* (Hor. C. 1.28.3–4). All of these were authors and works that Eliot had probably read.[14] If Eliot were alive, would he be able to name one of these as his source? If he could, would he also rule out all of the others? Might he have forgotten one or more of them? The futility of an approach that tries to link intertextuality with Eliot's intention is apparent.[15] Two possibilities remain. One is to say not that Eliot alludes to one or more of the places just cited but that *The Waste Land* does, and proceed to interpret the poem on this basis.[16] The other is to sidestep the question of allusion altogether and to say that "a handful of dust" is a topos.[17]

Whereas Eliot might have intended an allusion to one or more of the sources just named, even though his intention cannot be ascertained, one has also to take into account the case in which intertextuality is not intended at all but is perceived by the reader — intertextuality in spite of intention.[18] Searches in electronic databases often yield extremely subtle points of connection between one text and another, and some of these, one suspects, are unintentional on the part of the poet who is held to be making the allusions. Further, while it seems certain that no poet ever intended any particular phrase or line to be incorporated into a poem by a later poet — while no poet ever planned or could

---

13. Letters to the Editor, "Handfuls of Dust," *TLS*, Apr. 28, 1995, 18.

14. *TLS*, May 12, 1995, 15. And for yet another suggestion, see the article by Scott 1995.

15. For "the problem of determining when a reference is really a reference, and when it is merely an accidental confluence, inevitable between poets dealing with a shared or related language," Thomas (1986: 174), while conceding something to judgment, establishes "two absolute criteria": "the model must be one with whom the poet is demonstrably familiar, and there must be a reason of some sort for the reference — that is, it must be susceptible of interpretation, or meaningful." Even when both these criteria are satisfied, no conclusion can be drawn as to the author's intention to make the reference, which may yet be an accident.

16. Cf. the argument of Beardsley 1982: 200.

17. Philology's usual "reifying move," as Hinds 1998: 39 calls it.

18. Füger 1989: 180. Cf. more generally Beardsley 1970: 20: "A text can have meanings that its author is not aware of. Therefore, it can have meanings that its author did not intend. Therefore, textual meaning is not identical to authorial meaning."

plan for the intertextual repetition of his work — such repetition affects the way later readers read it. Parody is the most obvious example. Vergil's echo of Catullus's *lumen ademptum* (68.93), an example of damaging, if not exactly parodistic, retroactive intertextuality, is discussed in Chapter 8.

Authorial intention as a critical principle has also been argued for in another way, different from Hirsch's, which I have called external. Whereas both the New Critics and Hirsch, despite their differing views of the matter, thought of intention as external to the poem, it can also be seen as internal.[19] In a well-known and much discussed essay, Steven Knapp and Walter Benn Michaels argued the impossibility of intentionless meaning, maintaining that Hirsch had been wrong to separate meaning and intention in the first place.[20] Because intention is always copresent and coextensive with meaning,[21] it is internal to language: "Intention cannot be added to or subtracted from language because language consists of speech acts, which are also always intentional."[22] If language consists of speech acts, a fortiori poems and literary works in general are speech acts, and this premise then soon becomes a conclusion. Knapp and Michaels want to illustrate their concept of intention with the example of a poem (Wordsworth's "A slumber did my spirit seal") traced on the seashore by a receding wave. The words, they argue, will have to be taken either as accidental, nonintentional marks or as the products of an agent capable of intentions. I do not analyze this argument but only point out how the premise concerning speech acts returns as a conclusion. They say, "Either the marks [on the shore] are a poem *and hence a speech act,* or they are not a poem and just happen to resemble a speech act."[23]

The question remains of whether a poem is a speech act like any other in ordinary language. If it is not, then Knapp and Michaels's case for intentionality is lost. In order to address this question, a historical context for speech act theory is needed. In this context, in which the essay under discussion curiously refrained from locating itself, the difficulties of the literary application of the theory become apparent.[24]

19. For the internal-external distinction, see Carroll 1992: 101.

20. Knapp and Michaels 1985.

21. A similar argument has been developed along Wittgensteinian lines by Lyas 1992, again with a critique of Hirsch.

22. Knapp and Michaels 1985: 24.

23. Ibid. (my emphasis). For the tendency to concede Knapp and Michaels their equation, see, for example, the move made by Iseminger 1992b: 86–87.

24. In this connection, Knapp and Michaels cite only Searle 1977. For them, it is clearly a given

The foundational text is J. L. Austin's *How to Do Things with Words* (first edition 1962). The main purpose of the lectures from which this book was drawn was not to establish a new category of utterances called speech acts but to use this new category as a means of criticizing the prevailing philosophic view that the fundamental unit of language use was the declarative sentence, a true or false proposition about the world. In his first lecture, Austin swiftly established the distinction between such propositions, which he called "constatives," and another kind of utterance, which he called "performatives." These were cases "in which to *say* something is to *do* something; or in which *by* saying or *in* saying something we are doing something."[25] These were utterances that were not true or false; they were of another kind. Two of his favorite examples were "I do" uttered in the wedding ceremony and "I bet." He then proceeded, in the following lectures, to break the distinction down, showing various overlaps between the two categories. New terms became necessary, and in his eighth lecture he introduced "locutionary" (uttering a certain sentence with a certain sense and reference), "illocutionary" (utterances that have a conventional force), and "perlocutionary" (what we bring about *by* saying something as distinguished from *in* saying something). His project was then to distinguish the illocutionary from the other two. In passing, it is ironical that, even if one granted that, because perlocutionary in effect, a poem must be a speech act, one would not yet have secured a basis for the intentionality of the poet, because some of the consequences may, on Austin's theory of the perlocutionary, have been unintentional.[26]

The most important discussion of Austin's theory took place not in literary studies but in linguistics and philosophy. The principal names and events are well known and only a brief survey is necessary.[27] Émil Benveniste replied to Austin in 1963 in an essay called "La philosophie analytique et le langage," which looked back to Benveniste's earlier essays on personal pronouns and other "instances de discours" by means of which the speaking subject can

---

that a poem is a speech act. They do not cite Searle 1974, where it is argued that the author's illocutionary intentions are in fact what determine the fictionality of a text.

For critiques of Searle 1974, see Fish 1980: 231–44 and Petrey 1990: 59–69. For a comment on the relation of Knapp and Michaels to Searle, see Petrey 1990: 158 and Henkel 1996: 120–21.

25. Austin [1962] 1975: 12.

26. Austin [1962] 1975: 107.

27. The genealogy that I here offer is to be distinguished from another genealogy, also beginning in Austin, which shows how speech act analogies influenced theories of reading and interpretive communities. For such a genealogy, see Henkel 1996: 105–9.

appear in language.[28] Benveniste proposed a stricter grammatical definition of the performative (a first-person singular declarative-jussive verb in the present tense) and also stressed the importance of the speaker's authority. In *Speech Acts* (1969), John Searle, on the hypothesis that "talking is performing acts according to rules," systematized speech act theory and showed how it could be applied to current problems in linguistic philosophy.[29] In 1972 Jacques Derrida made a critique of Austin's assumption concerning the speaking subject's intentionality in the production of meaning. Derrida focused on Austin's distinction between "parasitic" (poetry was one of Austin's examples) and serious uses of language. He argued that the supposedly intentional speech act is always iterable and thus in principle nonunique. Contaminated by parasitism, it is never the full presence that could guarantee intentionality. In 1977, when Derrida's essay was published in English translation, Searle (who had repeated Austin's parasitic-serious opposition) defended Austin against Derrida. Searle's reply was followed by Derrida's reply to Searle, also in 1977.[30]

Derrida radicalized the linguistic side of Benveniste's critique of Austin, removing the speech act from its social context (which he considered inexhaustible and undecidable) and reducing it to a function of language. The linguistic approach was continued in Paul de Man, who in *Allegories of Reading* (1979) shifted attention from *parole,* the particular instance of language use (emphasized in Benveniste's critique of Austin), to *langue,* the system of language in which and through which particular instances are possible. In particular, de Man showed in his readings of Rousseau how the speaking subject's illocutionary act subverts the locutionary system that ought to have guaranteed the speaker's meaning.[31]

Literary application of speech act theory, contrary to the implications of Derrida's and de Man's positions, proceeded on the assumption that fiction and poetry constituted a separate class of utterances. In so doing, it preserved

28. Benveniste 1966: 267–76 (first published in 1963). The earlier essays are 226–36 ("Structure des relations de personne dans le verbe"); 251–57 ("La nature des pronoms"); 258–66 ("De la sujectivité dans le langage").

29. Searle 1969: 22.

30. See Austin [1962] 1975: 22 for his distinction. Derrida's essays are collected in Derrida 1988. See pp. vii–viii for the publication history of each of them. Searle's paper is Searle 1977. For *parasitic* in Searle, see Searle 1969: 78: "we need to distinguish normal real world talk from parasitic forms of discourse such as fiction, play acting, etc."

31. De Man's formulation: "Performative rhetoric and cognitive rhetoric . . . fail to converge" (1979: 300). For a critique of de Man's reading of the episode of Marion and the ribbon in the *Confessions* (276–301), see Petrey 1990: 153–57.

the age-old distinction between fiction and poetry, on the one hand, and serious, real-world utterances, on the other, but at the same time it went counter to the founders of speech act theory, Austin and Searle, who had explicitly excluded poetry and fiction from their undertaking.[32] At first glance, the literary scholar's attraction of speech act theory is difficult to understand. The obstacle to its application to literature has been well described by Richard van Oort:

> It must be remembered that speech act theory, rebellious though it was toward its logical-positivist precursors, is still hewn from the same philosophical tree, and that tree understands language as primarily referential, not fictional. Literary theorists are therefore inevitably plagued by the fact that they are theorists of fictional speech acts, not pragmatic functional ones.[33]

If the fictional speech act is a poem, the most obvious asymmetry between it and a real-world speech act is its lack of pragmatic context and thus of conventions governing the utterance. Benveniste's emphasis on the authority of the speaker, noted earlier, was in line with Austin's emphasis on convention and context.[34] Another asymmetry between a poem and a real-world speech act lies in the former's not being subject to the same "infelicities," as Austin called them, or "defects," as Searle called them. Poems do not succeed or fail in the same way as speech acts.

Literary scholars were accordingly drawn to longer works, plays, novels, and narrative poems, which provided a context for their characters' speeches and thus allowed these speeches to be analyzed as speech acts.[35] It was more difficult to take short poems like Wordsworth's "A slumber did my spirit seal" as speech acts, and, in 1994, a theoretically sophisticated scholar of English literature could still say, "It is less obvious than in the case of the drama or novel that speech-act theory is even relevant to the interpretation of poetic texts."[36] Knapp and Michaels's premise that speech acts are intentional may or

32. Austin [1962] 1975: 22; cf. 9, where writing a poem is an example of the opposite of being serious; 104–5, 122; Searle 1969: 78 (quoted note 30).

33. Van Oort 1995.

34. Convention: Austin [1962] 1975: 14, 26 (repeated from 14), 105, 109, 115 (n.b.), 117, 119 (n.b.). Context: Austin [1962] 1975: 100.

35. For useful surveys of speech act theory in literary studies, see Magnusson 1993 and Rabinowitz 1995.

36. Esterhammer 1994: 16. Note that Petrey (1990), in an extensive vindication of the relevance of speech act theory to literary criticism, says practically nothing about short poems. He refers only to Walt Whitman's *Leaves of Grass* (111–12).

may not be correct;[37] their assumption that a poem is a speech act is badly in need of argument, and their conclusion concerning the intentionality of poems, even if their premise is correct, remains unsubstantiated.

The most prudent course would be to say that poems are sometimes representations of speech acts.[38] While poems may represent or dramatize speech acts that have illocutionary or perlocutionary force (prayers, entreaties, warnings, exhortations, etc.), they are not speech acts on the part of an empirical poet in relation to an empirical addressee. And yet the main strategy that has been used to defend the intentionalism of Knapp and Michaels is to find examples of works generally acknowledged to be literary that are not fictional representations of speech acts but performances of an illocutionary act or acts. Lucretius's *De rerum natura* (*DRN*) has been one such example. Of this poem, Noël Carroll said that it appears to be an illocutionary act of assertion. "It does not seem correct to attribute to Lucretius the intention of representing the illocutionary acts of an Epicurean philosopher — he was an Epicurean philosopher philosophizing."[39]

What does *DRN* have to say on the matter? In the proem, Lucretius calls upon Venus to aid his project:

te sociam studeo scribendis versibus esse,
quos ego de rerum natura pangere conor
Memmiadae nostro, quem tu, dea, tempore in omni
omnibus ornatum voluisti excellere rebus.
quo magis aeternum da dictis, diva, leporem! (1.24–28)

I am eager to have you as an ally in writing the verses
that I try to compose on the nature of things
for my friend, son of the Memmii, whom you, goddess, always

---

37. Precisely the opposite conclusion has been drawn from speech act theory: Petrey 1990: 79–80, 82–85, although in this context Petrey is trying to rescue the notion of "textual illocution," that is, the notion that a poem is somehow a speech act.

38. Beardsley 1970: 59; 1982: 191–93; Ohmann 1971: 14. Further references in Pavel 1986: 18 and Carroll 1992: 127 n. 24. Cf. Doležel 1980: 24: "The narrative speech act of world construction cannot be compared or identified with such speech acts as stating truth or falsehood, lying, imitating or pretending. All these speech acts presuppose the independent existence of the world to which the corresponding utterances refer or fail to refer. Basing literary semantics on any of these referential speech acts means completely missing the specific character of the world-constructing act." For world-constructing, see Chapter 6.

39. Carroll 1992: 106. Beardsley 1970: 59–61 had already discussed *DRN* as a counter-example.

have willed to be conspicuous as one embellished with every good quality.
All the more, then, grant, goddess, loveliness to my words.

The poet refers to himself as writing verses, and he asks not for whatever
virtue might attach to philosophical argument but for "loveliness" for his
words. *Pangere* is a metaphor, on one interpretation, from the pressing of the
stylus into the wax of the tablet, a metaphor that faded as the verb came to be
used regularly of poetic composition. The poet presents himself as composing
a poem in writing. His writing might, in theory, still be a speech act, but his
addressee is Venus, whose pragmatic role would be hard to describe. Any
reader, ancient or modern, will read this address as a conventional, proemial
one. When Memmius is the addressee, is there any better reason to perceive a
speech act? Memmius, unlike Venus, is a historical person who might be
conceived as somehow the empirical addressee of some parts of the poem, but
the fact remains that, in those parts, Lucretius's communication to the reader
is distinguishable from his communication to Memmius, which is thus iron-
ically contextualized and loses the impact of real-world illocution.[40] So, while
DRN provides good examples of the written representation of certain kinds of
speech act (diatribe, inspired revelation, exhortation), it is not an example of a
poem that is a speech act.

While the historical person called Lucretius may have given Epicurean
counsel to the historical person called Memmius, the speaker of *DRN* and his
addressee are not identical to the historical persons just named but have to be
understood as constructions of the poem. If the historical Memmius was the
patron of Lucretius, then the balance of illocutionary authority was probably
in his, and not Lucretius's, favor. As a poet, then, in the medium of *DRN*,
Lucretius would have to find a way to reconstrue the relation between him and
Memmius. He would have to represent or construct a Memmius in need of
Epicurean doctrine. It might, however, still seem that, in a situation in which
Lucretius read *DRN* aloud in the presence of Memmius, a real speech act was
taking place. But precisely this case shows that poetry preempts real speech
acts. Everyone present at this hypothetical historical event of Lucretius's reading knew, and was there because, it was the recitation of a *poem*. Everyone
expected a performance of something composed in advance, not on the spot.[41]

Some poems are speech acts, however, in the opening centuries of Western

40. Cf. Chapter 4, note 4.
41. The resemblance between "performance" and "performative" seems to have led some to
the false conclusion that any verbal performance is a performative utterance.

poetry. While Vergil did not sing, despite *arma virumque cano,* archaic Greek poets did in fact sing certain kinds of poems.[42] Further, they composed these poems in performance. So a performance of this kind, often delivered to an audience known to the poet, can be considered a speech act. If Tyrtaeus delivers a verse exhortation to bravery before a band of Spartan soldiers about to go into battle, this kind of poem is tantamount to a command and meets Austin's conditions for a speech act, provided that the poet has a conventional authority in this situation. Likewise, if Archilochus's verse diatribes against Lycambes and his daughter caused them to hang themselves, one could not have a clearer example of the perlocutionary effect of "shame on you." In the examples of Tyrtaeus and Archilochus it matters little whether the poems are composed on the spot or recited from memory. The force of the utterance is what is at issue. It would be possible to go through all the genres of archaic monody, too, and classify them as speech acts of one kind or another. Choral lyric would be another matter. As for epic, Richard Martin has shown that the speeches called *muthoi* in Homer are classifiable as speech acts. They are all what he calls "performances of self."[43] In what sense, however, the performance of epic poetry itself can be considered a speech act remains obscure.[44]

In any case, it is, in general, only for as long as poetry is oral and performed that poems can be considered speech acts. Writing is the turning point. For a certain time, from its first appearance in Greece until about 550 B.C.E., alphabetic writing remains under the spell of performance and is the equivalent of performance. The earliest written poems are what Gregory Nagy calls "figurative performances," relying on the reader's voice.[45] This golden age of poems, even inscribed ones (like those discussed in Chapter 1), as speech acts ends

---

42. And thus my answer is no to the question posed by Johnson (1980: 60): "When Virgil says 'Arma virumque cano', is he not doing what he is saying?" Johnson (1980) has two goals, to interpret Mallarmé partly with reference to Austin, and to make a critique of Austin with reference to a prose poem by Mallarmé, "La Déclaration foraine." In passing, I observe that this prose poem is about, and quotes, the delivery of a sonnet in a merchant's booth (thus "foraine") at a fair. If poems are going to be speech acts, then it would be necessary to explain not only the sonnet but also the prose poem as speech acts. But does not the commercial nature (parodistic, obviously) of the delivery of the sonnet implicitly point back to the communication of the prose poem to the reader, that is, in writing, in print, as a commodity to be purchased by a reader? For an ancient poet's self-irony concerning the commercial aspect of his poetry book, see Hor. *Ep.* 1.20.

43. Martin 1989: 12–42 for *muthoi* as speech acts; 225 for "performances of self."

44. In what sense is such a performance illocutionary (what does it *do*?) or perlocutionary? As Nagy (1996: 119) says, "the outermost narrative frames of the *Iliad* and the *Odyssey* . . . give us for all practical purposes no information whatsoever about the context of performance, let alone occasion." Cf. note 41 on the nonequivalence of "performance" and "performative."

45. Nagy 1996: 35–36.

when writing begins to be used for transcription and is definitively over when it is used for composition, with the resulting text destined for a readership. Thereafter, the poem replaces the performer, and, as will be argued in Chapter 4, the "performer" is now the *persona loquens* internal to the text.

The ad hoc use of a written poem as a speech act is always possible, and a poem may have a practical effect even if it had no such perlocutionary intent, as when Octavia swooned upon hearing Vergil read *Aeneid* 6.860–86, the lines on her deceased son Marcellus (*Vita Donati* 32–33). Or a poet may pretend that his poems are speech acts, as Catullus does (35; 42).[46] But it should be remembered that when Catullus attacked Caesar in epigrams on Mamurra (29; 57) and then apologized, Caesar invited him to dinner the same day (Suet. *Jul.* 73).[47] Would Caesar have forgiven him if he had expressed the same opinions to Caesar's face or in some other context of speaking, instead of putting them in the form of epigrams? These poems seem not to have had the perlocutionary (e.g., anger) and illocutionary effects that a real speech act would have had. *Epistola non erubescit* (Cic. *Ad fam.* 5.12.1). So Catullus was apologizing for poems, not for speech acts. Further, if Catullus's apology was verbal (it is unclear from Suetonius's report), one can contrast its instant perlocutionary effect, forgiveness on the part of Caesar, with the far different effect of the poems, which Caesar described as "a lasting stain" (*sibi . . . perpetua stigmata imposita*). Unless one wants to say, most improbably, that the poems are continually repeated speech acts, one will have to understand the lasting effect to which Caesar referred as owing to their publication as written texts. His shame comes not from the direct effect of the poems on him, even though he is addressed in one of them (29), but from the judgment on him that is conveyed to others. The poems do not tell others, in the manner of a

46. Selden (1992: 503 n. 99) accepts Johnson's critique of Austin, and states that "the majority of Catullus' poetry is in fact performative and not constative" (481). Selden makes this statement in the context of a discussion of Cat. 16, in which "Catullus asserts the performative power of his compositions" (484). Selden concludes, however, with the same tension between the biographical and the textual that he well demonstrates in several other poems: "the reduction of the authorial persona to the text is matched simultaneously by the textual production of the same persona" (486). If the author remains textual, then how can the poem be a speech act in Austin's sense? Cat. 16 affirms the effects of other Catullan poems. What does Cat. 16 as a poem do or effect?

47. Usener 1900 showed that Cat. 42 is an imitation of a *convicium;* cf. Fraenkel 1961, and for a historical-sociological reflection of the role of insult in Roman life, Veyne 1991: 57–87. Of course, nothing can prevent a reader from believing that a poem or other fiction is a speech act and feeling illocutionary effects. The American novelist David Graham Phillips was murdered (1911) by a reader who saw an insult to a relative in one of Phillips's fictional characters.

speech act, what they must believe concerning Caesar. They put forth a shameful picture of Caesar and his relations with the reprobate Mamurra.

The Roman institution of the *recitatio,* the poet's reading of his work before his patron or friends or in a public place, might encourage the belief that Roman poems were, if not always in fact, at least potentially speech acts.[48] The notion of Lucretius reading aloud *DNR* to Memmius has already been discussed. For the *Georgics,* there exists a record, apparently historical, of its initial "publication" in the form of a reading to Octavian.

> Georgica reverso post Actiacam victoriam Augusto atque Atellae reficiendarum faucium causa commoranti per continuum quadriduum legit, suscipiente Maecenate legendi vicem, quotiens interpellaretur ipse vocis offensione. (*Vita Donati* 27)

> When Augustus [still at this time Octavian] returned after his victory at Actium and was tarrying at Atella to heal his throat there, Vergil read the *Georgics* to him over a four-day period, with Maecenas taking a turn whenever Vergil strained his voice and had to stop.

It is curious that Maecenas, who is the primary recipient of the agricultural teaching (1.2; 2.41; 3.41; 4.2) — that is, the one who should feel the illocutionary force of the poem — can play the role of the poet and, in effect, address himself.[49] Further, when the historical Vergil reads the opening lines of the poem and prays to Octavian as the deity that he will become (1.24–42), the illocutionary force of the prayer is qualified by its intertextuality with Callimachus and Catullus. In this way, the Octavian of the poem is a poetic creation, even if the real Octavian is present.[50]

The only speech act that took place was the *recitatio* itself, which was already defined by Roman social and literary conventions.[51] The speech act was not the activation of the enunciative properties of the poem (the implied speaker addressing the named addressees), which, paradoxically, were fic-

---

48. For what is probably the standard view on recitation, see the quotation from Kenneth Quinn in Chapter 7 (pp. 109–10).

49. He is formally the primary recipient, but, as Schiesaro (1994: 134–35) well observes, there is no privileged addressee. (Maecenas, Octavian, the *agricolae,* and a wider public are all addressees.) Sharrock (1994: 13–14) has made the same point.

50. Thomas 1988: 74: "Virgil's reminiscence [of Callimachus] . . . constitutes a literary, as much as a political, acknowledgement."

51. On which see Dupont 1997, esp. 52–55, on the *recitatio* as an expression of clientelism.

tional, as is shown by the fact that the role of the real poet was fungible and that Maecenas could play Vergil. A comparable *recitatio* is recorded by Pliny. Because he was a poor reader of verse, he used one of his freedmen as *recitator* of his work.[52]

The purpose of this discussion of speech act theory was to refute the notion that a poem is a speech act like any other in ordinary language and thereby to counter Knapp and Michaels's argument for intentionality. The possibility remains, however, that a poem is a special kind of speech act (and therefore that a poem might convey the intention of the poet in some sense other than the internal one, coexistent with meaning, proposed by Knapp and Michaels). In order to explore this possibility, the distinction between speech acts contextualized in longer works and short poems like Wordsworth's "A slumber did my spirit seal" as speech acts again provides a starting point. Is there any theoretical basis for considering such short poems speech acts, as, by the way, some classicists have wished to do?[53]

Samuel R. Levin's *The Semantics of Metaphor* begins to provide an answer to this question. This book addresses the problem, in linguistic philosophy, of "deviant expressions" and in particular the problem of metaphor. One of Levin's strategies is to ask if such expressions could be taken literally.[54] If so, would they have meaning? He concludes that a metaphoric sentence like "The stone died" can in fact be meaningful even if it cannot be satisfied in the real world. It is enough that the conditions under which the sentence might be satisfied be comprehensible (in this case, that the stone be animate). Everything depends on our having a place in which to put the metaphor, and, to describe that place, Levin uses the concept of possible worlds. The entrance to possible worlds is an indirect or attitudinal or "oblique" context established by an underlying "I (etc.) imagine, believe (etc.)." Extending his conclusions from metaphor to whole poems, Levin argues, in an article from the same period as the book, that poems also have an implicit, topmost, "higher" sentence with which they begin: "I imagine (myself in) and invite you to conceive of a world in which (I say to you) . . ."[55] This implicit sentence makes a poem a speech act, and the act is one of creating a possible world.

52. *Ep.* 9.34.2. Cf. Dupont 1994: 254–63.
53. Cf. Selden 1992; Oliensis 1998: 4–5 (who is well aware of the difficulties).
54. Levin 1977: ch. 6.
55. Levin 1976: 150. (Adjustments in this sentence are to be made for poems that begin with questions, requests, etc. For example, instead of "[I say to you]," "[I ask you]" would be understood.) Cf. Ohmann 1971: 17: "In inviting the reader to constitute speech acts to go with sentences,

In the terms of speech act theory, this topmost sentence is doubly performative. First, the act implied by "I imagine" has been performed, and the result is the poem. Second, "I invite you" is also performative. If the illocutionary force of the two performatives is successful, "then the perlocutionary effect on the reader is just what Coleridge called 'the willing suspension of disbelief,' the condition that constitutes poetic faith."[56] In this way, Levin's overriding concern, growing out of philosophy of language, was the truth value of poetry.[57]

What should be added to Levin's notion of the perlocutionary effect on the reader is the reader's willing acceptance of the historical, generic, and other modes of poetic language, which include intertextuality. Levin only glances at the intertextual dimension of the contract between poet and reader.[58] And yet this dimension is, in Roman poetry, especially important for the kind of illocutionary act that Levin has in mind. "What kind of illocutionary act," he asks, "must have the perlocutionary effect of exciting poetic faith, a faith which consists in entertaining as meaningful a set of statements that may make claims counterfactual to conditions in the real world and for whose warrant we have only the testimony of a speaker projected from the mind of the poet?" He answers: "It is the kind of act . . . that we associate with the seer, the *vates*, the vessel, the sibyl."[59] It is an act with which readers of Roman poetry are well acquainted.[60] In poetry composed in the Judeo-Christian tradition, the paradigm for this kind of poetic speech act is divine creation by the word. Angela Esterhammer, in a study of John Milton and William Blake, has used the term

---

the literary work is inviting him to participate in the construction of a world." Cf. also Doležel 1989: 237: "A non-actualized possible state of affairs becomes a fictional existent by being authenticated in a felicitously uttered literary speech act." And in the footnote to this sentence he explains: "If we want to express the authenticating illocutionary act by an explicit performative formula, then we could suggest the prefix: *Let it be.*" He does not refer to Levin. And Esterhammer 1994 does not cite Doležel, though *Let it be* expresses perfectly the speech act that she calls "the phenomenological performative."

56. Levin 1976: 152. Levin calls his topmost sentence a contract entered into by poet and reader. "If the contract is entered into by both parties, then the truth criteria for the statements made in the poem are altered. The truth conditions are not those that would obtain if the statements were taken to be making claims about the actual world; they are those that would obtain given a world of the imagination" (Levin 1977: 119).

57. Levin 1976: 145–46.

58. Levin 1976: 155: "the invitation [to the reader] is made atttractive by the inlay of the conventions in the language of the poem."

59. Levin 1976: 154.

60. Newman 1967. See Lowrie 1997b: 73 n. 56 for further references and her general index, s.v. "vates," for her own remarks.

phenomenological performative to refer to this paradigm, contrasting it with *sociopolitical performative*. The distinction, she shows, corresponds to the distinction between speech acts in the text, on the one hand, and the text as speech act, on the other.[61]

Levin's parenthesizing of "(myself in)" is a way of indicating that the top-most sentence has two different readings. The distinction between the two is fundamental in the argument of the present book. Levin states: "In the higher sentence that we are positing for poems . . . the *I* refers to the poet, in this world, but the *myself* which the poet imagines (images) is in another world, the world created by the poet's imagination. In that world, it is no longer the poet who moves; it is a projection of himself." In Levin's view, then, the empirical author belongs to the most implicit dimension of the poem, whereas the poet's projection of himself is a *persona*, a term that Levin also uses.

Levin's theory provides for a deeply implicit, external, and indeed a priori intentionality. The *phenomenological performative* can, of course, be made explicit in a poem, in which case it will be the act of a persona or of the *virtual poet* (see Chapter 4). But the kind of intention that Levin's theory rescues is of no practical use to anyone who wants to interpret a poem. Once one has identified, say, the *Eclogues* of Vergil as poems, and so, putatively, established an intention, what more does one know about them either individually or as a collection?[62] If, at the end of one's interpretive labors, one says, "And this was the intention of the poet," what has one gained? Nothing for the interpretation, which stands or falls on its own merits. Intention is an add-on that, in classics, satisfies the discipline's need for an objective criterion of historical truth. But, at the same time, paradoxically, it must remain inconclusive if, as all or many in the academy hope, each new generation of scholars is to have work to do.[63]

O F   W H A T   U S E is the historical poet for the understanding of intertextuality? Michel Foucault's concept of "authorial function" helps to provide some an-

---

61. Esterhammer 1994: ch. 1.

62. And so the proclamation of Searle (1974: 325) sounds hollow: "At the most basic level it is absurd to suppose a critic can completely ignore the intentions of the author, since even so much as to identify a text as a novel or a poem, or even as a text is already to make a claim about the author's intention."

63. Cf. the analysis of this ambivalence concerning intention by Shusterman 1988: 400–401. For a concise statement of the anti-intentionalist view in an official and institutional context, see Tarrant 1995a: 1: "I would suggest that it is precisely the student of classical literature who is in the best position to know that the meaning of works of art is not fixed (certainly not by their creators), and that each reader or viewer brings something unique to the act of interpretation."

swers to this question.[64] The author is a function that has been ascribed variously to texts by different institutions (e.g., religion, copyright laws, the business of publishing) at different times. The author is never linked spontaneously and naturally to a text but only by some construct or other that has emerged in scholarly and critical discourse. The author is thus the projection of the work that scholars and critics do on texts. For this reason, the "same" author can have two different projections at the same time.

The two Horaces of the 1990s are an example. The more familiar one is the historical person who can, it is believed, be discerned here and there in his poems and about whom one can write a biography. This Horace even appears in the *New York Review of Books.* Apropos of the poet's love life, B. M. W. Knox wrote: "He mentions a whole galaxy of ladyloves . . . and the only one that sounds at all real is Cinara, whom he twice mentions as an early love of his in a tone that sounds sincere."[65] Another Horace appears in the introduction to a book on the *Odes,* the same poems to which Knox was referring. Michèle Lowrie states: "I am happy to use proper names as metonymies for texts: Horace stands for everything that has come down to us under his name. But I balk at the study of personality, the subject of historians or psychologists."[66]

For the scholar for whom "Horace" is a metonymy for the texts ascribed to him, the poet's name has become what Foucault called classificatory.

A name permits one to group together a certain number of texts, define them, differentiate them from and contrast them to others. In addition, it establishes a relationship among the texts. Hermes Trismegistus did not exist, nor did Hippocrates — in the sense that Balzac existed — but the fact that several texts have been placed under the same name indicates that there has been established among them a relationship of homogeneity, filiation, authentication of some texts by the use of others, reciprocal explanation, or concomitant utilization.[67]

Precisely this use of the author's name underlies the history of Roman literature. With reference to a poet or poets, findings concerning one text can be brought into relation with another text by the same or another poet; comparisons can be made between examples of the same genre. In this activity lies the value of statements like the one quoted earlier (that Vergil "seems, after the *Eclogues,* to have avoided polemical or other reference to contemporary po-

64. Foucault 1984; Barthes 1977b.
65. Knox 1998: 47, col. 4.
66. Lowrie 1997b: 7.
67. Foucault 1984: 107.

ets"). Barthes's notion that the author's "only power is to mix writings, to counter the ones with the others, in such a way as never to rest on any one of them" seems to presuppose that one or more of the mixed writings can be discerned in, and as partially constituting, the mixture.[68] Indeed, in Roman poetry, elements of the mix can often be discerned, and it is useful to have a way to designate them. One way of identifying the ingredients in the mixture is with reference to authors.[69]

Although a history of Roman poetry might be organized in other ways, for example, by genre, or with reference to determinants, like ideology, as powerful as individual poets, the poets have retained a leading role in the spate of histories of Roman literature seen in the past decade. In his review of Gian Biaggio Conte's *Latin Literature: A History,* Charles Martindale sees these histories as the field's response to a crisis of authority brought on by literary theory.[70] They provide a view of things to which the majority of scholars can still assent and which thus becomes authoritative for the field. Further, for outsiders, the very existence of these histories is a sign of the field's vigorous health. The name of the poet has remained a favorite tool for the organization of this kind of authority.

It is also to the poet's name that the aesthetic pleasure of the text is ultimately referred. If one or more poems attached to a particular name are perceived as having compelling aesthetic value, they will be reread, included in reading lists for degree candidates, written about, discussed, and taught to students. In this process, some poems and poets have always remained and will apparently always remain; others have come and gone and may return. Canon formation and transformation are keyed to the poet, whether to his oeuvre as a whole or to individual works. The latter may change from time to time while the name remains. Thus "Horace" may designate one set of poems today, another tomorrow. Further, the canon is constructed on a prior principle of authenticity: A distinction is made between works rightly and works wrongly attributed to a particular author. Sometimes, a further distinction is made, within individual works, between authentic and spurious parts. The

68. Barthes 1977b: 146.

69. I believe that no more than the name of the poet is required to satisfy the desideratum of Hinds 1998: 48–50 and Hinds 1997: 119. The alluding author is not, contrary to Hinds, "good to think with" if this notion is in flat contradiction, as it is, to the position, also held by Hinds, that "the only author to whom we have access is a figure whom we, as readers, find in (or read out from) the text" (Hinds 1997: 119).

70. Conte 1994b; Martindale 1994: 155.

passage about Helen in *Aeneid* 2 (567–88) is contested. Sometimes it is by Vergil, sometimes not.

Poets are useful, then, for canons and for literary history but, perhaps paradoxically, not useful for the interpretation of the poems that they write. In particular, the intention of the poet is useless. As for external intention, it is only the implicit sentence posited by Levin. As for internal intention, it is only the "intention" of the speaker or persona.[71] The attempt, for the sake of rescuing the intention of the poet, to equate poems with ordinary speech acts is especially pernicious. The ontological status of poems is determined by various conventions that separate them from ordinary language.[72] In passing, and prospectively, I suggest that it is in the first place the poet's adoption of a persona, his speaking in a fictional voice, that gives a poem its special status outside the ordinary uses of language. Gérard Genette has argued that the distinction between author and narrator is the distinguishing characteristic of fiction, and the same can be said, mutatis mutandis, of poetry.[73] Further, to interpret a poem is to understand and reperform the speaker's role, which is an activity far different from the reaction to a speech act. While it might be argued that the authors of nonfictional works also speak through a persona, these works expect and require an identification of the persona with the author. Cicero wants to be recognized as Cicero in his speeches, his essays, and his letters, no matter what voice he adopts. But is the speaker of *Satire* 1.8 (*olim truncus eram ficulnus, inutile lignum*) to be identified with Horace?

71. As Dowling (1985) argues, against Knapp and Michaels.

72. Smith 1974: 173, without explicit reference to speech act theory but as if in reply to Searle 1974: "Poems are not utterances, nor historically unique verbal acts or events; indeed a poem is not an event at all, and cannot be said to have occurred in the usual sense. When we read the text of a poem or hear it read aloud, our response to it as a linguistic structure is governed by quite special conventions, and it is the understanding that these conventions are operating that distinguishes the poem as a verbal artwork from natural discourse."

73. Genette 1990. Iser (1978: 63), in the context of a discussion of speech act theory, formulates the difference between fiction and ordinary speech (the domain of speech acts) thus: "The parting of the ways between literary and ordinary speech is to be observed in the matter of situational context. The fictional utterance seems to be made without reference to any real situation, whereas the speech act presupposes a situation whose precise definition is essential to the success of that act. This lack of context does not, of course, mean that the fictional utterance must therefore fail; it is just a symptom of the fact that literature involves a different application of language, and it is in this application that we can pinpoint the uniqueness of literary speech." Iser, on the other hand, works as hard as possible to accommodate speech act theory to his theory of reading. Even so, the element of the performative is transferred to the reader ("This process of discovery [by the reader] is in the nature of a performative action"), and, when he refers to fiction, he puts "performance" in quotation marks (61).

In a determinedly intentionalist and indeed psychological study of influence in modern English poetry, Harold Bloom traces a succession of English poets starting from Milton. His *The Anxiety of Influence* provides the starkest possible contrast with the concept of the poet argued for in this chapter. Each of Bloom's poets feels the influence of his predecessor(s) as anxiety, which is understood in a mélange of specifically Freudian terms, of which Bloom's favorite is the "Family Romance." Strong poets find ways, "ratios of revision"—Bloom names and defines six of them—of overcoming the burdensome priority of the predecessor(s).[74] In general, the later poet deliberately misreads and misunderstands. His achievement is a "misprision." The ratios, neither strictly historical in sequence nor always linked to particular poets, are in the nature of laws of poetic anxiety. Criticism, then, takes poems as documents of these laws. So, as Bloom says, "The issue is reduction and how best to avoid it." Bloom's response to this dilemma is to deal in the relations of whole poems or at least of whole passages, which he refrains from discussing in detail. "We reduce to another poem."[75]

The question then arises of how Bloom as critic finds the meaning of one poem in another poem, a "parent poem." This question can be answered only by observing his own practice. It is hortatory and prophetic, and necessarily so, because the most essential thing, the poet's anxiety, is hidden at a level beneath the reach of explication and ordinary interpretation. It is psychological. For Bloom, then, proper names are not metonymies for texts, but vice versa, and names become metonymies for a definable class of revisionary moves. Paradoxically, the quest for the poet arrives at one or another of these typical moves. Bloom's project, in the terms of the distinction made by Lowrie, belongs to psychology more than to literature. The present book discusses the particular relations between Roman poets (in Lowrie's metonymic sense) that are referred to by "intertextuality."

74. Bloom 1973. Working on the same assumption as Bloom, that the psychology of the poet is discernible in the poem, Smith (1997) arrives at the diametrically opposed position of "poetic embrace."

75. Bloom 1973:94.

THREE

Reader

The very word *reader* implies interpretation or literary criticism and therefore forms a contrast with *philologist*. That contrast indeed goes back, as Daniel L. Selden has shown, to the origins of classics as a discipline at the end of the eighteenth century and is a recurring theme.[1] From the point of view of the philologist, the reader is someone else, either in the past, and an object of historical interest, or in the present, and an object of professional annoyance. For the literary critic, the reader is someone engaged in interpreting literary works. It is likely that *reader* also implies a contrast with *text*. The text on which the classicist works is often assumed to have an objective existence — "the text itself" — to which "empirical" access is possible and concerning which positive results may be obtained. The reader, especially in the practice of "reader-response" criticism, is seen as violating the sanctity of the text thus conceived.

The Reader as Viewed by the Philologist; the Reader-Philologist

Michael von Albrecht, in his contribution to *The Interpretation of Roman Poetry: Empiricism or Hermeneutics?*, states that "it would be wrong to give up all hope to find the historical truth. It is still a fascinating task to reconstruct the patterns of reality that meant something to our authors and readers."[2] Sometimes "the Roman reader" is appealed to as the standard against which the findings of the modern critic must be judged.[3] But, as I argue in more detail in Chapter 5, the original audience is a problematical concept. A poem may

---

1. Selden 1990. And, as he shows, it has an even earlier history.
2. Von Albrecht 1992: 177.
3. As in Kenney 1994, on which see Edmunds 1998.

have had a different meaning for those who read it ten years after its first publication, and even in the first year, for readers in different places, not to mention readers of different genders, social classes, and philosophies.[4] To focus on changes over time, at what point, one could ask, does the original audience cease to be the original one and become a "later" one? It seems that difference of meaning is coeval with origin, and "our readers" therefore have to be imagined as not only plural but pluralistic.

Philology sometimes softens the strict historicist criterion of the ancient reader's understanding of the text and assumes a general, transhistorical human subject as reader. Often the first-person plural is used to refer to this reader: "we" experience such and such when "we" read a Roman poem. (Cf. von Albrecht's use of "our" in the quotation in the preceding paragraph.) This reader as human subject satisfies the demands of historicism (it is the ancient reader) and also the claim or assumption, entailed in the very word "classic," of the lasting significance of ancient literature (it is the modern reader at the same time).[5] The first-person plural is conveniently vague, however, and may only mean "the ancient reader and we philologists."

Conte, whose text-centered approach is discussed in Chapter 1, insists on a "reader-addressee" who is somehow in the text and constitutes a standard of historical accuracy:

> The model of the reader in my studies is quite simple, and it is only the current situation of literary criticism which obliges me to comment on it. I could define my operative notion as the idea not of a *reader-interpreter* (which seems to have become prevalent in contemporary hermeneutics), but of a *reader-addressee*. The reader-addressee is a form of the text; is the figure of the recipient as anticipated by the text. To this prefiguration of the reader, all future, virtual readers must adapt themselves.[6]

---

4. On this problem, see the discussion of Hexter 1992: 342–44.

5. The position is perfectly expressed by Knox 1957: 1–2: "This book is . . . a study of . . . *Oedipus Tyrannus* in terms of the age which produced it, an attempt to answer the question, 'What did it mean to them, there, then?' But it suggests also an answer to the question, 'What does it mean to us, here, now?' And the answer suggested is: the same thing it meant to them, there, then. For in this case, the attempt to understand the play as a particular phenomenon reveals its universal nature; the rigidly historical method finds itself uncovering the timeless."

6. Conte 1994a: xx (emphasis as in original). Cf. 133: The "ideal readers" that he describes "belong to the form of the text; they are a strategy of the text. And they are also the model that empirical readers of the text learn to resemble while they progress in understanding it."

One notes the tone of annoyance (at "contemporary hermeneutics"). As already noted, the philologist's reader is someone else, here a figure in the text, one put there by the poet, as Conte proceeds to explain. This figure is the one the poet had in mind, the one that the poet intended. So the reader-addressee stands in for the intention of the poet that Conte elsewhere repudiates.[7]

As a confirmation of this point, one can consider the link between Conte's "intentionality of the text" and his reader-addressee:

> Certainly, it will often be difficult to rediscover the text's true historical intentionality, but even the attempt provides us with an enormous benefit: for without a decisive tension, like that produced by the search for the literary work's original intentionality, our very relation with these works loses its genuine interest. Searching for the text's intentionality — which is not a naïve recourse to the author's intentions — will mean searching for the semantic energy that binds a work's diverse and apparently incongruous elements into a significant whole, that energy which invests, motivates, and shapes the reader-addressee originally programmed by the form of the text.[8]

The search that Conte here proposes may not be a naive recourse to the author's intentions; it may well be a sophisticated one; but it is still a recourse, under another name, to those intentions. Conte nowhere explains how a text could acquire intentions such as he describes if not from its author.

Conte's standard is strictly historicist, admitting nothing like the compromise of the first-person plural. Anyone who now reads a Roman poet will be at best a "virtual" reader. A question immediately arises: How does Conte gain access to this figure of the reader? The reader-addressee appears only through the initial response of an empirical reader, Conte himself. The same point has been made about Umberto Eco's "Model Reader."[9] This empirical reader has

---

7. Conte 1986; 127; 1994a: 133. Farrell 1991: 23 and 64–65 showed the latent intentionalism of Conte's position.

8. Conte 1994a: xix = Conte 1991: 5. When Jauss (1982a: 142) speaks of "intentionality of the text," he means something completely different from what Conte means. He is using the phrase in the context of a distinction between the allegorical reading of a text and the reading that remains within the text's "horizon of meaning." The "intentionality of the text" is synonymous with this horizon, which has nothing to do with authorial intention. Jauss's usage is almost technical, looking to the phenomenological sense of "intention," which refers to the structure of consciousness generally as consciousness *of something*. The text's horizon or intentionality is that something that would be forsaken by an allegorical reading.

9. Jouve 1993: 32: "La difficulté avec les différents lecteurs théoriques . . . c'est qu'ils ne sont pas aussi 'théoriques' qu'il y paraît. Leur 'réalité objective,' censée garantir le pertinence et la

to interpret the text in order to arrive at the figure of the reader. So Conte must first be the reader-interpreter in order to know who the reader-addressee is, and one suspects that the two readers are really the same.[10] In any case, Conte provides no comment on the transition from the one to the other, whereas the contemporary hermeneutics that he repudiates has concentrated on the process of reading and has proposed several models.

Conte, one could say, is the reader-philologist, who possesses a "neutral instrument of philological analysis" and therefore supposedly knows who the reader-addressee is without ever being a reader-interpreter.[11] This attitude leads to detachment and to what Joseph Farrell has called a concentration on "philological discovery," at the expense of interpretation.[12] Here is an example of the reader-philologist at work in the domain of intertextual studies. Richard Thomas observes that, in the description of the plague at the end of *Georgics* 3, Vergil twice uses prosaic adverbs in *-im*, once at 485 and then again seventy-one lines later at 556. Lucretius, he points out, had used two such adverbs, first at 6.1144 and then forty-seven lines later at 6.1191, in his description of the plague at Athens. "Virgil uses the two [adverbs] only here, and their sole function is to recall Lucretius and thereby enrich our reading of the Virgilian version."[13] The stylistic and morphological pecularities and the parallelism are matters of fact, and they are data that the philologist provides concerning the passage in the *Georgics*. They are data worth having, but would they be noticed by a nonphilological reader, and, if so, how is it that they contribute to "our" understanding of the passage? It seems to me that, for most readers, they are subperceptual and that Thomas's first-person plural reaches out to other philologist-readers.

The best philologist-reader is the one who knows or can discover the most examples, and the subtlest examples, of intertextuality. The detection of examples is a criterion for ranking readers of this kind. This criterion is completely at odds, however, with what I take to be the fact of the matter for

---

généralité de l'analyse, est loin d'aller de soi. Pour décrire les réactions du Lecteur Modèle, Eco est obligé de passer par les réactions d'un lecteur empirique qui n'est autre que lui-même." As Iser said, the reader-addressee is a "fictional inhabitant of the text" (1978: 33).

10. Cf. the critique of Conte's reader-addressee in Laird 1999: 18–25.

11. Cf. Conte [1974] 1985: 117 n. 6: "un neutrale strumento di analisi filologica"; cf. Conte 1986: 29 n. 11, where the phrase is softened in translation to "a more neutral instrument suited to philological analysis." Conte (1994a: 130) states that he is astonished that none of the reviewers of Conte [1974] 1985 and Conte 1986 noticed the change, over the course of his work up to that point, from formalism to concern with how a text communicates.

12. Farrell 1991: 18.

13. Thomas 1986: 179.

anyone reading a text in the aesthetic perspective: "The test for allusion is that it is a phenomenon that some reader or readers may fail to observe."[14] In the realm of nonphilological reading, allusion has a different status. As something that may go unobserved, it can hardly serve as a criterion for ranking readers. The best reader will not be the one who misses the most allusions. The two kinds of reading, philological and aesthetic, are, from the point of view of allusion, heterogeneous and incompatible. Their respective positions are the result of the different status of allusion in their presuppositions. For philology, allusion is material that is objectively there in the text. For aesthetic reading, allusion is something that requires the participation of the reader and, if noticed, is integrated into the developing meaning of the text being read.

But philology tacitly recognizes the truth of the aesthetic perspective. In the matter, for example, of Augustan poets' allusions to their contemporaries, both philologists and interpreters are often in the position of a reader of *The Love Song of J. Alfred Prufrock* who has not read *Hamlet* and cannot get the allusion in "I am not Prince Hamlet nor was meant to be."[15] Thanks to Macrobius and Servius, some allusions in Vergil to the poetry of his friend Varius Rufus are known, but, as Pasquali said in "Arte allusiva," it is very certain that most such allusions to his contemporaries escaped the twentieth-century reader, and no doubt many of them were already lost on Macrobius and Servius, because the relevant poems were already lost.[16] Ignorant of these allusions, all kinds of readers still find Vergil and other Augustan poetry meaningful. While philologists postulate lacunae, mark cruces that defy conjecture, and diagnose anomalies that defy exegesis, with profound calm they pass over undiscerned and undiscernible allusions.

Reader-Interpreter; Reading

The reader appeared in various forms in twentieth-century hermeneutics and reader-response approaches. Hans Robert Jauss presented a theory and a

14. Miner 1994; cf. Füger 1989: 184; Stempel 1983: 92–93. Allusion, therefore, does not, contrary to Lyas 1992: 142, constitute an example of a feature of a work that requires knowledge of intention for its recognition.

15. Wimsatt and Beardsley (1946: 486) discuss another line from this poem. Perri (1978: 297) argues that the line can be meaningful even if the allusion is not grasped. Her position, with which I concur, is thus 180 degrees from that of Riffaterre, who in nearly all his articles listed in the Works Cited in this book speaks of intertextuality as indicated by gaps and "ungrammaticality" in the text.

16. Pasquali 1968: 278–89. Notorious evidence of our ignorance is Servius on Vergil *Ec.* 10.46ff. (and here the vague "ff." is for once justified): *hi autem omnes versus Galli sunt de ipsius translati carminibus.*

method of reading in an essay on Baudelaire's "Spleen II" (first published in 1980). He demonstrated a series of readings, the first aesthetic, the second interpretive, and the third historicist, attempting to recapture the original audience's reading. In the first reading, the reader reads from beginning to end, line by line, in the anticipation that the poem will end by impressing itself on him as complete and meaningful, even if he does not fully understand that meaning. And this is the difference between the first, aesthetic reading and the second interpretive one. It is quite possible to have a preunderstanding, an incomplete understanding of a poem, as common sense shows. Everyone has had the experience of reading, say, a sonnet by Shakespeare, which, upon an initial reading, seems complete and meaningful, even if one did not understand every phrase and even if one could not yet, on the basis of a first reading, interpret the poem. That is the Jaussian first reading. It corresponds very closely, I believe, to the experience that many persons have when they read a novel for pleasure.

The sequential character of the discovery of the text's (provisional) meaning is the rule of the first reading. "That which the poetic text, thanks to its aesthetic character, provisionally offers to understanding proceeds from its process-like effect; for this reason it cannot be directly deduced from a description of its final structure as 'artifact', however comprehensively this might have construed its 'levels'"[17] — and, one could add, its divisions or segments. These will have to have emerged in sequence. Not only Jauss and Iser, but also Barthes, Ricoeur, and Riffaterre have spoken of this kind of reading in terms of musical performance: The reader performs the meaning of the text.[18] While the first reading could be many readings and need not be empirically and absolutely the first, it will remain a process.[19] What is required is the *perspective* of the first reading.[20]

The poem constitutes the primary hermeneutic whole that is to be read. In

---

17. Jauss 1982a: 140.

18. Barthes 1977c: 162; Iser 1978: 27; Jauss 1982a: 145; Ricoeur 1981: 159: "reading is like the execution of a musical score"; Riffaterre 1983: 4. Cf. Johnson 1992: 209–10. Also Smith 1974: 179: "The text of any poem is to be interpreted, in the first instance, as, in effect, a score or stage directions for the performance of a purely verbal act that exists only in being thus performed." Conte (1994a: xx) also uses the same metaphor, but with a different view of the matter, speaking of "correct" performance.

19. Cf. Iser 1978: 108–14 on the "wandering viewpoint" (wandering because the text can never be grasped as a simultaneous whole) and the synthesizing activity of the reader. Indeed all of Iser 1978 is, in one way or another, on the process character of reading.

20. Jauss 1982a: 148.

the case of Horace, this whole is a single ode, not a book of odes, still less the total oeuvre of Horace.[21] And yet, reading through collections of poems, like the books of Horace's odes or of Propertius's elegies, the reader will create new wholes. The distinction between the individual ode as a whole and the larger wholes that readers stitch together as they read one ode after another lies at the heart of Michèle Lowrie's book on narrative in Horace.[22] The poem as hermeneutic whole is not a pretense[23] but the fact of the matter for anyone who reads in the hope of aesthetic and cognitive experience, as distinguished, say, from the mere desire to participate in scholarly debate or for some other strictly professional goal. Even if my goal is to understand Horace in general, for the purpose, say, of a history of Roman literature, I first have to understand each poem on its own. Because each poem is a single and unique artifact, it cannot be subsumed under a rule or a concept but requires the individual act of understanding here called reading.[24] Further, the reader who in reading "performs" the meaning of the poem submits himself to the conditions of any performance. He knows that his will be replaced by some future performance, perhaps even by his own, for why should his performance be the same at age sixty as it was at age thirty-five?[25] The reading is not the reader, any more than the poem is the poet. Once again, the difference between reading and various strictly disciplinary approaches to a poem is apparent.

Although it might seem that intertextuality destroys the whole of the individual poem, creating a new and indeterminate whole in the relation between two or more texts, the process of reading will in the first place — that is, in the aesthetic perspective — make the effort to reconstruct a fuller text as it actualizes unfixed, unpredictable intertextual patterns.[26] Of course, something may be left over, apparently "undecidable," that will open the way to a new reading in a new whole or in a new indeterminacy. But the reading of intertextual quotations undoubtedly poses obstacles to the process just described, though ob-

21. Some may wonder why it was necessary to state what seems an obvious point. See Syndikus 1993.

22. Lowrie 1997b: 30 n. 26.

23. Contrary to Nauta 1994: 223.

24. On the distinction between rule-based subsumption and individual act of understanding, see Edmunds 1998.

25. Consider the anecdote told by Barchiesi (1997: 211–12) on the appearance and disappearance of intertextuality in the same poem at different periods of the same reader's life.

26. Ben-Porat 1976. I have adopted some of the diction of her concluding paragraph. What is true of intertextuality is also true of "seriality," self-reference, and recurrence in the *Odes*. On these features, see Mauch 1986: 184–85.

stacles in principle no greater than nonintertextual poetic phenomena might pose — hyperbaton, morphological oddity, figures of speech, rare words, and so forth. All of these retard reading[27] and call for rereading. Even the separate readings that, following Jauss, I am distinguishing here will each consist of multiple readings.

Who is the reader who consents to the conditions of reading?

> The first reading, limited to the horizon of aesthetic perception, is not literally first but is rather a reconstruction of a first reading. *The reader is not naive* but has read other lyric poems, in Latin and in other languages, and is, by the standards of his own culture, an educated man or woman. Certainly he or she can read Latin well enough to read the poem. In the first reading, however, this reader suspends detailed historical information, and refrains from interrupting the reading to do research. Standard grammars, commentaries, and dictionaries will be the only supports, and information from such sources will have been absorbed in the actual readings that go to make up the idealized first reading.[28]

Nothing precludes the possibility that the reader, so defined, of a Roman poem will already know, say, a Greek poem to which the Roman poem alludes. He will either simply be aware of the intertextual relation or he will have more precise knowledge of it.[29] In either case, intertextuality belongs to the experience of the first reading, and the reader will attempt to integrate the allusion(s) into his perception of the poem as an evolving whole. If the reader is ignorant of the Greek poem, a first reading can still be successful, because, for reasons just given, the perception of intertextuality is not absolutely necessary to the meaningfulness of the poem. Intertextuality would, in this case, be a matter for the second or third reading.

The intertextual dimension of a Roman poem is, then, in the first place historical information that the reader may or may not possess at the time of the first reading,[30] and intertextuality thus, as said, discriminates between one

---

27. Compagnon 1979: 72.

28. Edmunds 1992: 3. I have now added emphasis. The phrase "suspends detailed historical information" I now regret. It has caused misunderstanding. I did not and do not mean that the reader uses no historical information of any kind in the first reading.

29. For the distinction between awareness and knowledge, see Riffaterre 1990: 56–57.

30. Denis Feeney at the meeting of the American Philological Association, on December 28, 1993, especially complained about the sophistication of the reader who knows the Anacreontic intertext of Hor. *Odes* 1.23 (about which I had been speaking) and the references to the various editions, believing that I had somehow contradicted my definition of the reader.

reader and another.[31] The same is true of other kinds of historical information. Every reader of an ancient text needs a considerable amount of it — "aesthetic perception is intertwined with historical experience"[32] — but not all educated readers will have the same historical information, and thus one first reading will differ from another. If I know or think that I know that Roman houses did not have windows, this information or misinformation may shape my first reading of Horace *Odes* 1.9 (*Vides ut alta*). It is the kind of thing that a reader brings to a first reading.[33]

First readings differ from one another not only because of differences from one educated reader to another with respect to historical information. Different readers will perform the meaning of the text differently, to use the musical metaphor previously evoked. In particular, they will differ in the way they fill in the "virtual dimension" of the text.[34] As an example of performance, one can cite the Horatian scholar Eduard Fraenkel. He says of his interpretation of *Odes* 1.27 (*Natis in usum laetitiae scyphis*):

> To bring into relief the dramatic character of the ode, I have inserted into my summary, as it were, stage directions. I have not, however, invented anything but only made explicit what is implied in the text itself. Although the ode contains nothing but the words addressed by the poet partly to the *sodales* in general and partly to the brother of Megilla, Horace's consummate skill enables him to make us see what is going on round the speaker and even to hear some of the utterances of the others. This subtle and consistent building up of a dramatic structure in a lyric poem is certainly not in the manner of Anacreon or, for that matter, any archaic poet, but bears the stamp of a later age.[35]

31. Nauta (1994: 227–28) presupposes that, on Jauss's view, there would be a homogeneity of the horizons of readers at any given time, and observes that interpreters "negotiate" their horizons. Nauta thus, in the somewhat abrupt conclusion of his essay, leaves a large theoretical question open. I would say that there will be some degree of homeogeneity, which will be clearer to future generations, and some degree of difference from one reader to another, which will partly derive — and here I agree with Nauta — from "what they know or think they know about the horizon of the past."

32. Jauss 1982a: 148.

33. To conform with the conventions of classical scholarship and indeed with the demands of editors, it will be necessary, in the published form of a first reading, to cite one's source(s) for things like Roman windows (and also the editions that one has used, etc.). Unfortunately for the method I am describing, the first reading then looks like a conventional scholarly presentation in which evidence and authority for positive results are being stated.

34. Edmunds 1992: 28. The phrase is Iser's.

35. Fraenkel 1957: 181. He cites Wheeler 1934: 204–5 on Catullus for the same practice. Cf. Lowrie 1997a: 26 on *Odes* 1.27.

Fraenkel as philologist must insist that he has invented nothing, referring to "the text itself," but his procedure is that of the hermeneutical reader as here defined. Another reader might perceive the "dramatic structure" differently. For example, while Fraenkel imagines the brother of Megilla whispering in Horace's ear, someone else will imagine the boy as making his confession to the whole company of guests.[36] To take a concise example from another ode, the position of the speaker and his interlocutor at the opening of Horace *Odes* 1.9 is not described by the poet and must be inferred. "The text itself" gives no help. According to H. P. Syndikus's stage directions, the speaker and Thaliarchus are outside, looking at the winter landscape (stanza 1), and then go indoors (stanza 2). According to my reading, they are already indoors. But, although each of us has given an interpretive reading, Syndikus believes that he is stating a fact that "Parallelstellen" and authority ("so Bentley") confirm.[37] My reading was influenced by the intertextual relation of the opening of *Odes* 1.9 to Alcaeus 338 (Lobel and Page) with its indoor setting.

A First Reading of Tibullus 1.1

The position of the speaker or persona of a Roman poem, that is, as represented in the poem, can be curiously vague, leaving much unsaid, and readers' efforts to fill in the blanks, the *virtual dimension*, will result in quite different but sometimes equally plausible readings. In Chapter 4, difficulties posed by the detachment of the persona in some poems are considered, and that discussion will be anticipated here in a first reading of Tibullus 1.1. Duncan Kennedy has offered a reading of this poem that takes its departure from the question of representation.[38] He begins by asking what the "facts," the "realities" are that underlie the series of hopes expressed in the opening lines? My answer to this question is somewhat different from his, and is offered as an illustration of how varying first readings can emerge from the same, or almost the same kind of, observations.

The speaker of Tibullus 1.1 begins by dismissing the accumulation of gold,

---

36. Fraenkel 1957: 181; cf. Quinn 1980: 174 on lines 17–20.

37. Syndikus 1993: 216: "Wenn man wie E. [Edmunds] mit Nisbet-Hubbard *vides ut* als Frage auffaßt, kann sie, wie die Parallelstellen zeigen, nur im Angesicht der Landschaft ausgesprochen sein. Aber auch eine Feststellung (so Bentley) kann nur unmittelbar nach dem optischen Eindruck geäußert werden."

38. Kennedy 1993: 13–15.

the holding of large estates, and military campaigning (the source of the gold?). He leaves it to others. Content with a stay-at-home, humble, inactive way of life, he prefers to be a farmer, working with his own hands (1–10). He tells of his scrupulous piety, point by point. When he comes to the Lares, an autobiographical "fact" emerges. His Lares are the guardians of an estate that was once prosperous but is now reduced. They will get a lamb instead of the heifer they got before (19–24). Why have things gone badly? What happened? No answer is forthcoming. Another, more important change has taken place in the speaker's life, which he signals with *Iam . . . iam* (25). Now he hopes to be able to be content with the little that he has and not always to be committed to the long march (as he apparently was committed in the past) (25–26). He is in some life passage, as yet unspecified. He returns to his hopes, or rather now his plans, for farming. He refers to customary practices of his: Here (*hic*) it is my wont to perform the rite of purification for my shepherd every year and to win the favor of Pales by sprinkling him with milk (35–36).

The theme of reduced means and humble life returns, but now, rather obliquely, appears the change that was signaled by *Iam . . . iam* (25): He has his mistress to share his bed with him (46), and that, it now appears, is why his days as a soldier are over. The bonds of a pretty girl hold him at home. Let Messalla decorate his house with the spoils of war (51–55). The opposition of the opening lines between the rich landholder and the humble farmer, the military man and the homebody, is now reformulated: On the humble side, it is now the farmer-lover. At this point, the speaker proceeds to identify himself in a series of topoi from elegiac poetry: He is the *exclusus amator* (56); he sets love above his good name (57–58); he imagines Delia mourning for him at his funeral (59–68); let's live and love while we may, he says (69–72); now is the time to break down doors and get into brawls (73–74). Messalla, to whom this elegiac dossier is addressed (53–54), does not, then, lack evidence for the speaker's new life-style and rejection of the military life, to which he returns in conclusion (75–77). Because much of the elegiac lover's behavior seems to require an urban setting, the dossier has to be taken as symbolic, not as belonging to the "real" setting of the speaker, which is the small farm. He seems to reassert his rusticity in the closing lines, when he says that he is "carefree with the heap of goods that he has collected" (*composito securus acervo*, 77).

In comparing my first reading with Kennedy's, I find that the greatest difference between us is in our understanding of the situation of the speaker, whom Kennedy takes to be abroad on military service, so that everything the speaker says is in the nature of a revery. To state the matter in terms of the theory of persona that I propose in Chapter 4, Kennedy sees a consistently detached persona, while I see a movement from a detached to an engaged persona, or a juxtaposition of the two, as in the examples from Ovid and Catullus that I discuss. Our readings were comparable in the first place, however, because Kennedy's was *temporal*, not *spatial*. He did not begin from the perspective, often found in discussion of this poem, of two "halves." Nor did he begin with the text, followed, for example, by Paul Murgatroyd in his commentary, in which lines 25–32 are transposed to follow line 6.[39] It proved possible to read the poem without this transposition.

Second Reading

To continue now with the series of readings, the first is the basis for the second, which looks to questions posed by the first and to "significance still left open," "still unfulfilled significance."[40] It is a reflective rereading of a kind familiar to anyone who reads lyric poetry. Here I am speaking of a reader contemporary with me, though rereading was also familiar to Roman readers, as Horace *Satires* 1.10 shows. The questions to which the reader returns in the second reading come from the first reading. These questions may be replaced by new ones, but they all go back to the first reading. There is thus a crucial difference in starting point between philology and hermeneutics. Philology proceeds either from problems already defined in the scholarship on the text or from the observation of particular problems, and it typically proceeds in defiance of the hermeneutic circle. Omitting reading from its method, it tends to neglect the whole.

There is also a crucial difference in starting point between hermeneutics, on the one hand, and formalism or structuralism, on the other. The latter approaches, far from neglecting the whole, determine the whole retrospectively as a pattern (e.g., of images) or in terms of the paradigmatic (in contrast to the syntagmatic) or some other structure. The hermeneutic first reading is prospective, not retrospective, and therefore the hermeneutic second reading, while it answers the need for retrospection, is grounded in a dynamic, aesthetic perspective.[41] Formalist, structuralist, and now deconstructive approaches all

39. Murgatroyd 1980.
40. Jauss 1982a: 141, 145.
41. Cf. the critique of structuralist plot models by Ronen 1990.

depend, implicitly or explicitly, on an Archimedean stance of the reader, who somehow knows what he has to know about a poem before he begins to read it and can therefore supposedly read backward as well as forward. This reader is a *sujet connaissant*, for whom the poetic text is an object posed for scientific inquiry.[42] The text is conceived of spatially and analyzed in visual terms.[43] For the first two hermeneutic readings, which are performances, the poem evolves in time, and is apprehended as sound, not as space.

As for a second reading of Tibullus 1.1, which will not be executed here, I would want to return to the apparently contingent "autobiographical" references by the speaker to the decline in his fortunes (19–22, 41–42). Why is the speaker not just poor but poor though once rich? What do his *reduced* fortunes have to do with the rest of the poem? Another question concerns the series of elegiac topoi with which the poem ends. They define the farmer or would-be farmer as a lover, but how are these two identities linked? Does being a lover require him to be a farmer? Or is it that love of Delia makes hardscrabble farming attractive?

Third Reading

The third, historical reading tries to establish the original audience's horizon of expectation. Jauss's formula for this reading is as follows: It begins "by seeking out the questions (most often unexplicit ones) to which the text was a response in its time." He continues: "An interpretation of a literary text as a response should include two things: its response to expectations of a formal kind, such as the literary tradition prescribed for it before its appearance; and its response to questions of meaning such as they could have posed themselves within the historical life-world of its first readers."[44]

An obvious objection to this procedure is that one's access to "the original

---

42. For *sujet connaissant*, cf. Chapter 1, note 53.

43. Cf. Edmunds 1992: 107–8. One of the first major steps away from (I would say: beyond) New Criticism was Stanley Fish's critique (1970) of the spatial conception underlying the New Critical "poem itself," reprinted in Fish 1980: 21–67.

44. Jauss 1982a: 146. Bruno Gentili states the link between the first and the third readings with characteristic perspicuity: "Uno dei princìpi fondamentali dell'ermeneutica è quello di leggere un testo inanzitutto nei termini della nostra esperienza personale perché abbia senso: solo partendo da questa comprensione iniziale si può arrivare ad un'interpetazione del significato e della funzione che il testo ebbe o doveva avere nel suo contesto originale e nell'orizzonte d'attesa del pubblico cui era destinato" (1999: 26).

audience's horizon of expectation" is no more direct than to the text one is trying to interpret.[45] One will have to use other texts, and these will have to be interpreted, with the same importations from one's own historical situation as in the case of the first reading of the target text. No "objective" reconstruction, against which one could measure one's reading of the target text, seems possible.[46] The answer to this objection is quite simple. Although the reconstructed horizon may not be objective, it is, in the first place, inevitably different from my own horizon of expectation, and the difference can usually be grounded in an expanded context of inferable ancient reception. Vengeance on the Parthians is no concern of mine, but a good many poems of Propertius and Horace and one of Vergil (*G.* 3.30–31) show that it was a concern of their readers, even if only because it was a concern of Octavian.[47]

I can complete a first and second reading of Horace *Odes* 1.36 (*Et ture et fidibus iuvat*) without knowledge of its literary tradition, which in fact has to be mainly reconstructed from poems written *after* it was published and which very few readers are now likely to have firmly in mind on a first encounter with *Odes* 1.36. The third reading of this ode attempts to establish the expectations of its first readers as regards this literary tradition. In the case of Tibullus 1.1, I can get a sense of its meaning for its first readers, quite different from anything that occurred to me in my first reading, by reading it in the context of other renunciations of traditional Roman values, or of urban tastes, in favor of rustic life: Vergil's *Georgics* (see 2.495–99 for the theme); Propertius 2.19 (to Cynthia in the country); and Horace *Epodes* 2 (the attitudes expressed by Alfius) and 16 (the golden age vision of "happy fields"). I might also, for example, try to figure out how much humor the poem once had. Its humor, if any, which was more or less lost on Kennedy and me, might emerge from comparison with Horace *Epistles* 1.4, where one hears about a certain Tibullus's riches. If it is Albius Tibullus and if Horace is reliable on this point, then one can imagine how the incongruous self-representation of Tibullus in 1.1 would have affected the poem's first readers.

Example of a Third Reading: Ovid's *Metamorphoses*

Ovid in the *Tristia* calls the attention of a particular reader, Augustus, to a particular aspect of the *Metamorphoses;* and Quintilian and both Senecas

---

45. Fowler 1993: 88.
46. Cf. the articulation of this objection to Jauss's method by Nauta 1994: 214–15.
47. "A pretext in his policy": Syme 1939: 302.

offer comments on the poem. These various responses, solicited and un-solicited, reveal that, in the case of this poem, the two questions posed by Jauss are the same, or, rather, that the answer is the same. More fundamentally, the discussion of these responses shows that a reading, at least in outline, contemporary with the ancient poem can be reconstructed, one that departs from the norms of twentieth- and twenty-first-century reading, whether scholarly or interpretive.

Tristia 2 is a plea to Augustus for forgiveness of the two crimes that caused Ovid's exile. Of these two crimes, *carmen et error* "a poem and a mistake" (2.207), the latter is notoriously vague, and the former is certain — it is the *Ars amatoria*. In referring to this poem, Ovid is led to refer to another poem, which Augustus has not, apparently, yet seen, the *Metamorphoses:*

> quid referam libros, illos quoque, crimina nostra,
>   mille locis plenos nominis esse tui?
> inspice maius opus, quod adhuc sine fine reliqui,
>   in non credendos corpora versa modos:
> invenies vestri praeconia nominis illic,
>   invenies animi pignora certa mei.   (61–66)

Why should I mention that my books, even the ones that are held against me, are full of your name in a thousand places? Consider the greater work, which until now I have left unfinished, the bodies changed in incredible ways: you will find there declarations of your name, you will find sure pledges of my loyalty.

The phrase *maius opus* echoes Vergil's invocation to the Muses at the beginning of the second half of the *Aeneid* (*maius opus moveo,* 7.45). My new poem, Ovid suggests (with a bravado that is unstifled even in his present circumstances), is comparable with Vergil's epic (an already established classic), and Ovid thus makes a generic distinction between this and the earlier books of poetry (i.e., the *Ars amatoria*), even as he stresses the continuity in his loyalty to Augustus. But it is difficult for me to see how Augustus, if he did in fact read the finished *Metamorphoses* at some point in the five years or so remaining to him after the date of *Tristia* 2 (9 C.E.), could have missed Ovid's hybridization of Vergil's epic with amatory poetry in the part of the *Metamorphoses* in which Ovid's relation to Vergil is closest, his "Aeneid" (13.623–14.608). Is there a way to know if Augustus or another contemporary would have perceived this feature of Ovid's poem?

A clue is provided by *lascivia* (wantonness), Ovid's trademark as a love poet. Later in the plea to Augustus just quoted from, Ovid asks

> at cur in nostra nimia est lascivia Musa,
>   curve meus cuiquam suadet amare liber?
> nil nisi peccatum manifestaque culpa fatenda est.
>   paenitet ingenii iudiciique mei.   (313–16)

But why is there is so much wantonness in my Muse? Why does my book persuade anyone to love? There is nothing for me to do but confess my sin and my obvious guilt. I am ashamed of my wit and my judgment.

The word *lascivia* was in fact programmatic in the *Ars amatoria,* where Apollo dubbed Ovid *lascivi praeceptor amoris,* "a teacher of wanton love" (*AA* 2.497). Elsewhere Ovid said, *Nil nisi lascivi per me discuntur amores,* "only wanton loves are taught by me" (*AA* 3.27).

The clue that I am following leads first to Quintilian, not a contemporary of Ovid but still within the same century as the *Metamorphoses.* He gives a summary evaluation of the poet:

> Lascivus quidem in herois quoque Ovidius et nimium amator ingenii sui, laudandus tamen partibus.   (10.88)

Wanton, to be sure, is Ovid, even in his hexameters, and too much a lover of his own wit, though praiseworthy in parts.

The hexameters are, of course, the *Metamorphoses,* and Quintilian implicitly makes the same distinction between the amatory poetry and the epic that Ovid made in *Tristia* 2, in the passage just quoted.[48] In Quintilian's view, there is no doubt that the love poet is still present in the epic.

Would Augustus have failed to perceive the same thing? And if he objected to the *Ars amatoria,* would he not have objected, in particular, to Ovid's "Aeneid" in the *Metamorphoses* on the same grounds? The answers to the question of the literary tradition of Ovid's "Aeneid" and to the question of its meaning, at least for Augustus, would have been the same: wantonness.

The moral fault, as it would have been perceived by Augustus, is, under

---

48. Cf. Martial 3.20.6: "Wanton in elegiac verse or severe in heroic [epic]?" *(lascivus elegis an severus herois?).*

another aspect, an aesthetic one. The conflation of the moral and the aesthetic in matters of literary style is not instinctive for the modern reader but is normal for Romans in theory of oratory. "As the man, so his speech" (*Qualis autem homo ipse esset, talis eius esse sermonem;* Cic. *Tusc.* 5.47). Seneca argues at length in *Epistle* 114 that literary style is a sign of moral character. The tradition goes back at least as far as Plato's *Republic* (400d6–7). Poets did not want to be held to the same principle.[49] To take up the clue of *lascivia* again, already in book 4 of the *Institutio Oratoria,* in his discussion of the structure of the oration, Ovid had occurred to Quintilian as a negative example:

> Quotiens autem prooemio fuerimus usi, tum sive ad expositionem transibimus sive protinus ad probationem, id debebit in principio postremum esse, cui commodissime iungi initium sequentium poterit. illa vero frigida et puerilis est in scholis adfectatio, ut ipse transitus efficiat aliquam utique sententiam et huius velut praestigiae plausum petat, ut Ovidius lascivire in Metamorphosesin solet, quem tamen excusare necessitas potest, res diversissimas in speciem unius corporis colligentem.   (4.1.76–77)

> However on all occasions when we have employed the *exordium,* whether we intend to pass to the *statement of facts* or directly to the *proof,* our intention should be mentioned at the end of the introduction, with the result that the transition to what follows will be smooth and easy. There is indeed a pedantic and childish vogue in the schools of marking the transition by some epigram and seeking to win applause by this feat of legerdemain. Ovid is given to this form of affectation [*lascivire*] in the *Metamorphoses,* but there is some excuse for him owing to the fact that he is compelled to weld together subjects of the most diverse nature so as to form a continuous whole.[50]

Here *lascivia* is Quintilian's way of characterizing the transitions in the *Metamorphoses.* These have often attracted the admiration of modern critics for their skill and cleverness. Quintilian mostly disapproves.

The same aesthetic fault is pointed out by Seneca in the third book of his *Natural Questions,* in which he discusses the waters of the earth. In the last four chapters, he explains how the "fatal day of deluge" (*fatalis dies diluvii,* 27.1) will come about, the cyclical deluge that destroys all life on earth. It begins, says Seneca, with rain; then snows melt; rivers leave their banks; the

49. Cat. 16.5–6; Ov. *Trist.* 2.353–58; Plin. *Ep.* 4.14.5.
50. Butler 1921: 47–49 (the emphasis is Butler's).

sea overflows its shores; men flee to the tops of mountains. Here he quotes Ovid's *Metamorphoses* by way of illustration, but not without criticism of his source:

Ergo insularum modo eminent

montes, et sparsas Cycladas augent,

ut ait ille poetarum ingeniosissimus egregie. Sicut illud pro magnitudine rei dixit:

omnia pontus erat, deerant quoque litora ponto,

ni tantum impetum ingenii et materiae ad pueriles ineptias reduxisset:

nat lupus inter oves, fulvos vehit unda leones.

Non est res satis sobria lascivire devorato orbe terrarum.   (3.27.13–14; *Met.* 2.264; 1.292; 1.304)

So mountains rise up like islands

"and they increase the number of the scattered Cyclades,"

as the most ingenious of poets says beautifully. Just as he also said this, appropriate to the magnitude of his theme:

"All was sea, and the sea had no shores."

Yet he reduced his great inspiration and subject to childish silliness:

"The wolf swims among the sheep, the wave carries tawny lions."

It is not a sufficiently serious attitude to make fun of the whole world now swallowed up.[51]

The unrestrained cleverness of Ovid was all too conspicuous. Even those who obviously enjoy it have to censure it as *lascivia*.

51. The translation is that of Corcoran 1971, with slight changes.

Seneca's comments well illustrate the difference between the perspective, on the one hand, of the third, historical reading that I am reconstructing, and, on the other, any first or second reading that might now be performed. Anyone who now reads the *adynata* in Ovid's description of the flood in book 1 of the *Metamorphoses* will be intrigued by the subtle, elaborate pattern of allusions that link this passage to *adynata* in Vergil's *Eclogue* 8, and, through Vergil, to Theocritus.[52] The other example that Seneca takes from the flood in book 1 (line 292) is, if anything, an even more explicit allusion to Vergil, this time to the *Aeneid* (3.126–27).[53]

Ovid's lack of self-restraint is also pointed out by the Elder Seneca, a contemporary of the poet. He tells an anecdote: Some of Ovid's friends asked if they could suppress three of his lines, and he asked in return to exempt three lines. Each wrote out the three lines he had in mind; when the choices were examined, the three lines were the same in every case. (Seneca quotes two of the lines, which are both from Ovid's elegiac poems.) What his friends liked least, Ovid liked most. Seneca concludes:

Apparet summi ingenii viro non iudicium defuisse ad compescendam licentiam carminum suorum, sed animum.   (*Contr.* 2.2.12)

It is clear that to a man of consummate wit, not judgement but the will to restrain the licence of his poems was lacking.[54]

Once again, the gift is recognized. The closely related fault is here characterized as *licentia,* which can apply just as well to morals. This term had long since marked the difference between orators and the poets. The latter used *verborum licentia liberior* — "a freer license in the use of words" (Cic. *De orat.* 1.70).

For a final example of how Ovid was read by contemporaries or by the next generation, I return to the Younger Seneca, in particular to a place in his

52. With *Met.* 1.292: *omnia pontus erat,* cf. Verg. *Ecl.* 8.52: *omnia vel medium fiat mare* ("let all become sea, even mid-sea") and note the singular verb; with *Met.* 1.304, cf. Verg. *Ecl.* 8.52 and context; Theocritus 1.132–36.

53. Seneca's third example, from *Met.* 2.264, is, apparently without Seneca's realizing it, inconsistent with the other two: It describes the drying up of, not the flooding of, the ocean, which was caused by the wild course of Phaëthon's chariot. Mountains that were invisible before rose up as the ocean contracted.

54. In *Contr.* 9.5.17, he says that Ovid *nescit quod bene cessit relinquere* and quotes an example from *Met.* 13.503–5.

Apocolocyntosis. At a council of the gods, Juppiter, in the manner of a Roman senator, declares:

> censeo uti diuus Claudius ex hac die deus sit ita uti ante eum quis optimo iure factus sit, eamque rem ad Metamorphosis Ouidi adiciendam.   (9.6)

> I propose that from this day forth Claudius be a god, to enjoy that honor with all its appurtenances in as full a degree as any before him, and that a note to that effect be added to Ovid's *Metamorphoses.*[55]

The joke presupposes that Seneca's reader recalls the several apotheoses of book 15 of the *Metamorphoses,* which, in Seneca's conceit, can be added to as if in the official *tabulae pontificum.* It suggests that the prolixity of Roman themes in the final book of the poem was already felt,[56] not to mention the humorous treatment of the apotheoses that modern readers perceive,[57] and, to return to the passage from the *Tristia* quoted at the beginning of this section, Ovid's declarations of Augustus's name and the sure pledges of his loyalty to the emperor are not likely to have carried conviction.

The negative Augustan reading that has been inferred here, and "read back" from later sources in the first century C.E., has little or nothing to do with "Augustanism" or "non-Augustanism" as these terms are usually employed in discussion of the *Metamorphoses.* One has to think not of politics, political ideology, or support for the regime, but of taste, life-style, and world view. As for the *Amores* and the *Ars amatoria,* these poems "portrayed the normal habits of high society in everything that was distasteful to Caesar Augustus."[58] The salience of the spirit of these poems in Ovid's "Aeneid," that is, in the most refractive context imaginable, would have had an unmistakable Hellenistic look that connected Ovid with a counterculture, of which the foremost representative was Tiberius, whose taste in poets ran to Euphorion, Rhianus, and Parthenius.[59]

Not only did the apotheoses and the name of Augustus in book 15 fail to

---

55. Translated by Rouse in Heseltine and Rouse 1987.
56. Cf. Galinsky 1975: 210–17.
57. Tissol 1993: 77.
58. Syme 1978: 192. Other formulations of the same idea: Fabre 1986: 182; Due 1974: 60 ("But Augustus had not saved the state in order to enable Ovid and his kind to practise *la dolce vita.* Of course people were supposed to be satisfied with the New Order, but Ovid was too satisfied and in a thoroughly unsatisfactory way").
59. Suet. *Tib.* 70. Cf. Syme 1978: 107–8, 189.

make amends, but when Ovid, in the speech of Pythagoras, ostensibly repairs the absence of prophecy and Roman destiny in his reworking books 3 and 6 of the *Aeneid,* he puts Rome, now rising on the banks of the Tiber, in a list of cities that are nothing but another category of things "changed into new forms" (*in species translata novas;* 15.420). Rome is the last city in the list; the others — Troy, Sparta, Mycenae, Thebes, Athens — are now little but names. The prophecy of Helenus that Pythagoras proceeds to quote, culminating in the apotheosis of Augustus (15.439–49), is therefore implicitly qualified: Rome will someday meet the same fate as the other great cities.[60] Metamorphosis, a constant feature of Ovid's "Aeneid," returns as a cosmic principle in the speech of Pythagoras — "all things change" (*omnia mutantur;* 15.165) — the foundation of the aesthetics and ethics of *lascivia.*[61]

Questions of literary tradition and of meaning would not have been distinct for Ovid's first readers. Quintilian's phrase "subjects of the most diverse nature" (*res diversissimas*) need not refer to contents alone. These are heterogeneous not only in themselves, simply as stories, but also with respect to genre, as would have been at least as obvious to Quintilian as it is to readers at the beginning of the twenty-first century. Genres are not merely artistic but carry ideological weight. The elegiac in the epic was yet another example of the unquenchable *lascivia* of Ovid, and the meaning of the *Metamorphoses* would have been taken by Ovid's contemporaries as counter to official Augustan values. Ovid had already pointed out to Augustus that Vergil himself, "your blessed author of the Aeneid," had "put 'arms and the man' in a Carthaginian bed" (*ille tuae felix Aeneidos auctor / contulit in Tyrios arma virumque toros; Tristia* 2.533–34).[62]

The Philologist's Reader and the Philologist-Reader Again

I return to the philological reader discussed at the beginning of this chapter and in particular to Conte's definition of the reader as reader-addressee. Conte demonstrates this notion in his essay on Lucretius, "Instructions for a Sublime

60. Though perhaps there was sanction for this pessimism in the proverbial status of *Il.* 4.164–65 (= 6.448–49), which Scipio was said to have quoted, with reference to Rome, as he gazed on the ruins of Carthage (App. *Pun.* 132): "The day will come when holy Troy perishes and Priam and the people of Priam, him of the goodly ashen spear."

61. On the amorality of the *Metamorphoses,* see Solodow 1988: 157–76.

62. See Casali 1995: 66–69 on *Met.* 14.78–81, Ovid's summary of *Aen.* 4, which, Casali shows, brings out an "embarrassing," anti-Augustan or non-Augustan aspect of Aeneas.

Reader: Form of the Text and Form of the Addressee in Lucretius' *De rerum natura.*" He informs the reader of the translation that "the prophetic voice of Empedocles . . . reechoes in the verses of Lucretius."[63] But can the reader of the translation hear this voice, as Conte impressively demonstrates that he has heard it? Can the reader of the translation become the ideal, sublime reader?

A more serious objection to Conte's notion of the reader concerns Conte's own relation to the reader-addressee of *DRN*. Is he that reader? He gives no sign that he could be the Epicurean catechumen that he describes. "Put into the state of receptivity by appeals and invectives, the reader is ready to admire and receive the description as a privileged revelation."[64] This is not Conte, who reads from a privileged, neutral third position, that of the philologist.[65] "I am a philologist."[66]

He sees it as his task not to become but to define the reader-addressee. Consider once more the sublime reader whom Conte defines as the reader of *DRN*. If this reader is to be sublime, he must not be distracted by the literariness of a densely intertextual surface. Conte allows that "Lucretius ends up making different discursive structures collude with one another,"[67] and he mentions in particular the philosophic diatribe, with its sarcasm and moralism and its favorite themes of misery, exile, old age, and death.[68] But Conte's desire to define a certain kind of reader-addressee causes him to rule out the force of the diatribe in *DRN*. The diatribe is "a field of expressive counterforces that dissent from the sublime but almost always end up being cancelled out by it."[69] For the sake, then, of a particular "figure of the recipient as anticipated by the text," Conte makes choices within the "structures" (note the plural) of the text. This "prefiguration of the reader" in the text is, then, an interpretation, not a positive finding about the text, and Conte is a reader-interpreter even when he thinks that he is a philologist.

The resemblance of Conte's philologist or "philologist-reader" to the her-

---

63. Conte 1994a: 9. This essay was originally published as the introduction to a translation of *DRN* published in the "Classici Rizzoli" in 1990.

64. Conte 1994a: 10.

65. Cf. note 11.

66. Conte 1994a: 131. The whole sentence: "I am a philologist who is happy with his job and is only trying to explain what he encounters in texts."

67. Conte 1994a: 31.

68. Conte is in fact the author of an important article on the diatribe in Lucretius: Conte 1966.

69. Conte 1994a: 32. The diatribe is precisely the aspect of *DRN* that causes engagement with this text at the end of the twentieth century. Consider, for example, Nussbaum's (1994) chapters on love, anger, and aggression in Lucretius.

meneutical reader that he repudiates emerges from a curious piece of intertextuality that is found in more or less the same words in three of Conte's works. I quote the wording from *The Rhetoric of Imitation*: "Readers . . . who approach the text are themselves already a plurality of texts and of different codes, some present and some lost or dissolved in that indefinite and generic fluid of literary language."[70] In the contexts in which Conte makes this statement, he is always insisting on the text as opposed to the author and on the distinction between the philologist and the historical addressee. It is odd, then, that Conte is alluding to a passage in the opening of Barthes's *S/Z*: "This 'I' which approaches the text is already a plurality of other texts, of codes which are infinite or, more precisely, lost (whose origin is lost)."[71]

Barthes's concept of the reader is, of course, diametrically opposed to Conte's. His manifesto in *S/Z* is that "the goal of literary work . . . is to make the reader no longer a consumer, but a producer of the text."[72] The effect of Conte's allusion to this alien position is to make Conte's readers think of him as a Barthian reader, though one would refrain from identifying him with Barthes's dissolved subject of reading. Indeed, the impact of Conte's work comes from his engagement as a particular reader (not a philologist) with Roman poetry in its subtler and more complex intertextual aspects. His success as a reader-interpreter is in spite of, not because of, his theoretical views on readership.

Text and Reader

The desideratum of a text-object stated in Chapter 1 is satisfied by the reader *in reading*. The interaction of text and reader creates the text-object. (Bennett's notion of reader-formations is apposite.) This is not a free creation. The reader described here belongs to a class or community, Stanley Fish's "interpretive community," to which the reading must make sense, whether or not the reading is accepted.[73] An absolutely arbitrary reading that could only be related to

---

70. Conte 1986: 29. Cf. Conte and Barchiesi 1989: 88; Conte 1994a: 137. Cf. Fedeli 1989: 377.

71. Barthes 1974: 10 = Barthes 1970: 16: "Ce 'moi' qui s'approache du texte est déjà lui-même une pluralité d'autres textes, de codes infinis, ou plus exactement: perdus (dont l'origine se perd)."

72. Barthes 1974: 4.

73. Fish 1980: 10–11, 147–73 ("Interpreting the *Variorum*"); cf. Jonathan Culler's "literary competence" (1980). For reception of Fish's notion in the field of classics, see Wills 1996: 32–33 and n. 55.

the individual psychology of the reader would not be countenanced except for special reasons, like those which cause parents to admire and display their children's artworks.[74] Furthermore, the hermeneutic sequence of readings provides a check on possible arbitrariness or error in the first reading: the second reading may entail historical research; the third, historicist one certainly does.[75] Ultimately, however, time is the test. Readings that are arbitrary or merely clever will fall by the wayside and will not go into the "formation and transformation of the aesthetic canon,"[76] which, in the case of Roman poetry, has a long, definable history wherein the relative value assigned various texts and poets has changed considerably and is still obviously changing. Readings that are successful will demonstrate, if not to the reader and his contemporaries, at least to later readers, the horizons of expectation within which these readings took place.[77]

Reading is constrained by interpretive communities. It is not constrained by some unchanging essence in the text, some intention left there in the auroral moment when the author said what he meant once and for all, or by some ideal reader somehow inserted there (I have commented previously on Conte's reader-addressee), or by an unchanging structure or design to which univocal, imperishable meaning is attached. In my view, no binarism of text and reader is possible and therefore no either-or decision has to be made. Meaning, including intertextual meaning, emerges from the interaction between the two.[78]

74. Cf. Iser 1978: 23–27.

75. Jauss 1982a: 146.

76. Jauss 1982a: 147.

77. And this is the answer to Nauta 1994: 219. The reader reads. He cannot be expected to read and simultaneously to observe himself reading from some detached scientific point of view that would disclose the horizon of the reading. The horizon is implicit in the reading.

78. Laird (1999: ch. 1, sec. v) conceiving the interpretive community in ideological terms and the text as discourse (i.e., implicated in power relations), reaches the same conclusion as I. He says: "An intertext is constituted by whoever sees it; it does not make sense to talk about whether it is 'readable or identifiable enough'. In my own view, the very detection of an intertext — no matter how palpable, demonstrable and well attested — is in the end ideologically determined." The quotation within this quotation is from Lyne 1994: 200.

FOUR

Persona

If intertextuality is not to be understood in relation to the poet, that is, to the empirical, historical person who produced the poem, if this source of intertextual phenomena is abandoned, to what can scholarship and criticism attribute them? The answer is that intertextuality, like every other element of a poem, is activated by the speaker or persona of the poem, who speaks for, but is not identical to, the poet, and it is activated in a reader. In this chapter, however, not the reader but various kinds of persona are the subject. In a narrative poem, furthermore, another scenario of intertextuality may present itself. A character or audience internal to the poem is seen to be engaged in interpreting a message of one kind or another. The question then arises, which this chapter also addresses, of intertextuality in the communication thus represented.

The temptation is strong to identify the poet speaking in the first-person singular with the real poet, but, even when the *I* of the poem represents himself as the poet of the poem, and even when the poet refers to himself by name, this *I* is not identical with the real poet but is a speaker or persona. As Paul Veyne said of Catullus's self-naming, the poet takes his own name as his stage name.[1] As I suggest in Chapter 6, poems would be impossible if names had to carry exactly the same sets of properties in poems as in the actual world, and this principle applies to the poet's name as much as to the name of a mountain, like *Soracte*.

Beside the poet as the speaker of the poem, the poet as persona of the real poet, the poet may appear in another way, as the implied poet.[2] Even when the

---

1. Veyne 1988: 174; cf. Fowler 1994: 246.
2. The expression "implied poet" is a variation of Wayne C. Booth's "implied author": Booth [1961] 1983: 151. Cf. the distinction between "implicit speaker" and "overt speaker" in Perry 1965: 13–16 and also Nehemas's (1981: 145 n. 36) "postulated author," the similarity of which to Booth's "implied author" he remarks.

persona is already the poet speaking in the first-person singular, the *I*-poet, the implied poet may emerge at the same time. In Ovid *Amores* 1.3, the speaker is the poet-lover. He is without noble lineage and wealth, but Apollo and the Muses are on his side. To win the addressee as his mistress would be to have "happy matter" (*materiem felicem,* 19) for his poems. But even in the midst of the poet-lover's protestations, the implied poet emerges. John Barsby remarks that the poet "is addressing the usual protestations of love to his girl, who is supposed to believe what he is saying, but at the same time he is looking over his shoulder, as it were, at the reader with an occasional broad wink."[3] Gordon Williams generalizes the phenomenon: "This is the situation with all of Ovid's writings, with due adjustment made for different genres. The poet is a speaker who stands in a real sense detached from what he is saying and who communicates with the audience over the heads of his characters, whether those characters are mythic or friends *or even the poet himself.*"[4] The implied speaker, as Barsby and Williams indicate, entails an implied reader, who is different from the persona's addressee (see Chapter 5).

Although the temptation is great to identify the implied poet with the real poet, as Barsby and Williams appear to do, and to believe that the real poet is somehow there in the poem, the implied poet is nothing but implied, and is no more present to the reader than the *I*-poet, who is as fictional as any other persona.[5] From the days of the archaic Greek grave inscriptions, which presupposed a reader's vocalization of their utterance,[6] no poet's voice has ever been heard as such, speaking directly, in an unmediated communication, but has always depended upon an iteration by someone else. This rule applies also to the earliest Western poetry, in which the *aoidos,* even in the most creative of his live performances, still reiterates in large measure someone else's (one says: the tradition's) voice. And it applies, too, to those archaic poems that can be considered speech acts, in which conventional force relies on conventional language. When poetry comes to be something for reading, the sequence of its

3. Barsby 1973: 55. For this interpretation, Barsby cites Curran 1966.

4. Williams 1992: 139 (my emphasis). Cf. Mitsis 1994, who refers, apropos of Lucretius, to the reader's "winking with the poet behind the back of" the addressee (128); see also (in the same volume) Schiesaro 1994: 133; and Williams 1973: 277: "we could say that Virgil's battle-scenes present his own self in the scenes of pathos and an 'anti-self,' a 'mask,' in the scenes of horror."

5. Cf. Booth [1961] 1983: 151: "This implied author is always distinct from the 'real man'—whatever we may take him to be—who creates a superior version of himself, a 'second self,' as he creates his work."

6. Svenbro 1988: 33–52; Nagy 1996: 35–36.

iterations becomes the history of its reception. But this very condition of iteration, though it means changes of understanding over time, is the background of a powerful fiction discovered by poets: the fiction of their immediate, unchanging presence, which can of course be enhanced by the construction of what Ellen Oliensis has called a "coterie-effect," luring the outsider to try to look in on a privileged intimacy from which he or she is excluded.[7]

In Chapter 2, I started a history of poetic performance, describing a first phase in which at least some poems were speech acts by poets and performers presented to their audiences. Even inscribed poems were "figurative performances," requiring vocalization. That phase came to an end at the somewhat arbitrary date of circa 550 B.C.E. Thereafter, I proposed, in written texts the poet or performer could have a new status as the *persona loquens* internal to the poem (not that performance simply came to an end). In other words, poems continued to have speakers or voices even if the living poet or performer was no longer present. An elegiac couplet inscribed on a bronze statuette of the late sixth century B.C.E. has been taken to symbolize the change.

πᾶσιν ἴσ᾽ ἀνθρώποι[ς] ὑποκρίνομαι ὅστις ἐ[ρω]τᾶι,
ὥς μ᾽ ἀνέθηκ᾽ Ἄνδρων Ἀντιφάν[ου]ς δεκάτην.
(*CEG* 286 = *IG* I² 410 = *IG* I³ 533 = 131 Friedländer)[8]

To all men, whoever asks me, I answer (verb *hupokrinesthai*) the same things, that Andrōn son of Antiphanes dedicated me as a tithe.

This inscription is, Jesper Svenbro points out, the first one to use the metaphor of the voice with regard to itself.[9] The metaphor is implicit in the verb *hupokrinesthai* "to answer." The conceit of the inscription is that it speaks on

---

7. Letter to author, Aug. 13, 1998. Consider, for example, the apparently autobiographical *Epistles* 1.19, usually taken as a record of the historical Horace's disappointment at the reception of his *Odes,* can more plausibly be read, Gordon Williams has argued, as a declaration of pride in his achievement. "The core of reality is a shadowy centre around which flicker the lively wit and the play of ideas" (1968: 27).

8. The editors of *IG* I³, David Lewis and Lilian Jeffery, say that Ἀντιφάνος (Ἀντιφάνους) cannot be read and is an impossible emendation. So for the second line they read: ὅς μ᾽ ἀνέθηκ᾽ ἀνδρῶν· ᾽Ἀντιφάνης δεκάτην᾽. My interpretation is not fundamentally affected. I have, for convenience of exposition, continued to use the reading of *IG* I² and *CEG* and so to refer to the "Andrōn inscription."

9. Svenbro 1990: 374. Cf., for the semantics of *hupokrinesthai,* Nagy 1990: 168 n. 95. My discussion relies on Svenbro, but I differ from him in regarding the silent reader not as "passive" and a "spectator" but as active and a performer.

its own, anticipating the question of imagined interlocuters; it does not require someone else's vocalization. Svenbro placed this inscription in a history of reading: It is an evidence that at least some readers were already capable of silent reading. He brings this evidence into relation with the well-known article by Bernard Knox on silent reading in the fifth century B.C.E. and also presents new arguments.[10] For Svenbro, silent reading means that the reader hears an inner voice when he reads, unlike the traditional reader, who needs the sound of his voice in order to grasp what a text is saying. For present purposes, in a discussion of the persona in Roman poetry, it is not primarily the reader or the history of reading but this inner voice that is of interest. What is this voice? It is a mental repetition of the voice perceived in the text, the voice that refers to itself as such in the inscription just quoted.

But still more is implicit in the Andrōn inscription. If the reader is a performer, the text is a "space," to borrow Svenbro's metaphor. "Scriptural space is a 'scene,'" he says.[11] The reader also has to imagine this scene as the one occupied by the persona. These two conditions for the reading of poetry, the persona and the dramatic setting, already implicit in the Andrōn inscription, were perhaps from the beginning in conflict with something explicit in that inscription: the claim that it always says the same thing to whoever comes along, to whoever asks. As suggested already, this claim managed to create the powerful fiction that the written text remains the same through all its iterations. Must one believe it? The inscription under discussion assumes that the question will always be the same: Whose statuette is this and why was it dedicated? But as the present comments have shown, these questions are now of slight interest. Readers like Svenbro have put new questions to the text and it has yielded new answers. What began on the statuette dedicated by Andrōn was not a history of self-identity but a history of reading. Another phase in this history of reading will be reached in Chapter 7.

While the implied poet, when present, speaks simultaneously with the persona, the latter may be varied within the same poem in other ways. Consider the opening of *Amores* 1.3, cited earlier for the implied poet:

10. Knox 1968. As Gilliard (1993) points out, there was already in Clark 1931 a good explanation of Augustine's apparent surprise when he saw Ambrose reading silently (*Confessions* 6.3.3–4). Gavrilov (1997) has reinterpreted the passage and maintained that silent reading was actually an everyday phenomenon well known to Augustine (62–66). Appendixes in Gavrilov's article (69–73) provide lists of evidence for silent reading in antiquity. New evidence for silent reading came from Burnyeat 1991, 1997, and also Gilliard 1997.

11. Svenbro 1990: 375, 378, 381.

Iusta precor: quae me nuper praedata puella est,
    aut amet aut faciet, cur ego semper amem.
a, nimium volui — tantum patiatur amari;
    audierit nostras tot Cytherea preces.
Accipe, per longos tibi qui deserviat annos;
    accipe, qui pura norit amare fide.   (1–6)

Just is my prayer. May the girl who has lately taken me as her prey either love me or give me cause to love her forever. Ah, I have asked too much — only let her endure to be loved. Let Cytherea hear my many prayers. Take one who would be your slave through long years. Take one who knows how to love with pure faith.[12]

The implied poet does not emerge until later in the poem. Here, at the outset, it is only a persona who describes himself in terms of a prayer. The first two lines are not, however, a direct prayer to Venus (e.g., "Venus, I pray that . . .") but a statement of his petition, in which the beloved appears in the third person ("It is my just prayer to Venus that my beloved . . ."). The speaker declares his desire. Except for a hint of urgency in the jussive subjunctives of line 2, the speaker's tone is declarative. In lines 3–4, a modulation begins, with the exclamation *a*, though the beloved remains in the third person, and Venus is not directly addressed. In lines 5–6, however, the speaker bursts out (note the repetition of *accipe*) in an entreaty addressed to the beloved in the second-person singular.[13] Lines 1–2 and lines 5–6 are two different modes of the persona, for which it might be useful to have two different names, and lines 3–4 are transitional, with the speaker's reflection on what he has just said.

The opening lines of Catullus 8 provide another example, this time of a rather stark juxtaposition of two modes of the persona:

Miser Catulle, desinas ineptire,
et quod vides perisse perditum ducas.
fulsere quondam candidi tibi soles,
cum ventitabas quo puella ducebat
amata nobis quantum amabitur nulla;
ibi illa multa cum iocosa fiebant

12. The translation is that of Showerman 1986: 325–27, with slight changes.
    13. Quite different, I think, from the abrupt shift to the second person that C. O. Brink associates with the Greek diatribe and the Latin *sermo;* see Brink 1963–82: 2:138 on Hor. *AP* 47.

> quae tu volebas nec puella nolebat,
> fulsere vere candidi tibi soles.   (1–8)

Hard-luck Catullus, stop making a fool of yourself and count as lost what you see is lost. Once, fair days shone for you, when you followed where the girl led, she who was loved by me as none will ever be loved; there, when those many playful deeds were done that were your wish, and she did not refuse, truly fair days shone for you.

In contrast with the lines of Ovid discussed previously, this poem opens with an already impassioned persona. The poet-lover Catullus, in an interior monologue, reproaches himself for continuing to love Lesbia when the affair is clearly over. At line 5, however, the speaker's stance shifts abruptly: With *nobis,* the interior monologue is momentarily interrupted, as the speaker ceases to address himself in the second-person singular and makes a comment on the affair in the first-person plural. The shift in perspective is not only grammatical. At line 5, the speaker views his whole life, past and future, aoristically, whereas, up to and after this point in the poem, he obsessively concentrates on the past and its unhappy outcome in the present.[14] With *tu* (7) and *tibi* (8), the persona of the monologue returns. (Curiously, the poet-lover also speaks of himself later in the poem in the third person, representing Lesbia's point of view.)[15]

Although this poem has often been taken as a simple, direct expression of the emotions of the historical person Catullus, the shifts in self-reference are indicative of an underlying ambiguity that cannot be resolved by reference to any real or reconstructed situation. This ambiguity can be described partly in terms of the specifically comic persona that the speaker of the poem takes on.[16] He is in some ways the Plautine *adulescens.* Daniel Selden has described the effect in this way:

14. Kroll 1989 ad loc.: "wo man tibi erwarten sollte; eine ähnliche 'Entgleisung' Prop. 2, 8, 17 sic igitur prima moriere aetate *Properti?* . . . exagitet *nostros* manes. Vgl. 4, 14. 64, 144." Fordyce 1961 ad loc.: "the illogical change of subject is natural enough." He, too, cites Prop. 2.8.17–19. Cf. Cat. 14b: *si qui forte mearum ineptiarum / lectores eritis manusque vestras / non horrebis admovere nobis.* These lines are apparently from a second preface.

15. Compare the notorious shift in perspective at Cat. 51.13 (*otium, Catulle, tibi molestumst*), and, for that matter, the shift after the first two lines of the envoi introducing the book of poems (Cat. 1).

16. Skinner 1971.

Catullus may be genuinely distressed . . . or he may be detached and ironic, satirizing the blind infatuation of an otherwise trivial romance, but these options do not allow him to be both. Since the pathos of the first reading is precisely the target of the second, the two possibilities have to engage each other in direct confrontation. . . . Is the piece attempting . . . to dignify an affection (*amor*) which Roman culture traditionally scorned as superficial, or does it deliberately savage the deluded pretensions of the undisciplined and mawkish lover? To decide the issue one would have to know the context for the composition, but the context is precisely what the composition makes it impossible for us to decide.[17]

If the poem, in fact, presents two options, two possible descriptions of its persona, and if, furthermore, these are mutually dependent and at the same time irreconcilable, then it cannot be the direct outpouring of the historical Catullus's despair that it has often seemed to be. Is it then a reflection of the historical poet's ambivalence? But would not real self-irony undercut real despair? If so, the poem might then be a document of the former but not, or not to the same extent, of the latter. But the poem's persona was said to comprise two mutually dependent, contradictory descriptions. One has to conclude that this persona and the possibility of reference to the historical Catullus are mutually exclusive. The "Catullus" of the poem, who calls himself "resolved" (*destinatus*), remains fundamentally unresolved for readers. As *destinatus* in the general sense of projected toward the future, this "Catullus" remains forever in the play of a textually constructed dilemma, and this dilemma, not the identity of the historical poet, in fact preserves "him" for future readership.

Tibullus 1.1 presents a changing persona who for long stretches simply describes his situation and his hopes, raising his voice now and then, especially toward the end of the poem, when he addresses Messalla and Delia. The monologue of the more detached persona includes statements in the indicative (not prayers or entreaties) to Ceres (15) and to the Lares (20, 23). Then he addresses a command to thieves and wolves (*parcite,* 34) and a prayer to the gods to be with him (*adsitis,* 37), and soon follow two exclamations (45–48, 51–52) and then the addresses to Messalla and Delia. On a broader scale, the poem moves in the same way as the opening of *Amores* 1.3, from one mode of the persona to another, with very little but (inferred) tone of voice to orient the reader to the change.

17. Selden 1992: 470–71.

Another, distinct mode of the detached persona is a third-person observer or commentator. In elegy, in which the speaker is usually the lover, this detached persona speaks not of his own but of others' love affairs. (Thus, Cairns refers to this persona as a "vicarious speaker.")[18] Three of the poems in "Sulpicia's Garland" are written from this third-party stance,[19] as are three poems of Propertius addressed to Gallus: 1.10 (the speaker was sleeping in the same room [7] with them when Gallus and his mistress made love the first time); 1.13 (to Gallus, with again the speaker as witness, this time more specifically); 1.20. Another Propertian example is 3.12, a *propemptikon* addressed to Postumus from the point of view of his wife Galla.[20]

An especially interesting example of a detached persona is in Horace *Carmina* 1.36. This poem concerns the return from Spain of a certain Numida. An ex voto sacrifice is taking place or about to take place. It precedes the customary *cena adventicia,* the preparations for which are described.[21] The poem thus belongs to a group of poems that celebrate the return of a friend, usually with reference to sacrifice or to a cena or to both (Cat. 9; Hor. C. 2.7; 3.14; Juv. 12). There are also two *propemptika* in which a future return is imagined.[22] In all of these poems, as might be expected, the persona is strongly engaged: "You have come! Thank God for this news!" (Cat. 9.5). "Corvinus, today is sweeter than my birthday!" (Juv. 12.1). What of the speaker of Horace *Carmina* 1.36?

> Et ture et fidibus iuvat
> placare et vituli sanguine debito
> custodes Numidae deos,
> qui nunc Hesperia sospes ab ultima
>
> caris multa sodalibus,   5
> nulli plura tamen dividit oscula
> quam dulci Lamiae, memor
> actae non alio rege puertiae

18. Cairns 1972: ch. 8 ("Speaker-variation").
19. Tib. 3.8 = 4.2; 3.10 = 4.4; 3.12 = 4.6.
20. Discussed by Cairns 1972: 197–201.
21. For references for this custom, see Nisbet and Hubbard 1970: 401.
22. Ov. *Am.* 2.11.37–56; Stat. *Silv.* 3.2.127–43. Cairns (1972) conceives of these poems in terms of a very broadly based genre called the *prosphonetikon* (20–31). But Hor. C. 2.7, 3.14 are not included in his list of examples. It is not my intention to enter here into the question either of genre or of this genre in particular. I return to genre in Chapter 8.

mutataeque simul togae.
　　Cressa ne careat pulcra dies nota,　　　　　　　　　　10
neu promptae modus amphorae
　　neu morem in Salium sit requies pedum,

neu multi Damalis meri
　　Bassum Threicia vincat amystide,
neu desint epulis rosae　　　　　　　　　　　　　　　　15
　　neu vivax apium nec breve lilium.

Omnes in Damalin putris
　　deponent oculos, nec Damalis novo　　　　　　　　　20
divelletur adultero
　　lascivis hederis ambitiosior.

It is a delight to placate with incense and the lyre's strings and with the blood of a votive bull calf the gods that have protected Numida, who now, returning safe from the ends of Spain, imparts many a kiss to his friends but to none more than to Lamia, remembering a boyhood spent under no leader but him and the toga virilis that they assumed on the same occasion. That this fair day may not lack its white chalk-mark let there be no stint in bringing out the amphora; let there be no rest for feet dancing à la Salii; let heavy-drinking Damalis not defeat Bassus in the Thracian sconce; let roses not be lacking to the banquet nor ever-green celery nor the short-lived lily. All will look with melting eyes on Damalis, but Damalis, more embracing than the wanton ivy, will not be torn from her new lover.[23]

To whom is it a delight to placate? To the speaker or to someone else? To put the same question differently, who vowed the bull calf? Who is giving the banquet? What is the relation of the speaker to Numida? Does the speaker receive the kisses of Numida? To whom are the instructions for the banquet given (lines 10–16)? Another set of questions concerns the time of the occasion. Does "It is a delight . . ." (line 1) refer to a sacrifice that is under way or does this statement refer to plans for a sacrifice? Unlike the first set of questions, these can be answered. The "now" of line 4 must refer to a general present and not to the banquet, which has not yet begun, cannot begin, until after the sacrifice. The instructions are prospective. In the last stanza, the speaker shifts to the future tense (*deponent*, 18; *divelletur*, 19).

23. For this translation, some phrases were stolen from the commentaries of Nisbet and Hubbard 1970; Quinn 1980; and Smart 1855: 36.

The speaker of Horace *Carmina* 1.36 is as disengaged a persona as one can find, while the ode's link to a real occasion is overdetermined by the exceptional naming of more than one real person.[24] Here three are named. The final stanza is, as Kenneth Quinn said, a "fade-out." The speaker abandons his own already detached point of view for that of "all" (*omnes*), and the intensity of feeling that might have been expected to be directed to Numida by the speaker comes instead from Damalis, and the feeling is erotic (if one assumes that the *novus adulter* is Numida — the speaker leaves the question open!).

To return to intertextuality, any of the personae here defined may activate it. The one just observed, or looked for, in Horace *Carmina* 1.36 clearly depends, even though I cannot say how, on a set of conventions (those of the *cena adventicia* itself; probably the recitation of a poem or poems by the honorand's friends; undoubtedly the established literary version of that occasional poem). Another detached persona, as in Catullus 45, may be using intertextual reference as a way of accentuating ironic distance. This persona refers to "those rosy lips" of Acme (*illo purpureo ore*, 12; cf. Simonides 585 Page: πορφυρέο ἀπὸ στόματος / ἱεῖσα φωνὰν παρθένος).[25] Further, the implied poet, in distinction to the persona, may be the one who activates allusion, as I argued in the case of Horace *Carmina* 1.9.[26]

Sometimes, it is difficult to decide between implied poet and persona. In Horace *Carmina* 2.14 (*Eheu, fugaces*), which has a strongly represented persona, lines 21–24 alludes to Lucretius:

> linquenda tellus et domus et placens
> uxor, neque harum quas colis arborum
>   te praeter invisas cupressos
>   ulla brevem dominum sequetur

you will have to leave your land and your house and your pleasing wife, nor will any of these trees that you cultivate follow their short-term master except the hated cypresses

24. See Citroni 1995: 338, 352 n. 24.

25. The context of the Simonides passage in Athenaeus suggests that the adjective is a way of describing the beauty of the maiden. Cf. pseudo-Acro on Hor. C. 3.3.12, which also alludes — in the same line as in Catullus (12) — to Simonides 585 Page.

In terms that I shall use later (Chapter 8), Catullus's *illo* may present the allusion as a *citation*, suggesting "as Simonides said."

26. Edmunds 1992: 4–5.

The passage in Lucretius is:

> iam iam non domus accipiet te laeta, neque uxor
> optima nec dulces occurrent oscula nati
> praeripere et tacita pectus dulcedine tangent.   (3.894–96)

Now no more shall your glad home welcome you, nor will your good wife and
sweet children run up to snatch the first kisses, and touch your heart with a silent
thrill of joy.[27]

The deictic *harum* in Horace dramatizes the situation. The speaker gestures
toward the trees as he speaks to Postumus. The allusion to Lucretius might
then be intended, that is, by the persona, for Postumus. But, if so, Postumus
has not only to grasp the allusion but to grasp it also as a critique or misappropriation of Lucretius (for the sake of convenience I refer to the persona of
DRN as Lucretius). In book 3 of *DRN*, Lucretius counters the fear of death by
showing that the soul is material and does not survive death. The lines just
quoted are what mourners say, who believe that there is some part of you left
to regret these things. Lucretius argues against the mourners. But Horace's
speaker uses the mourners' point of view in order to persuade Postumus —
implicitly — to enjoy life because death is to be feared. The allusion to Lucretius, if intentional on the part of the speaker, obliges the reader to imagine a
background. For example, the Horatian speaker might be challenging the
known adherence of his friend Postumus to the views of Epicurus as ex-
pounded in Lucretius. It would also be possible to understand the allusion as
communication between the implied poet and the reader. Ultimately, the
reader in fact will decide, and the decision will depend upon how he manages
to integrate the allusion into his reading.

The distinction between poet and persona, while it is now associated with
the New Criticism and might thus seem passé, has a particular relevance to
Roman poetry. Ancient Roman rhetorical education trained the young Roman
to assume, in effect, the persona that would carry his point or win his case.
Roman poets had had this education, and its effects are always more or less
palpable in their work. Whether real performance is intended, the poet verbally performs a role, and, I shall argue, to read a Roman poet is to reperform
(and so to reinterpret) that role. In the case of the satirists, their "masks" or

27. Bailey 1947: 349.

personae have long been central to interpretation,[28] even though satire is in some ways the most realistic genre, the closest to life, and the presumption of the real poet's presence might accordingly be strong. In the other poets, too, I have argued in this chapter, what is present is a persona.

But sometimes poets present characters as speakers. Some of the most memorable passages in Roman, and also Greek, epic are speeches. If an allusion to another poet occurs in a speech — that is, not in the voice of the poet's persona or in that of the virtual poet — then the allusion is coming in the first place from the character who gives the speech. It bears on the situation: the outlook of the character, the point that he or she is trying to make, his or her relation to the addressee(s), and so forth. Or the allusion is a kind of irony on the part of the poet: The character is unconscious of the allusion (unlike the speaker of Hor. C. 2.14), which thus says something, metapoetically, about the character as a character in a poem. For example, in Statius's *Achilleid* 2.110–16, when Achilles describes his training by Chiron, he alludes extensively to the Parcae's predictions concerning him in Catullus 64.340–41.[29] Statius alludes to Catullus, yes, but in the first place Achilles alludes to the Parcae. His allusions thus in themselves, without any awareness on Achilles' part, enact a fulfillment of the prophecy: I have become the one whom the Parcae prophesied. But the enactment of the allusion by Achilles is also Statius's trope: My character, Achilles, is the fulfillment of Catullus's character, the Achilles prophesied by the Parcae.

The distinction between poet as speaker and character as speaker has often proved difficult to grasp, though it has a venerable history in literary theory.[30] In the *Republic* Plato distinguishes three kinds of poetic style: simple narrative (*diēgēsis*), imitation (*mimēsis*), and a mixture of the two (392D–394C). In the first, the poet speaks consistently in his own voice, as in dithyramb. (Plato did not make the distinction between poet and persona made earlier in this chapter.) When the poet uses imitation, he has another character speak for him. Tragedy and comedy are completely in the mode of imitation. In the mixed form, of which Homer is an example, the poet sometimes speaks in his own voice and sometimes has other characters speak. These distinctions are as important to Socrates as the content of poetry, and become criteria for the

---

28. See most recently Braund 1996.

29. I took this example from Hinds 1998: 125–26 and have interpreted it somewhat differently from him, though I think in his spirit.

30. See Laird 1996; Clay 1998.

admission and rejection of poets in the city that he and his interlocutors are planning. (The minimum of imitation — and that only of the good — is what is wanted; consistent imitation, as in drama, is inadmissible.) Aristotle, in the *Poetics* (1448a19–25), made a similar division. Although the relevant passage is controversial, it certainly distinguishes between the poet as narrator and characters as speakers acting their own parts. Again, Homer is the example of the combination of these two modes. The notion of tragedy as the completely enacted, unnarrated mode is fundamental to Aristotle's theory and is the basis of the six parts of tragedy.[31] Appropriately enough, the distinction between poet and speaking character was soon applied in antiquity to problems in the interpretation of Homer, in particular to contradictions between statements by the poet and statements by characters. Aristarchus was apparently the source of the "solution from the character speaking" (λύσις ἐκ τοῦ προσώπου): Not Homer, but the character, is the source of inconsistency — that is, the inconsistency is artistic. James J. O'Hara brought this ancient critical concept into interpretation of Vergil's *Aeneid*.[32]

The distinction just discussed ought to be all the clearer, but is sometimes forgotten, when the poet recedes from view and the speaker takes over the narrative, as when a story is embedded in a frame story. The concept of embedded narrative was elaborated by Gérard Genette in *Narrative Discourse: An Essay in Method* and then further explained in *Narrative Discourse Revisited*.[33] In the second of these books, he introduced a diagram to clarify the relations of levels of narrative (Figure 1).[34]

If one applies this scheme to Ovid's "Aeneid" in the *Metamorphoses* (Table 1), then narrator A is the poet and the addressee or narratee, to use Genette's term, is the reader. The poet represents several characters as narrators (level B) and two of these include a narration or song (level C) in their narrative. Following Genette, I have counted Ovid's ecphrasis (the cup given by Anius to Aeneas at 13.685–701) as a narrative: Ovid puts the iconography of the cup's maker, Alcon, into words.[35] I have also included the Cyclops's song (13.789–869). Although it is not a narrative, it is as extensive a quotation, within a level

31. Else 1967: 97.
32. For references to Aristarchus, Homeric scholia, and modern scholarship, see O'Hara 1990: 123–27.
33. Genette 1980 (first published in French in 1972); 1988 (in French in 1983).
34. Genette 1988: 85.
35. Genette (1980: 231) includes the couch coverlet in Cat. 64 in his examples; he does not use the term *ecphrasis*.

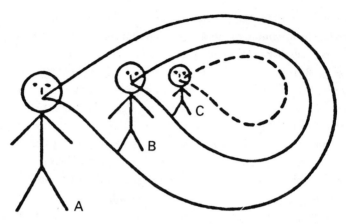

Figure 1. Levels of narrative

B narrative, as most of the B narratives. It is remarkable that about three quarters of Ovid's "Aeneid" consists of embedded narratives, including the song just mentioned (685 of 954 lines, or 72 percent, to be exact). Clearly, Ovid's extensive intertextual program is affected by this narrative scheme, and the reader has to consider not only the level of narrative, but also, to refer to two of Genette's elaborations, the type of narrative (explanatory, thematic, etc.)[36] and especially the relation of persons (subnarrator talking about self or about someone else, etc.). "Relations of person freely cut across the relations of level." A subnarrator can talk about himself or herself; can become the narratee of a sub-subnarration (level C); include some other subnarrator in his or her narrative; and so on. Any intertextual allusion will be qualified by its position in the scheme.[37]

In the first place, by consigning most of the metamorphoses that he weaves into his retelling of the *Aeneid* to subnarrators, Ovid obviously maintains a certain decorum, a certain respect for his model. He wrote what the subnarrators say, but, as a narrative, Ovid's "Aeneid" seeks what might be called "justification from the character speaking." If this principle is correct, one might expect Ovid's more extreme intertextual ventures to be in sub-subnarrations, which is what one finds, for example, in the anonymous nymph's story in book

36. Genette 1988: 92–94 offers a typology.
37. See Barchiesi 1989 for the distinction between "ironic" reading, attentive to narrator and situation, and literalist reading, cutting across such differentiae to an authorial voice (esp. 55–56, 64, 73–74, 87 n. 36).

TABLE 1. *Levels of Narrative in Ovid's "Aeneid"*

Lines	Number of Lines	Level	Narrator	Narratee
Book 13				
644–74	31	B	Anius	Anchises; Trojans
685–701	17	A/B	Ovid/"Alcon"	Reader
740–45; 750–897	54	B	Galatea	Scylla
789–869	81	C	Cyclops	Galatea
917–65	49	B	Glaucus	Scylla
Book 14				
30–53	24	B	Sibyl	Aeneas
167–222	56	B	Achaemenides	Macareus
233–440	208	B	Macareus	Achaemenides
318–434	117	C	Nymph	Macareus
464–511	48	B	Diomedes	Venulus

14 (Table 1). The Vergilian inspiration for the story is a three-line explanation of the phrase "palace of Picus," which is where Latinus receives ambassadors sent by Aeneas (*Aen.* 7.189–91). Picus, Vergil explains, was an early Latin king who was transformed into a woodpecker by his wife Circe. In Ovid, the story, which becomes 117 lines, is prompted by a question of Macareus concerning a statue that he sees: a young man with a woodpecker on his head. Macareus, in his narration to Achaemenides, proceeds to recount the explanation given him by one of Circe's nymphs. She begins by saying that the young man was the son of Saturn, a king of the Ausonian territory, fond of war-horses, and

> Forma viro, quam cernis, erat: licet ipse decorem
> adspicias fictaque probes ab imagine verum.   (14.322–23)

The hero's appearance was what you see. You can perceive his beauty and infer the true from the likeness [molded image].

A theme (the relation of likeness to original) is established. Picus goes hunting. Circe sees him and is smitten. She sends the image of a boar to lure him away from his companions: "she makes the incorporeal likeness of an illusory boar" (*effigiem nullo cum corpore falsi / fingit apri;* 14.358–59). At this point, the theme of fiction becomes metapoetic, reflecting on Ovid's own composition, because at this point the nymph's story is modeled on a likeness in the *Aeneid,* which in turn is modeled on a likeness in the *Iliad.* In the Greek epic, Apollo removes Aeneas from the battlefield, substituting an image of him over which the two sides fight (5.445–53). In Vergil, the image of Aeneas returns, this time created by Juno as a way to lure Turnus from the battlefield and save him from death (10.636–88). The nymph, or Ovid, hardly echoes the diction of the passage in the *Aeneid* (perhaps only 14.364 ~ *Aen.* 10.648) but the prototype is unmistakable. So Circe makes the likeness of a boar; Ovid makes the likeness of an earlier poetic likeness — of Aeneas! To continue the story, Picus rebuffs Circe because he is in love with the nymph Canens. (So Circe was not the wife of Picus as in Vergil.) Circe transforms him into a woodpecker and his companions into various monsters. Canens then literally dissolves in grief on the banks of the Tiber. The nymph concludes:

> fama tamen signata loco est, quem rite Canentem
> nomine de nymphae veteres dixere Camenae.   (14.433–34)

> But her fame is marked by the place, which the old Camenae duly called Canens from the name of the nymph.

The symmetrical line-final positions of *canentem* and *Camenae* suggest that Ovid is suggesting an etymological connection. How seriously? How alike does the reader believe that Ovid believed that they were? Or, to put it another way, how false is *Canens* as a verbal image of *Camenae*? At this point, with the typical marks of the "Alexandrian footnote" (*fama, veteres*), with the learned "etymology," with the *aition*, the voice of the poet has just about supplanted the voice of the nymph.[38] No such place in Rome as Canens is known. It is apparently an invention, a place that exists only in Ovidian verse. A new watery muse is added to the group of those spring nymphs, the Camenae, the original Italian Muses, and this new one is a muse of metamorphosis, in that her grief, caused by a metamorphosis, ultimately causes her own. All of these points, unconscious on the part of the narrator, the nymph, are lost on her addressee, Macareus, whose only comment is: "I heard and saw many such things in the course of a long year" (14.435–36). The nonfunctionality of the narrative qua narrative in these respects shows that it must serve some other purpose, in short, the thematic one that appeared at the very beginning of the nymph's story. So the type of subnarrative here is thematic; and the theme is the metapoetic one of imitation and invention. The story was really about Ovid.

For Ovid's appearance in the nymph's story, everything depends on the

---

38. On the "Alexandrian footnote," see Chapter 8. On these two lines, see of course the useful materials assembled by Bömer 1986: 143.

degree of intertextual difference from Vergil that he has achieved. Vergil's voice is replaced by the nymph's. She is as good as an eyewitness to the metamorphosis of Picus. She is a better authority, then, than Vergil. Her version of the story ought, in this conceit, to be the true one. In this way, Ovid sheds responsibility for the story and preserves the decorum of his relation to Vergil that he displays at the level of his own narrative.[39] The relation of narrative levels B and C provides the occasion for the nymph's thematically pregnant comment about the statue (n.b. *ficta . . . ab imagine* and *fingit*). When Circe's boar then dashes from the pages of Vergil across Picus's field of vision, the metapoetic aspect of the allusion is hard to miss. Ovid, from a safe distance, makes an ironic comment on what he is doing. Circe's boar may be the perfect likeness of a boar, but this illusory creature is not a good likeness of its model, which is another likeness, the likeness of Aeneas in Vergil. Thus at level C the virtual poet appears, with characteristic *lascivia*. Not content with the implications of the boar, Ovid, in the voice of the nymph, proceeds to add a new muse of metamorphosis to the number of the Camenae. Canens is there in Rome, perpetually lamenting the metamorphosis of Picus and testifying to her own metamorphosis.

Any scene in a narrative poem in which a character or audience internal to the poem is described as interpreting a message, of whatever kind, will inevitably have an effect that corresponds to the metapoetic one just discussed. The reader will become self-conscious about his interpretation of the interpretation that he encounters. A much-discussed example is Aeneas's response to the depictions of the Trojan War on the temple of Juno in Carthage (*Aen.* 1.441–93). Aeneas has been called the reader's "textual surrogate," and it has been said that in this scene "Aeneas offers us a kind of model for reading text."[40] The notion of Aeneas as reader is, of course, beset with difficulty. "Reader" is a metaphor or even allegorization created by Vergil's reader, who has only "is inscribed" (*inscribitur;* 478) as a prompt, and, on this interpretation, the word would have to be taken as a metaphor for both the action depicted (Troilus's spear leaves a line in the dust) and the depiction itself (where the line is "inscribed"). Any appeal to Aeneas as reader calls attention to the point of transition between the interpretative situation represented in the narrative and the interpretative situation as between reader and *Aeneid*.

39. It is often said that Ovid will not compete with Vergil. Cf. Bömer 1986: 45.

40. Hexter 1992: 353; Smith 1997: 27. I have not attempted to cite the extensive literature on this ecphrasis, hoping that a renunciation of any claim to originality will suffice. For references, see Hexter 1992: 381 nn. 122, 129, 131; Smith 1997: 26 nn. 1–2; 27 nn. 3–7.

If, however, one concedes that Aeneas is a reader of what he sees on the wall of Juno's temple, one can ask what help he offers the reader of his reading. In the first place, Aeneas and Achates are concealed in a cloud, and view the scenes on the wall from a radically private vantage point (440). The reader might take this perspective as an ideal for reading, but then Aeneas and Achates view "reality" in the same way, as they become spectators of their fellow Trojans' supplication of Dido (516–19), asking the same question about *fortuna* both times (454; cf. 517). What, then, is the difference between reading a text and observing a nontextual reality? When the cloud bursts and an Aeneas embellished by Venus emerges, Dido reacts to him in the same way that he had reacted to the artwork, with stupefaction (*obstipuit,* 613; cf. *stupet,* 495). Dido does not know that she is beholding an artistic version of Aeneas. Her response to Aeneas may be a clue to his response to the artworks. Although he, unlike her, knows that he is looking at art, he reacts to it as if it were reality, the reality of the Trojan past. Unless one wants to say that Vergil already holds the notion that "there is nothing outside the text," one will have to begin to suspect that his representation of Aeneas's reading is critical.

Does Vergil in fact offer his reader, through his Aeneas, the same privileged perspective, the same total, unreflective absorption in mimesis? Does he at all suggest that Aeneas's way of reading is ideal? On the contrary, Vergil has done everything to distance his reader from Aeneas as reader, beginning with the fact that Aeneas can see much more than Vergil's reader: the immediate context of the Trojan scenes (implied by 453–56); the whole sequence of battles (*ex ordine pugnas,* 456); the division of the scenes, which remains doubtful to this day, though it was presumably not so for Aeneas; the nature of the artwork, likewise obscure to Vergil's reader (fresco, painted mural, relief?). Vergil even plays on the difference between the reader's and the spectator's perspective, referring to Aeneas's sight of himself in the midst of the Achaean chiefs (488). The reader struggles to connect this observation with the story of the Trojan War. In a two-dimensional representation or bas-relief, however, as in the central panel of the Tabula Iliaca Capitolina, Aeneas can see himself in the midst of the Achaeans, while, in the event narrated by the artwork, he is distant from them.[41]

For Aeneas, furthermore, the artwork has a simple, powerful message of hope (463) and an overwhelming emotional effect of grief (459, 465, 470, 485). Vergil denies his reader this kind of response, calling the picture "empty"

41. For this panel, see Bömer 1951: pl. II, facing p. 17; Horsfall 1979: pl. II.

(464), and present-day readers tend to share this ironic view of the matter, finding Aeneas's reading inept, especially in its disregard of the broader context—that is, the temple of the goddess bent on the Trojans' destruction. A more profound disregard is entailed in Aeneas's stopping before the Trojan scenes (*constitit*, 459). Vergil leaves it open to his reader to imagine that Aeneas had seen other artworks, but they remain a complete blank. If Tyre had a past, if this was the artworks' subject, it is forgotten. As Ralph Hexter has shown, the Dido who built this temple is already Romanized. She "already believes that Rome's history is the only history."[42]

Intertextuality is, of course, lost on Aeneas, and so becomes another means of distancing him as reader from any reading undertaken by Vergil's reader, who perceives a particular selection of scenes from the *Iliad* and Cyclic Epic and particular condensations of these scenes. As a list, the ecphrasis inevitably employs appropriate devices that resonate with earlier Latin and Greek poetry.[43] In rereading, a whole dimension of intratextuality emerges, which is again unavailable to Aeneas. The scenes that he beholds prefigure, unbeknownst to him, the battles that lie ahead in Italy. Gauged by allusion that inevitably escapes him, Aeneas's ignorance is deepest, however, in his perception of Athena's refusal of the Trojan women's supplication: "the goddess, hostile, kept her eyes fixed on the ground" (*diva solo fixos oculos aversa tenebat;* 482). The line is both intertextual (with *Il.* 6.311) and also intratextual, to be applied, with only slight variation, to Dido when Aeneas meets the jilted queen in the underworld and she refuses to speak (6.469). The tragedy of Dido is in this way already included in the fall of Troy and in the already Romanized Carthage in which Aeneas encounters his city's history. The Trojans are at this point, as Aeneas views the scenes on the wall, still victims, but Dido is already a victim of the victims. Vergil's reader, enticed to share Aeneas's linking of the *lacrimae rerum* to Trojan misfortune (461–63), nevertheless becomes aware of another loss, which, unlike the Trojan one, is without hope. This broader perspective on mortal things is available to the reader by way of allusions that are denied Aeneas, who must read as a Trojan and proto-Roman.

---

42. Hexter 1992: 357.

43. Wills (1996: 286–87) cites 448–49 (*aerea . . . aere . . . aënis*) as an example of triple repetition, and gives both intratextual and intertextual parallels (the device is rather common in Greek poetry). He (1996: 356) puts repetition of *ut* (486–87) in the category of allusive anaphora and compares Prop. 2.14.24 (where two of the three items in Vergil's list appear) and three places in Ov. *Am.*

To conclude, intertextuality may be activated by the speaker or persona of a poem, by the poet as persona, the *I*-poet, or by a narrator or a subnarrator. Whenever an allusion makes no sense, or has no dramatic or narrative function, coming from one of the voices just named, then the implied poet is the likely suspect. The implied poet may turn up anywhere, next to any of the voices. This figure is like the Cheshire cat that Alice encountered in the duchess's house, "grinning from ear to ear," and then again, outside in the woods, where it appeared and disappeared three times. The third time, "it vanished quite slowly, beginning with the end of its tail, and ending with the grin, which remained some time after the rest of it had gone."[44] The grin of the *implied* poet is as close as the reader ever comes to the *real* poet (the empirical, historical person who was the source of the psychophysiological activity necessary to the production of the poem). In this book, the name of the poet is a metonymy not only for any or all of the works or texts of the real poet but also for the implied poet and sometimes even for a persona.

In the next chapter, I turn to a recent book by Mario Citroni that, for all its many original observations on a large body of Roman poetry, remains mired in a mimetic concept of poetry, according to which the poet's feelings about particular persons and situations are the key to interpretation. In order to argue my case in two ways simultaneously, thematically and by way of example, I have used the form of a dialogue. Of the three speakers, one is deceased; another, Citroni, is someone I have never met. In the dialogue, I refer to other parts of this book, which my interlocutors have never read. To whom are such references directed and who is making them? The views expressed by me and my interlocutors are, however, our real views.

44. Carroll 1946: 75. The grin reappears in the air above the queen's croquet ground (97–100).

FIVE

Addressee
A Dialogue

M. C. Mario Citroni
L. E. Lowell Edmunds
R. H. Richard Heinze

R. H. I gave a five-part definition of "die Horazische Ode" in an article by this name.[1] First, it is an address or speech [*Ansprache*], by the poet himself, to some second person or other. The addressees are usually definite individuals, human or divine, and usually named. Second (and from now on I refer mainly to books 1–3 of the *Odes*), the poems present themselves as quite literally directed to these persons, spoken or sung to them, destined to be heard by them. An address to a person who is to be thought of as present—that is, the type not only of Horatian but of ancient lyric in general, I mean monodic lyric, whereas modern lyric poetry is monologic. Roman elegy, for its part, preserves in Tibullus and Propertius the dialogue form, but the tendency of these two is toward monologue.[2] Third, the Horatian ode is voluntaristic. The poet addresses a second person in order to exert an influence, to decline a request, or to express his own will. Fourth, because of the characteristics already named, the Horatian ode is public, not private. An expression of the inner life of the poet, as in modern lyric poetry, is not to be expected, and, indeed, the odes are a poor source for the personality of Horace. In sum, the publicness of the delivery [*die Öffentlichkeit des Vortrags*] is the presupposition of the odes. I warn you that the fifth and final part of my definition introduces a notion that drastically qualifies the

1. Heinze [1923] 1938.
2. Heinze [1923] 1938: 190.

apparent realism of the first four parts. The fifth part has to do with delivery. Whereas Horace presents himself as the *lyricus vates* with lyre always at hand and implies that his poems are improvised, there is no reason to believe that he knew how to play the lyre or that he sang his poems. In *Epistle* 1.19.4, he uses the verb *recitare* to refer to the expected delivery of his poems in public, and, as for improvisation, the admission of great toil and the description of his *carmina* as *operosa* goes against it (cf. C. 4.2.31–32). One has to conclude that the delivery of the poems as represented by Horace is a fiction. And, if this is a fiction, so is everything else that I have defined as characteristic of the Horatian ode — the direct address, the poet face-to-face with the addressee, the concrete purpose of the poem, its public situation. It is all fiction. So Horace expected much more of those in his audience than a grasp of the archaism of his odes' metrical form; he expected nothing less of their imagination than that it transport them into the times of an Alcaeus or Anacreon, to grasp the form in which the altogether modern content of his odes was offered them.

L. E. You do not put your final point in terms of readers or reading, but I think that, after Mario's work, it will have to be taken in that way. Mario showed that literary communication in Horace's time, beyond any importance that an oral-aural moment might have had, took place in the form of writing and reading. Horace's oeuvre coincides with, and also promotes, the growth of a new literary culture, which is a reading culture. This seems to me the most valuable part of Mario's *Poesia e lettori in Roma antica,* and it throws a wrench into Florence Dupont's book, which happened to appear at about the same time as his.[3]

M. C. But I take issue with Heinze's definition, which is both rigid and formalistic. As for its rigidity, Richard Reitzenstein, in his reply to Heinze in 1924, had already pointed out that there are some odes in which a monologue, interior or exterior, is sustained and that in others there are monologic passages.[4] A counterexample that I have used against Heinze is the proems and epilogues in the *Odes,* where the communication with the addressee takes place not within the poem, that is, as the representation of communication, but by means of the poem as a written text in which the addressee or interlocutor sees himself named.

3. Citroni 1995; Dupont 1994.
4. Reitzenstein 1924.

L. E. You mean that in *Odes* 1.1 (*Maecenas, atavis edite regibus*) or 2.20 (*Non usitata*), for example, the reader should imagine not Horace addressing Maecenas but Maecenas reading the poem in which he is mentioned? (You have made this point about Catullus 1, too.) [5]

M. C. Yes.

L. E. Your observation might provide one more piece of evidence for the Roman as reader, to be added to what I will be saying in Chapter 7.

M. C. However that may be, I believe that my discussion of the addressee amounts to a demonstration that there are degrees of presence of the addressee, just as there are degrees of presence of the speaker, as you showed in Chapter 4.

L. E. What about Heinze's formalism?

M. C. Most or all of one chapter in my book (chapter 6, "I piani di destinazione nella lirica di Orazio") is directed against this fundamental orientation of Heinze's approach to Horace. I call attention to the Horatian ode as a communicative moment in the ambit of a group of friends, often in situations very similar to those of the neoteric poetry that I discussed earlier in my book.[6]

L. E. Well, one would have to grant that Horace was a real person; that real persons are named in his poems; that the names have the same reference in the poem as in real life (cf. what I shall say about names as "rigid designators" in Chapter 6); that these persons were Horace's friends or acquaintances; therefore, that, at the time the poems were first presented or circulated, in many cases no doubt prior to the publication of the odes in books, they had particular, more or less personal, and, in this respect, restricted meanings. In this aspect, these poems would belong to the biography of Horace and to the social and political history of Roman literature (cf. what I said about the poet in Chapter 2).

M. C. But I want to apply the communicative moment to an analysis of individual poems, to show how the presence of a particular addressee can have conditioned the overall articulation of the poem, its language, its manner of

5. Citroni 1995: 276–77.
6. Citroni 1995: 279.

communicating with the public, and that is why I have distinguished three planes of destination: the person(s) directly coinvolved and to whom a message is transmitted that is determined with respect to the situation; the ambience of those who recognize persons and facts to which the poem refers (for the most part this plane tends to coincide with the first one); and extraneous readers. I want to see how and to what degree this doubleness or plurality of planes of destination is reflected within the composition of the poem.[7]

L. E. I'd like to return at some point to the extraneous readers, but, for now, I want to ask how you go about distinguishing these planes within a Horatian ode.

M. C. I start from the fact that 38 percent of the odes and epodes of Horace are addressed to real persons and that there are thirty-two such persons, not counting Augustus and members of the imperial family.[8] I look for places in which, because he is addressing a certain person, Horace departs from his usual style. These places are detectable through their greater expressive immediacy and more direct pathetic abandon. *Odes* 2.7 (*O saepe mecum*) and 17 (*Cur me querelis*) are my best examples. Another symptom of the communicative moment is a greater than usual elegance of composition, as seen at least once in the *Odes*, in 1.7 (*Laudabunt alii*), where Horace had a special desire to please Plancus.[9]

L. E. When you say "places," do you mean poems as wholes or passages within poems?

M. C. The latter.

L. E. In order to make a point about the relation of these supposed places to the poems in which they are found, I want to return to your most general statements about the relations between planes of destination, which are in section 3 of the chapter we are discussing, "Occasioni private e lettore generico." There you say that the private and the broader planes usually harmonize perfectly. You repeat this point several times in the nine pages of this section.

7. Citroni 1995: 290–91.
8. Citroni 1995: 279–80.
9. Citroni 1995: 321; cf. 299. Cf. Lowrie 1997b: 101–16 on C. 1.7.

M. C. Yes, but the particular poems I discuss in subsequent sections are in one way or another exceptions to this rule.

L. E. Are the exceptions aesthetically inferior?

M. C. No.

L. E. If they are not aesthetically inferior, that is, if they have the same degree of artistic finish as the completely integrated poems, then I find a theoretical and a practical self-contradiction in your approach. The theoretical one consists in a double view of what a poem is. On the one hand, it is a literary construct, as in your general statement on the harmony of planes of destination. On the other, it stands in a mimetic relation to real life, in such a way as to admit passages that reflect the real, historical situation of communication between the poet and a real addressee. Here I'd like to refer to one of your examples, the *propemptikon* for Vergil. You say that this poem "happily unites elegant literariness and warmth of affection."[10] But I do not see how the two are distinguishable. Warmth of affection in a poem is the product *of* poetry, it is not an imitation or reflection *in* poetry of an emotion external to the poem. Which is all the clearer here because of the generic and intertextual dimension of the poem, to which you yourself refer. The practical self-contradiction consists in the combination of the "affective fallacy" with a purportedly scientific philology. On the one hand, you appeal to the reader's intuition,[11] which must arise from the feelings provoked in him by the poet's expressive immediacy and direct pathetic abandon. On the other, you maintain the ideal of a "correct, univocal reading,"[12] and your own procedure is in every way in conformity with the scientific traditions of classical philology.

M. C. But I believe that I have shown, in some extreme cases, that we cannot understand a Horatian ode because we are not privy to the personal meaning that it had for the addressee and his friends. One of these cases is *Odes* 1.26 (*Musis amicus*), for Horace's friend Lamia. It is inconceivable that a poem in which the moment of homage and celebration for a real person is

10. Citroni 1995: 330–31.
11. Citroni 1995: 305 (bottom) "Il lettore intuisce. . . ." (There is also the more fundamental intuition from which Citroni's whole project proceeds: "la sensazione nel lettore di non disporre di elementi necessari per la comprensione del carme e riservati solo a un uditorio intimo" [1995: 438]).
12. Citroni 1995: 306.

so stark could be written without connection to a real situation, and this situation, for Lamia himself and for the restricted circles of friends who participated in this situation, surely constituted an essential part of the significance of the poem. It is his alienation from the situation that makes this poem appear to every other reader as singularly lacking in references to a situation that would justify and give coherence to its articulation.[13]

L. E. Probably because of recent discussion of the *prooimion* in Greek epic and lyric poetry, I read *Odes* 1.26 as a *prooimion*,[14] and I am encouraged in this approach by the fact that Alcaeus is known to have written one (Paus. 10.8.10; fr. 307 Lobel-Page = 307 Voigt). So, according to me, the reader needs to know more about ancient literature, not about ancient persons and occasions. But I am not offering this remark about the *prooimion* as an interpretation of the poem. I'd like to speak more generally about the reader's alienation, and so here I return to the extraneous readers who are your third plane of destination. (In fact, I was translating your *estraneità* by "alienation," to avoid "extraneousness.") Your presentation of the three planes of destination was implicitly synchronic. But you also recognize diachronic change in these planes, as in your remark about the readership of *Odes* 1.7 (to Plancus).

M. C. Yes, I said that we must admit that the significance that it will have had for those who read it in those years (just before or just after Actium) when Plancus had recently been the protagonist in a surprising volte-face was different from the meaning that the ode assumed in 23 B.C.E., when Plancus was about to crown his long career with the prestigious office of censor.[15]

L. E. I agree with you completely. A similar observation was made by Kenneth Quinn on *Odes* 1.35 (*O diva, gratum quae regis Antium*). In 26 B.C.E. the ode would have been taken as referring to military campaigns then imminent or believed to be imminent. "When the ode is published along with others that make up the collection, it will have a different reception: a new expedition to the Middle East is now imminent, an expedition to Britain still something which is talked about; the ode acquires a fresh topical rele-

13. Citroni 1995: 308–11.
14. As was argued by Kirkpatrick 1969.
15. Citroni 1995: 322. Quinn (1980: 136) observes that Plancus is spoken of as still a soldier but at the time of the publication of *Odes* 1–3 his military service was long in the past.

vance and is interpreted by its audience in that light."[16] He went on to say that the same was true of the Cleopatra ode (*Odes* 1.37) and of the Roman odes (*Odes* 3.1–6). It seems, then, that, whether or not for the first two planes of destination, certainly for the third, for the extraneous readers, an ode could have different meanings at different dates even within the poet's lifetime. So the personal meaning that, according to you determines the articulation of the ode —

M. C. I cannot help interrupting you to point out that in your Chapter 3 you often referred to "the" third, historical reading, as if there were only one. So, before you again point out that I have contradicted myself, I would like to point out that you have contradicted yourself: You have just observed, with reference to me and to Quinn, that there will have been more than one, no doubt several, historical readings even within the poet's own lifetime.

L. E. I accept your criticism; that part of Jauss's method needs to be refined. When one attempts a historical reading of a Roman poem, one must either name the year or brief span of years in which he thinks that the poem was read in a certain way or admit that he is presenting a generalized historical reading, for instance, one that includes observations or responses that any Roman living in the time of Horace could make, if we are still talking about the *Odes*.[17]

M. C. What were you going to say when I interrupted you?

L. E. I was going to say that, if a sequence of changing readings can be imagined for the poet's lifetime, why cannot it be imagined for the half century (or whatever length of time you like) after the poet's death, and then the next half century thereafter, and so on up to the present? After all, Horace could imagine a Horace who imagined readers of his poems in distant places and times (*Odes* 3.30.7–12). At each step of the way, readers will read a Roman poem within their own horizon of expectation, as you have well said that they did in the case of *Odes* 1.7, to Plancus, which would have been received differently in 23 B.C.E. than at the time of the Battle of Actium. As for the addressee, he becomes more obscure as time

16. Quinn 1980: 187–88.

17. Cf. Nehemas 1981: 148: If the attempt is made to recapture the experience of the original audience, how is this audience to be defined? Who, of an assumed plurality of candidates, constitutes this audience?

passes; the personal relationship between poet and addressee into which you think that the reader is called to enter disappears;[18] the personal meaning of the ode fades; and yet the ode remains meaningful and enticing. Even if I know nothing about Plancus except what can be inferred from the ode, I can read the ode with as much enthusiasm as the first and second planes of destination read it in whatever year it first appeared.

R. H. I deserve credit for my intuition about the demand of the Horatian ode on the reader.

L. E. Yes, you do. And this point brings me to the *Epistles,* about which you, Mario, also had something to say in the chapter of your book which we have been discussing. They ought to provide the best material for the analytical, historicizing interpretation that you favor. They are addressed, nearly all of them, to real persons, and the message of a given *Epistle* ought to arise out of the personal relationship between poet and addressee that you looked for in the Odes (not to mention the apparently autobiographical element of *Epistles* 1.1, where Horace speaks of his disappointment at the reception of his *Odes*).

M. C. In fact, I do regard the *Epistles* as continuing, and confirming, the tendency that I described in the *Odes.* One can say that the fact that Horace, after the publication of the first three books of the *Odes,* developed this epistolary modality, in which the relevance of the message for the single, individual addressee is a manifest and generally conceded presupposition, supports the idea that also in the lyrics the presence of an addressee presupposed as a rule the specific relevance of the message for this person.[19]

L. E. I cannot agree that "the relevance ... is ... generally conceded." Gordon Williams, in *Tradition and Originality in Roman Poetry,* not cited by you in this connection, presented a completely different view of the *Epistles.* Williams said that "the *Epistles* are poems, imaginative works, for which Horace invented a form that exactly suited his genius for writing in the context of personal relationships. They had no practical function as letters which should distract the reader, whose duty is to participate in the poet's imaginative setting and not attempt to construct a historical reality,

18. Citroni 1995: 306.
19. Citroni 1995: 345.

not revealed in the poem, but supposed, nevertheless, to lie somewhere behind it."[20]

M. C. But they are, after all, addressed to real persons.

L. E. As Williams said, this one element may be the only link to reality that the *Epistles* have. It is, on this basis, possible to speculate (but no more than to speculate) on Horace's motives. One of these would be literary. It was useful to him to maintain the pretense of address to a real person: It legitimated a certain casual style of composition. In other words, the real addressee is a literary device! "Another motive," as Williams said, "for addressing the Epistles to real people will certainly have been the wish to do them honour."[21] This motive, however, is hardly internal to the poem in any way that is useful for interpretation. It is an aspect of the intention of the author and therefore belongs to the biography of Horace and to the social history of Rome. But I don't want to belabor this point, and it probably isn't fair to cudgel you for what you said about the *Epistles,* which was in the nature of an addendum to your Chapter 6; and you expressed a certain doubt about your own thesis.[22] I'd like to turn now, in keeping with the theoretical aims of my book, to a more general discussion of the addressee, which I will approach by way of Ovid's *Amores.* You discussed the *Amores* and Ovid in general in the last chapter of your book, "Ovidio e la scoperta del 'lettore affezionato.' "

M. C. Yes. I regarded Ovid as the culmination of the development, starting from Catullus, in the relevant genres, from poetry written for a private or restricted audience to poetry written for a general reader, for the "gentle reader," as you say in English. Of the fifty poems of the *Amores,* only three bear the name of a friend, and the role that the friend plays in the poem is marginal. Indeed, in all of Ovid's preexilic poetry, no other contemporary persons are mentioned except members of the imperial family, who are public figures with whom Ovid does not suggest that he has any personal relationship. We know from the works written in exile that there is a biographical plane of the *Amores:* Ovid often refers to his poet friends, to recitation, to mutual criticism. And yet this plane hardly emerges in the

20. Williams 1968: 24.
21. Williams 1968: 22.
22. Citroni 1995: 347: "Il 'tu' cui si rivolge via via il discorso morale tende continuamente . . . a farsi indistinguibile da un generico interlocutore in cui può riconoscersi ogni lettore."

Amores. These poems had a privileged audience, like those of Catullus and Horace, but its presence in the text has been lost, in the face of the growing necessity of presenting poetry as addressed directly to the reader.[23]

L. E. I'd like to distinguish between real, named, external addressees and addressees that are only internal to poems. I'll take the first book of Ovid's *Amores* as an example. While it is true that the only named external addressee is Atticus (*Am.* 1.9.2; cf. *Pont.* 2.4; 7), the consistent tendency of these poems is to represent the speaker as addressing someone or something. The first poem begins as a monologue but in lines 6–20 addresses Cupid, who replies at line 24. The poem concludes with an apostrophe to the Muse (and I might add that apostrophe is a device that occurs several times in the first book of the *Amores* and might, for example at *Amores* 1.9.24 and 34, be regarded as compensatory for the paleness of the addressee). Again, in the second poem, a monologue (1–18) turns into an address to Cupid (19–end). *Amores* 1.3, the opening of which I discussed in Chapter 4, and 1.13 both provide a brief introduction followed by an address, the former to the mistress and the latter to Aurora. *Amores* 1.8 is the overheard address of the bawd Dipsas to the poet's mistress. *Amores* 1.6 is a *paraklausithuron* addressed to the doorkeeper, with apostrophes to the abandoned garland (67–70) and the doors and doorposts (73–74). The eleventh and the twelfth poems are a pair, the first addressed to Napē, who is to carry a letter from the poet to Corinna, and the second addressed to the rejected tablets. *Amores* 1.15, the final, poetological poem of the book, is addressed to personified Envy. The only poem that is consistently monologic—it stands out—is the fifth (which includes the description of the beloved's body, in detail unparalleled in elegy). The poems that I haven't mentioned are 4, 7, 10, and 14. I'll return to them. At this point, I'd like to propose a synchronic picture that I prefer to your diachronic, developmental one, and I will refer to the dissertation of Walther Abel.

M. C. But Abel's approach was no less diachronic than mine. He saw change from Catullus to Propertius, from the first to the subsequent books of Propertius's elegies, and so forth. He was especially interested in how an *I* could emerge outside of an address to a *you*. In Catullus, he thought, all self-expression was governed by an address to someone else, whereas in

23. Citroni 1995: 435–37.

Propertius the subjective stance of an *I* begins to detach itself.[24] Abel's findings support me.

L. E. I would still rely on Abel for the synchronic picture that I want to present, because his analyses of individual poems of Tibullus and Propertius again and again show how closely tied the poet's expression is to one form of address or another. In short, I would say that, in the relevant genres, which are practically all genres except epic, Roman poetry will demand that an addressee be imagined. Distinctions in degree of presence of the addressee must again be made (but these distinctions are to be understood as synchronically operative). As for these distinctions, Abel himself observed that the reader does not have to imagine the addressee as present; it is enough if the addressee is present in the conception of the speaker.[25] This point brings me to the poems in *Amores* book 1 that I did not mention earlier, 4, 7, 10, and 14. In each of these poems except 4, there is at least one change of addressee. Poem 7 begins with an appeal to "any friend who is present" and maintains a public address for sixty-two lines, at which point the speaker addresses the mistress whom he has beaten, and the poem ends with six lines addressed to her. Because he invites her to take corporal vengeance on him, it seems that she is to be imagined as physically present in the situation in which the speaker is speaking. There would be, then, what John Barsby calls a "dramatic setting."

M. C. What is a dramatic setting?

L. E. The term goes back to the New Criticism, in which it was used, as it is used by Barsby, to refer to the presence of a speaker and an addressee. It's something of a misnomer, because often, as in *Amores* 1.7, there is no indication whatsoever of the physical setting. (Indeed, Abel considered such indication an effective innovation in Propertius.)[26] So we should distinguish between "dramatic" and "theatrical." In theater, physical space is the primary requirement. Peter Brook's famous definition of theater in *The Empty Space* is: "I can take any empty space and call it a bare stage. A man walks across this empty space whilst someone else is watching him, and this

---

24. Abel 1930: 127, of Catullus: "alle Selbstäußerungen werden von der *Anrede* beherrscht" (his emphasis); 129: "Das novum bei Properz ist . . . die sich . . . von der Anrede ablösende subjektive Ich-Äußerung."

25. Abel 1930: 120.

26. Abel 1930: 121.

is all that is needed for an act of theatre to be engaged."[27] One sees how different poetry is. The reader is both the director who creates the space of the setting and also the spectator who observes it.[28]

To return to the remaining poems in *Amores* book 1, 10 and 14 both begin by addressing Corinna, and then move in another direction. Poem 10 moves toward a diatribe whose audience is all women. Poem 14 shifts at line 16 or 17 from the second to the third person, and then at 27, with *clamabam* (cf. *dicebam*, 1), returns to the second person until line 51, where the speaker describes the reaction of his mistress to what he has said. Despite the reference to her in the third person, she is, then, to be imagined as present. As regards dramatic setting, the fourth poem is the most obscure. The speaker gives his mistress instructions on how to behave at a dinner party to be attended by him and her husband. The speaker is clearly addressing her. If the poem is not an epistle (and there is no sign that it is), then the addressee, the mistress, is not mentally but physically present to the speaker and should be so imagined by the reader. But where are they? The reader has to create the space of the setting for himself or perhaps be satisfied that there is a spatial context of the address without being able to specify it.

In any case, I believe that all of the poems I have discussed, with the exception of 5, entail an addressee and some entail a setting. I would like to make an inductive leap and say that Heinze's findings concerning the form of the Horatian ode can be generalized and applied, mutatis mutandis, to most Roman poems (as always, excepting epic). Further, Heinze was right to stress the imagination of the reader as the means of the completion of the form of the poem. (This is, then, anything but an empty formalism.) As against a purportedly objective analysis (which lapses into affective criteria) of the real situations of Roman poems, which is guided by, and on which is therefore imposed, a historical-developmental presupposition, I would prefer to have your readings of these poems. What do they mean to you?

Tacent omnes.

27. Brook 1968: 9.

28. In Cat. 50, discussed in Chapter 7, the dramatic setting is the epistolary relationship between Catullus and Calvus. It is not a problem. But the setting of the previous day's encounter is a problem. Was it the house of Catullus, as *meis* (2) might imply? Or the house of Calvus or some third person's house, as *illinc abii* (7) might imply?

SIX

Possible Worlds

In Chapter 2 Levin's application of speech act theory to poetry includes, without discussion, the concept of possible worlds. This concept, which has been borrowed from philosophy by literary theory, is relevant to the interpretation of Roman poetry and, in particular, to the hermeneutic role of the reader. The reader's "intertextual encyclopedia," to use Umberto Eco's phrase, is one of the main things that enables him or her to participate in possible worlds.

The Theory of Possible Worlds

Introduced by Saul Kripke in the context of modal logic, the concept of possible worlds deals with propositions of possibility and necessity. In an article published in 1963, Kripke showed that such propositions could be considered true or false with respect to "model structures" or possible worlds. The key paragraph in this article began, "To get a semantics for modal logic . . ."[1] In short, possible worlds provided something for the formal language of modal logic to designate. The concept was soon borrowed by other fields, including literary theory, in which it was applied in theory and semantics of fictionality; genre theory and typology of fictional worlds; narrative semantics, including theory of character; and poetics of postmodern fiction.[2] Seldom, however, has the concept been applied to poetry.

Despite the welcome accorded possible worlds by theorists of prose fiction, which must have arisen from a sense that being fictional is somehow like being possible, the obstacles to the literary-theoretical projects mentioned in the

---

1. Kripke 1963: 84 = 1974: 804.
2. These are the four areas defined and discussed by Ryan 1992. Semantics here means: having to do with truth or reference.

preceding paragraph are many and great. Indeed, the possible worlds of philosophy are fundamentally unlike those discussed by theorists of fiction. Ruth
Ronen has formulated the difference:

> Literary theorists treat fictional worlds as possible worlds in the sense that fic-
> tional worlds are concrete constellations of states of affairs which, like possible
> worlds, are non-actualized in the world. Yet, it is obvious that possible worlds
> are indeed non-actualized but *actualizable* (an actualizability that explicates the
> very idea of possibility), whereas fictional worlds are non-actualized in the world
> but also *non-actualizable,* belonging to a different sphere of possibility and im-
> possibility altogether.[3]

What is true of fiction, however, that is, its nonactualizability, is not true of
most kinds of poetry. (Epic seems to be an exception, but, in the manner of the
historical novel, it presents worlds that were once possible.) Poetic worlds
usually present themselves as some possible state (wished for, demanded, ab-
jured, etc.) of the same world occupied by the speaker of the poem. The
possible world of a Latin poem overlaps that of the poet's contemporary
reader under some profile or perspective of the reader's actual world. The
problem will arise of the relation between possible worlds and the actual
worlds of historically remote readers.[4]

In order to explore the notion of a poem as a possible world, it is helpful to
return to an analogy for possible worlds that Kripke used in the preface to the
second edition of his *Naming and Necessity.*[5] At the time of the writing of this
preface, seventeen years after the publication of the article cited earlier, Kripke
was concerned to oppose the notion of possible worlds as "something like distant planets." He regretted the worlds terminology, recalling that already in
the first edition of the book he had recommended that " 'possible state (or history) of the world,' or 'counterfactual situation' might be better" than "possible world." To clarify his view, he used the analogy of a throw of the dice:

> Two ordinary dice (call them die A and die B) are thrown, displaying two num-
> bers face up. For each die, there are six possible results. Hence there are thirty-six

3. Ronen 1994: 51.
4. The problem of multiple actual worlds, as given in different descriptions of the actual world,
is separate and is not of concern in this chapter. For the distinction between multiple possible
worlds as alternatives to a single actual world, on the one hand, and multiple actual worlds, on the
other, see Goodman 1978: 2.
5. Kripke 1980.

possible states of the pair of dice, as far as the numbers shown face-up are concerned, although only one of these states corresponds to the way the dice actually will come out. . . .

. . . The thirty-six possible states of the dice are literally thirty-six "possible worlds," as long as we (fictively) ignore everything about the world except the two dice and what they show. . . . Only one of these miniworlds — the one corresponding to the way the dice in fact come up — is the "actual world," but the others are of interest when we ask how probable or improbable the actual outcome was (or will be).[6]

In his elaboration of this analogy, one of the points Kripke emphasizes is the counterfactuality of possible worlds.

Roman Poems as Possible Worlds

Roman poems typically present counterfactual situations, ways this world might have been or might be. The genres of Roman poetry in themselves provide directions to worlds. Conte instinctively employed the world metaphor in defining genre: "Genre must be thought of as a discursive form capable of constructing a coherent model of the world in its own image."[7] A view of Roman poems as genre-determined, counterfactual versions of the actual world fits neatly with Levin's proposal concerning the speech act that introduces poems. Levin said that poems begin with an implicit, topmost, "higher" sentence: "I imagine (myself in) and invite you to conceive of a world in which (I say to you) . . ."[8] The world to which the reader is invited can be considered a possible world and can be formulated as a counterfactual condition. "If we were shepherds, we would live a life of aesthetic fulfillment, without pain or danger" (pastoral); or, "If you loved me, I would have everything that I desire" (elegy); or, "If you would heed this teaching, you would understand how to lead a better life" (didactic); or, "If the social, ethical, and related problems of Rome are such as described by me (and I insist that they are), things are worse than ever before" (satire).[9] Poems rely on the same intuitive notion that Kripke

6. Kripke 1980: 16.
7. Conte 1994a: 132. In the Italian original, I noticed the definition of genres as "modelli articolati di mondi possibili" (Conte 1991: 167). This phrase somehow escapes me in the English.
8. Levin 1976: 150.
9. These counterfactuals are not foundational of their genres but typical. Clearly they will not apply to each and every poem in the genres indicated.

invoked: "I am just dealing with an intuitive notion. . . . We think that some things, though they are in fact the case, might have been otherwise."[10]

Such, however, is the sophistication of Roman poems, from the Augustan period on, if not from even earlier, that the counterfactuality of their worlds becomes matter for self-conscious reflection. The propensity of poets to this kind of reflection is, in some ways, relative to genre. It has been argued, for example, that in Vergilian pastoral, "the 'pastoral vision' is uttered by a speaker who has no hope of attaining the pastoral vision, which is always perceived by the speaker as out of his reach, contrary to fact, or defining someone else's situation."[11] Epic might seem to lie at the other end of the spectrum. As purportedly "historical," it would be the least counterfactual of genres, and also the least open to self-conscious reflection. But, from the beginning, Roman epic introduced councils of the gods, palpable divine intervention in human life, and other supernatural and superhuman features that, in effect, made the "historical" world dissimilar to the world of the poet and his audience and thus another kind of possible world. Further, already in Vergilian epic, to say nothing of Flavian epic, the poet has found many ways to introduce reflection on the poem that he is writing.

The difference between a fictional world and a poetic possible world can be summed up, in Ronen's terms, as the difference between a parallelism and a ramification. A fictional world has a distinct, autonomous existence, with its own modal structure, and makes no claim about the actual world, to which it is parallel.[12] A poetic world is a ramification of this world, or another perspective on the same dice that came up as this world. It is the poet's way of playing the game to look at other surfaces of the dice. The poet's account of the results is in an oblique relation to the actually existing state of affairs. For this reason, the notion of a poetic world is not a formalistic one and is not at all incompatible with the close relation between Latin poets and Roman life that scholars often seek and find.[13]

Paradoxically, poems, which are closer than fiction to the actual world, are formally and linguistically stranger. Whereas the fictionality of fiction is not easily linked to an intrinsic property of fictional texts and therefore depends for its recognition on a pragmatic definition, on an "official cultural categori-

10. Kripke 1980: 39 n. 11.
11. Cf. Perkell 1996: 135.
12. Ronen 1994: 61, 87, 89.
13. Griffin 1985 is a notable example.

zation,"[14] the poetic status of a poem, its aesthetic otherness, is immediately obvious from text-immanent and formal features, beginning (in the case of Roman poetry) with meter.[15] Further, a fundamental characteristic of the language of poetry is the trope, which changes the literal meaning of words and thus defamiliarizes—to invoke a well-known theory of poetic language[16]—the actual world in order to assert a new, possible world. Intertextuality is yet another defamiliarizing device, by which a poem uses the existence of other poems, often in very precise aspects, as a means of signaling its own poetic status. Tropes, defamiliarization, and intertextuality are not, of course, specific to poetry; all that is suggested here is that, within the already intrinsically given poetic status of the poem, they reinforce the otherness of the poem's possible world and strengthen its autonomy. To restate the paradox, the border between a poetic possible world and the actual world is more clearly drawn than between a fictional world and the actual world,[17] but the poetic world is closer to the actual one.

For all of their differences, the possible worlds of poetry and the fictional worlds of narrative fiction share a particular feature: incompleteness. For this aspect of Roman poetry, the testimony of an illustrious scholar has already been cited.[18] For fiction, the literature is extensive.[19] The incompleteness of possible worlds does not concern philosophers, who are interested in the rela-

---

14. Ronen 1994: 86–87, 143; cf. Pavel 1986: 75–85. One of the main arguments of Lamarque and Olson 1994 is that the distinction between fiction and the stories told by scientists and historians "is rooted in human practices whose institutionally based rules give them their salient features" (20). Cf. the quotation from Sir Philip Sidney at the end of Chapter 1.

15. And Levin's speech act can therefore be understood as secondary to (not as grounding) the perception of a poem as a poem.

16. Shklovsky [1917] 1965. Of course prose fiction may defamiliarize, too; Shklovsky takes examples from Tolstoy, Gogol, and even folklore. But poems, I think, always and consistently defamiliarize; prose fiction inconsistently and not always. Greetham (1999: 131) observes that the editorial principle of *lectio difficilior* acknowledges the principle of defamiliarization.

17. See again Pavel 1986: 75–85, on borders.

18. Fraenkel 1957, cited in Chapter 3 at note 35. Cf. Joseph Farrell, in an electronic communication to his Vergil course, posted September 25, 1995 ⟨http://vergil.classics.upenn.edu⟩: "*aënis* (1.449) and *inani* (1.464, 476) may not etymologize the hero's name, but the reader who 'recognizes' them as punning references to it and thus as it were 'reads' the word 'Aeneas' on the temple and in the pictures, may be making an interpretive leap parallel to that of the hero when he 'recognizes' himself in the scenes—and in his farther-reaching inference that the temple signifies that they will find safety in Carthage. Both the reader and the hero by adopting these interpretations . . . 'fill a gap' in the text with a meaning that may be 'wrong,' but to which they cling in their desire that the text make some sort of sense."

19. See the works cited by Ronen 1994: 114–43; Pavel 1986: 105–13.

tions *between* possible worlds, not in the structure of any single possible world. The incompleteness of a Roman poem—Horace *Odes* 1.36 is an example—means that gaps or blanks and "places of indeterminacy" have to be completed by the reader. At this point, hermeneutics and the concept of possible worlds come together, and it is notable that Ronen, in her chapter, "Fictional Entities, Incomplete Beings," in *Possible Worlds in Literary Theory,* and Wolfgang Iser, in his discussion of indeterminacy in *The Act of Reading,* begin with the same passage of Roman Ingarden.[20] The key sentence in this passage is: "Every literary work is in principle incomplete and always in need of further supplementation." Iser added the dynamic interaction between reader and text as the means by which the text is completed. Jauss took the further step of introducing the distinction between the first and subsequent readings and emphasizing the aesthetic character of the first reading.[21] In response to the dominant literary critical trends of the 1960s, which included the Marxist-semiotic approach of Kristeva and the Tel Quel group, Jauss maintained the aesthetic character of text, the genesis of the aesthetic object in the reader, and the grounding of literary history in an aesthetics of reception.[22]

Others have employed the notion of incompleteness. In *The Role of the Reader,* Umberto Eco spent considerable time on the development of a formal semiotics of the possible worlds of prose fiction. One of his principles was that "texts are lazy machineries that ask someone to do part of their job." In particular, the reader is asked to take what Eco called "inferential walks." These can even include the mental writing of "ghost chapters" that supply whole sections of narrative that must have taken place if such-and-such is the case.[23] While Eco focuses on prose fiction, this point applies equally well to poetry, even to lyric poetry. In Chapter 3, I observed that Syndikus has Horace *Odes* 1.9 begin outdoors. In the second stanza of the poem, however, the speaker and Thaliarchus are indoors, building a fire. So Syndikus's ghost chapter tells how the two decided to, and did in fact, go indoors. Eco maintains that intertextuality is what provides the cues for inferential walks, and, again, Syndikus is an example. Syndikus says, without specifying them, that "Parallelstellen" are the basis of his interpretation of the opening stanzas of Horace *Odes* 1.9. These are included in his "intertextual encyclopedia."

20. Ingarden 1973: 251; Ronen 1994: 108; Iser 1978: 170.
21. Jauss 1982a: 144–45.
22. Such is the thesis of "Literary History as a Challenge to Literary Theory" (in Jauss 1982b).
23. Eco 1979: 214.

But the relative closedness of poetic possible worlds to the actual world leads to the temptation to complete the meaning of a text with information drawn from the actual world. This temptation is all the stronger in the case of historically remote texts like Roman poems, for which it seems that missing information concerning references to the historical actual world is what is most needed. Commentators typically supply it. Soracte, the mountain named in Horace *Odes* 1.9, is "2,400 feet high, 20 miles north of Rome, 6 miles from Città Castellana (the site of the ancient Fallerii)."[24]

The Constructedness of Possible Worlds

But, just as philosophic possible worlds are stipulated, not discovered,[25] poetic possible worlds are constructed. Poems are what Lubomír Doležel calls "constructional texts":

> In the explanation of the origin of fictional worlds, constructional texts are sharply differentiated from descriptive texts. Descriptive texts are representations of the actual world, of a world existing prior to any textual activity. In contrast, constructional texts are prior to their worlds; fictional worlds are dependent on, and determined by, constructional texts. As textually determined constructs, fictional worlds cannot be altered or canceled, while the versions of the actual world provided by descriptive texts are subject to constant modifications and refutations.[26]

For *fictional* here one can read *poetic*. Information concerning the height of Soracte would belong to a descriptive text. The first stanza of *Odes* 1.9 is not, however, a description of the real Soracte but has primarily to do with the relation between the speaker of the poem and an as yet anonymous addressee. The speaker calls attention to a frozen landscape that implicitly refers to a similar situation in a poem of Alcaeus and perhaps also to a line of Ennius.[27] The reader does not, in the first place, have to know any facts about Soracte that are external to the poem. (The proximity of the Fallerii to Soracte might be relevant in the second or third reading.) Indeed, the first challenge to the

24. Nisbet and Hubbard 1970: 119.
25. Kripke 1980: 44.
26. Doležel 1989: 236.
27. De Marchis 1994: 63–64. The line is *constitere amnes perennes, arbores vento vacant* (Enn. *var.* 12 V = *Scipio* 4 Warmington).

reader is to make sense of the relation just mentioned, to complete the scene in the mind's eye, and to integrate the intertextuality of the scene into his or her reading.

A rejoinder to Doležel might be that, because the name *Soracte* refers to something real, that is, nonfictional, in the world external to the poem, this thing is in fact prior to, is not constructed by, the poem. This rejoinder makes an important assumption about names, namely, that they are sets of definite descriptions. On this assumption, Soracte would bring with it into the poem a set of properties assumed by the poet to be in the reader's possession, perhaps "2,400 feet high, 20 miles north of Rome, . . ." But in my opinion an equally strong claim can be made for the view of Kripke and others that names are "rigid designators."[28] On this view, a name designates the same thing in all possible worlds and in the actual world even if the thing does not have the same properties in all worlds. Indeed, "worlds other than the actual world can be imagined *only because* diverse descriptive conditions are associated with the same object in different possible worlds."[29] One could even go so far as to say that poems would be impossible if names had to carry the same sets of properties in poems as in the actual world.[30]

A further consideration arises from the paragraph of Doležel just quoted. While he was at pains to distinguish between different kinds of texts, representing different worlds, possible and actual, it would follow from what he says of descriptive texts that the actual world is also a constructed one, as the possible one is by definition. "The versions of the actual world provided by descriptive texts are subject to constant modifications and refutations."[31] Eco has made the useful point that the entirety of the actual world structure is never in play "but just a *profile* of it or *perspective* on it that we take as a determinant for the interpretation and generation of a given text."[32] Roman genres, as was pointed out, perform this function of selection and make life easier for the reader (though sometimes more difficult). For any counterfactual, possible world, only a few properties of the actual world are "blown up," and the rest are "narcotized."

28. This is the argument of Kripke 1980. For a survey, see Ronen 1994: 130–35.
29. Ronen 1994: 133 (my emphasis).
30. For example, Aristophanes' *Frogs* would be impossible if the character Dionysos has to carry all the attributes of Dionysos. Cf. Dover 1993: 40–41: "in *Frogs* the comic Dionysos is treated in isolation from the multifarious legends, cults, and functions of which a divine person, called in all cases 'Dionysos,' was the nucleus."
31. Doležel 1989: 236 again. The thesis is argued by Goodman 1978.
32. Eco 1979: 228 (his emphasis).

Possible Worlds and Hermeneutics

On the basis of a constructed world of reference, one can outline several relations between worlds and thus systematize some of the hermeneutic concepts that have emerged thus far in this book.

1. Whether I am reading an ancient text or one written in my lifetime, my world of reference (W_0) is not exactly the same as that of every reader contemporary with me. My perspective on W_0 is not the same as someone else's, though if I have the sense to respect my interpretive community, I do not lapse into solipsism. Eco did not face this problem of differences between one W_0 and another because he relied on his notion of the Model Reader. He could thus assume a symmetrical relation between "the interpretation and generation of a given text."

Even within a more or less united community of interpretation like classics, different readers will start from different W_0's. The feminist reader of Horace *Odes* 1.23 (*vitas inuleo me similis, Chloe*) might want to blow up the relation between Chloe and her mother and narcotize the relation between the would-be seducer and the girl, as Cynthia Damon once suggested at a panel on Horace.[33]

2. The W_0 of me and/or my contemporaries will not be the same as that of the contemporary readers of an ancient text — another problem of difference that Eco did not face, because he limited himself to examples from the nineteenth and twentieth centuries. Further, there is no reason to believe that all ancient contemporary readers had the same W_0. (Consider the various readerships proposed by Mario Citroni in the preceding chapter.)

3. But the relation between any ancient W_0 and any ancient possible world (W_1) was certainly more symmetrical than the relation between my W_0 and any ancient W_1.

In this world-based formalization, the conclusion becomes starker perhaps than it was in Chapter 3: The accessibility to me of an ancient W_1 depends neither on the resemblance of my W_0 to the ancient W_0 (there is no convenient "we" that embraces the horizons of the ancient and the modern reader) nor on my reconstruction of the ancient W_0, which will be partial at best.

The accessibility to me of an ancient W_1 depends in the first place on the

---

33. Presented at a meeting of the American Philological Association (Dec. 1993, Washington, D.C.).

extremely asymmetrical relation between my W_0 and the ancient W_1. This asymmetry, not readers' stupidity or lack of historical information, produces the history of reception. I find relations between this ancient text (W_1) and my W_0 and participate in this history.

To explain how I do so, I start from the principle of incompleteness. Texts require completion by readers. One of the resources that the reader has at his disposal for this task is his intertextual encyclopedia, to return to Eco's notion. To some extent, my intertextual encyclopedia overlaps with the (or an) ancient reader's, and, in this way, my completion of a text's meaning is something like his. What I share, to some extent, with the ancient reader, is what Paul Ricoeur has called "the quasi-world of texts or literature," which is the same as a referential worldlessness of texts. Ricoeur says:

> The suspense which defers the reference . . . leaves the text, as it were, "in the air," outside or without a world. In virtue of this obliteration of the relation to the world, each text is free to enter into relation with all the other texts which come to take the place of the circumstantial reality referred to by living speech. This relation of text to text, within the effacement of the world about which we speak, engenders the quasi-world of texts or *literature*.[34]

The accessibility to me of an ancient text W_1 is therefore aesthetic in the first instance, and intertextuality is an important means of access. It is not clear how those who wish to level poetic language to everyday language, who refer to a "Poetic Language Fallacy," deal with the quasi world created by a text's relation with other literary texts.[35]

Roman Intertextual Composition and the Quasi World of Texts

A particular habit of Roman poets, attested often enough and over a long enough period of time to be taken as normal, will have contributed to the creation of what Ricoeur called the "the quasi world of texts" — to the possibilistic, nonreferential status of the poetic text that has been described in this chapter. Roman poets describe themselves as depending on reading both as an

---

34. Ricoeur 1981: 148–49 (his emphasis). This view, of course, differs profoundly from the one that, assuming that a poem is nothing but the transcription of living speech, speaks of "that reference to life which must be demanded from the greatest poetry": Nisbet and Hubbard 1970: 229.

35. For a statement of the position to which I refer, see Petrey 1990: 77–80.

immediate stimulus to writing and also as a source of models for composition. The earliest evidence is Catullus 68, which begins as an epistle to the poet's friend Manius, who has asked for a poem. Catullus cannot write the poem:

> ignosces igitur si, quae mihi luctus ademit,
>   haec tibi non tribuo munera, cum nequeo.
> nam, quod scriptorum non magna est copia apud me,
>   hoc fit, quod Romae vivimus: illa domus,
> illa mihi sedes, illic mea carpitur aetas;
>   huc una ex multis capsula me sequitur.   (31–36)

Pardon me then if I do not, because I cannot, present you with those gifts which grief has snatched away. For as for my not having plenty of authors at hand, that is because I live at Rome: that is my home, that is my abode, there my life is spent; when I come here only one small box out of many attends me.[36]

"Here" is Verona. Catullus's excuse for not writing the poem that his friend wants is that he does not have his library with him. C. J. Fordyce observes that the excuse is "revealing evidence of the methods and the ideals of the *doctus poeta:* what is expected of him is Alexandrian poetry, translated from, or modelled on, Greek."[37]

What looks like Alexandrianism as long as Catullus is the only example before one's eyes persists into the next generation and is attested for another kind of poetry and for a set of sources presumably quite different from the ones Catullus had in mind. A certain Damasippus finds Horace at his Sabine estate, and chides him for his failure to write anything, even now that all the circumstances are favorable.

> quorsum pertinuit stipare Platona Menandro,
> Eupolin Archilocho, comites educere tantos?   (*S.* 2.3.11–12)

What was the point of packing Plato in with Menander, Eupolis with Archilochus, of bringing such companions here with you?

The question presupposes that Horace has brought these authors with him as a stimulus to his own writing. Indeed the relevance of this reading list to the

---

36. Cornish, Postgate, and Mackail 1988: 141.

37. Fordyce 1961: 348 on line 33. Quinn (1973: 380 on lines 33–34) holds that *scriptorum* is not from *scriptores* but from *scripta*, these *scripta* being Catullus's own writings.

second book of *Satires* has often been noticed,[38] and the existence of this book seems to be a confirmation in reality of the intertextual principle implicit in the fictional dialogue. One might, however, prefer to say that Horace is toying with the asymmetry between the W_1 of the text (Horace unable to write) and the reader's W_0 (which includes the finished second book of *Satires*, which reflects the reading list in *S*. 2.3).

Moving on another generation to Ovid, one finds him in Tomis complaining of, among other things, the loss of his poetic talent. He gives two main reasons. One is that in this barbarian place there is no one to exercise it, by which he means that he has no audience. The other is lack of books:

> non hic librorum, per quos inviter alarque,
> copia: pro libris arcus et arma sonant.   (*Tr.* 3.14.37–38)

Here I do not have a good supply of books to inspire and nourish me. Instead, I hear the sound of bows and arms.

Ovid's words are reminiscent of Catullus's *scriptorum non magna est copia apud me*. The poet's inhibition is exactly the same, although the reliance on books is perhaps unexpected in the case of the fluent and prolific Ovid.

The effacement of the world is almost programmatic in the poetics called for by a character in Petronius's *Satyricon*. Eumolpus, an elderly poet whom the hero, Encolpius, meets in the course of his adventures, has two main principles, of which one is that

> neque concipere aut edere partum mens potest nisi ingenti flumine litterarum inundata.

[and] the mind cannot conceive or bring forth its fruit unless it is steeped in the vast flood of literature.

In the same context, about to recite his own "Civil War," he repeats his principle with respect to this kind of epic:

> ecce belli civilis ingens opus quisque attigerit nisi plenus litteris, sub onere labetur. non enim res gestae versibus comprehendendae sunt, quod longe melius historici faciunt, sed per ambages deorumque ministeria.   (Petr. 118)

---

38. And in this connection commentators observe that the Plato mentioned here must be the philosopher, not the comic poet: The dialogue form is important for the second book of the *Satires*.

For instance, anyone who attempts the vast theme of civil war will sink under the burden unless he is full of literature. It is not a question of recording real events in verse; historians can do this far better. The free spirit of genius must plunge headlong into allusions and divine interpositions.[39]

My purpose here is not to gauge the degree of Petronius's irony toward Eumolpus but to set out the old poet's doctrine. The greatest mistake, according to him, would be to put history (*res gestae*) into verse. Poetry has a different purpose. "Steeped in the vast flood of literature," the poet defamiliarizes history. Even if "allusions" is too generous a translation of *ambages*, it is in the right spirit. The consequence of Eumolpus's principle is intertextuality.

Conclusion

Talk of nonreferentiality, of defamiliarization, of the effacement of the world, may have begun to give the impression that poems are autotelic and are related only to other poems in a "chain of poetic discourse," an autonomous poetic tradition. On the contrary, in "classical" possible-worlds theory, a possible world is a counterfactual state of this world, and any poem, as a possible world, will stand in an implicitly or explicitly critical relation to this world. The application of possible-worlds theory to poetry invites readers to reflect on the relations between the world of reference (W_0) and the possible world of the text (W_1), between the vastly and ineluctably different worlds of reference of ancient and modern readers, between one W_0 and another at any given time, now or then. Self-consciousness concerning my W_0 includes the reflection that my intertextual encyclopedia includes a great many texts in modern languages that could not have been anticipated by an ancient poet. For that matter, my encyclopedia includes Latin texts that could not have been anticipated by, say, Catullus. Thus, it can cause retroactive intertextual effects.

39. The text and translation are those of Heseltine and Rouse 1987.

SEVEN

Reading in Rome, First Century B.C.E.

In this chapter, I first offer an argument that reading in a sense like the one described in Chapter 3 — private reading for cognitive and/or aesthetic experience — was a new development in the function of Roman literature in the first century B.C.E.[1] This development is partly a reflex of the crisis in the aristocratic form of life, with new limits on the traditional expression of *virtus* and a consequent resignation and "melancholy" (Syme), which are especially owing to the principate but of which the signs appear already at midcentury.[2] In short, literature ceases to display and support aristocratic competition and acquires a private function. A symptom of this new function is indeed the representation in literature of the private (in bucolic, in elegy, in many of the *Odes* of Horace, and already in the Epicurean doctrines addressed to the busy Memmius). Cicero, in the *Pro Archia* and in his infamous request to Lucceius (*Ad fam.* 5.13), speaks for an older view of poetry, as does Horace in his literary *Epistles*.[3] In the *Pro Archia,* poetry is defended in its relation — that is, subordination — to the Roman political and military career. In particular, poetry either provides relaxation in the intervals between public exertion or it celebrates achievement. Horace in the *Ars poetica* gives a short history of poetry that makes poets the founders and preservers of civilized society. In this

1. New, that is, in the history of Rome. For Hellenistic literature, cf. the formulation of Hunter 1995: 139: "they wrote poems to be recited and subsequently read." For a thesis on the continuity of Roman reading with modern hermeneutics, see Eden 1997.

2. Such is the argument of Mauch 1986.

3. The theory of literature set out in *Ep.* 2 and *Ars* does not account for many of Horace's own odes. Thus Rudd at the end of his Cambridge commentary writes an appendix called "The status of the private odes" (1989: 230–33).

history, drama, the main subject of the *Ars poetica,* appears as a respite from toil; the point is the same as Cicero's in the defense of Archias. In conclusion, Horace turns to the elder of the Pisones and says, in effect: Therefore you do not have to be ashamed of writing poetry (391–407).

I also consider such evidence as there is for the act of reading. Some passages in the first book of Horace's *Epistles* not only show that reading belongs to the newly delimited area of the private but also provide description of the poet as reader. My topic entails the act of reading poems and philosophical works, among others, and not texts designed primarily to convey information, for example, inscriptions or the labels on wine jars.[4] My subject is different from research on literacy, on readership (who and how many read what), on the physiology of reading,[5] and on generic or ideal readers who are thought to be inferable from poems.[6] My goal is to define a particular "reading culture" — I borrow the term from William Johnson — in ancient Rome, undoubtedly a minority one and quite unlike both the *recitatio* and the performative reading of a text amongst friends at an elite dinner.[7]

Private Reading

Against the notion of private reading as a new development in the function of Roman literature in the first century B.C.E., one has to set all the evidence for public reading, and one has to acknowledge the common view, based on that evidence, that public reading was in every way primary — the normal, initial act of publication; the basis of aesthetic judgment; the fundamental mode in which literature was communicated to its audience. This view of the matter is still common. In a fundamental article in *Aufstieg und Niedergang der römischen Welt,* Kenneth Quinn stated: "In the Augustan Age it seems clear that the written text continued to be felt as no more than the basis for performance." "Performance is always implied. Even when contact with a writer takes place through a written text, that text was thought of as recording an actual performance by the writer; the published text may be the result of a series of drafts, but it is still offered as, so to speak, a transcript of a performance which the reader recreates for himself, by reading the text aloud or

---

4. Cf. Prop. 4.7.84.
5. On which see Horowitz 1991.
6. Citroni 1995: 243.
7. Johnson (forthcoming) well describes this social reading.

having it read aloud."[8] The same view, stated in different terms, and more strongly, has reappeared in Florence Dupont's *L'invention de la littérature*.

Quinn was thinking of the performance of new, hitherto unpublished poems, and the institution of the *recitatio* must have influenced his opinion.[9] Probably he would have conceded that Greek and older Roman literature was often read (whether aloud or silently is not at issue here) in private, not performed in public. But the fact is that Roman poets in the second half of the first century B.C.E. could imagine private reading as the primary reception of their work. One kind of evidence is found in prefaces and programmatic passages in which the *libellus* is expected to be held in the reader's hands and received visually.

Catullus 14b, apparently the fragment of a second preface to his book of poems, imagines the book held in the hands of the reader:

> si qui forte mearum ineptiarum
> lectores eritis manusque vestras
> non horrebis admovere nobis.

if perhaps any of you will be readers of my frivolities and will not shrink from putting hands to me.

"Me" (*nobis*) means the book. The "readers" whom Catullus addresses are not, I assume, paid professionals,[10] but private readers (who may, of course, have read aloud to themselves or have subvocalized). Horace in *Epistles* 1.19.33–34 says,

> iuvat immemorata ferentem
> ingenuis oculisque legi manibusque teneri.

It is my pleasure, bearing things hitherto untold, to be read by freeborn eyes and to be held by freeborn hands.

---

8. Quinn 1982: 144–45, 156–57.

9. But the *recitatio* could be regarded as in fact the symptom of, or reaction to, the trend of publication in writing. Cf. Habinek 1998: 107: "By reciting his compositions in public, the author seeks to reclaim the authoritative presence that is in danger of being dissipated by the proliferation of writing."

10. *Oxford Latin Dictionary*, s.v. "lector" (b). For this institution, see Starr 1990–91.

In *Epistles* 1.13.17–18, Horace gives instructions to a certain Vinius on the delivery of a book of poems to Augustus.

> carmina quae possint oculos auresque morari
> Caesaris

These are poems "that may give pause to the eyes and ears of Caesar." Augustus might have the poems read to him (ears) or he might read them himself (eyes).

Roman poets' expectations of private reading also appear in some explicit descriptions of readers. In Propertius 3.3.19–20, Phoebus tells the poet to forget about epic and write another kind of poetry:

> ut tuus in scamno iactetur saepe libellus,
> quem legat exspectans sola puella virum.

so that your book may often be cast down on the footstool, your book that a solitary woman reads while she awaits her lover.

The poems of Propertius provide many other indications that a reading public is being addressed.[11] Horace, in *Epistles* 1.19, already cited, expects a small, elite group of cultivated readers. He disdains recitation and the canvassing of approval.[12] Indeed, the Augustan poetry book, a major innovation, presupposes a reading public.[13] Implicitly admitting that his claim to exclusiveness was hollow, Horace links his reception to the book trade (*Epist.* 1.20). If successful, a book both earns money for the booksellers and also carries the poet to foreign lands (*Ars* 345–46; cf. C. 2.20.13–20).

Not only, as in the passages just cited, is reading imagined as the primary reception, but the physical mode of the writing, the look of the page, could be expected to convey meaning. In Ovid *Amores* 1.10.11–12, the poet looks forward to a written reply from Corinna to the letter that he is sending her.

> comprimat ordinibus versus, oculosque moretur
> margine in extremos littera rasa meos.

11. Fantham 1996: 105 and n. 12.

12. This is an attitude that he expresses in several other places, also. Cf. Citroni 1995: 247, 269 n. 76 for further references.

13. Fantham 1996: 64–65.

> Let her compress the lines in rows, and let a letter erased on the outmost margin detain my eyes.

As apart from whatever Corinna may say in the letter, the very fullness of the page, with closely spaced lines, one after another (*ordinibus*), will be a positive message to the poet; and what he cannot read, an erased letter, will be as intriguing to him as what he can read. The domain of the bibliographical, in Jerome McGann's sense, has been reached: The textual medium in its very materiality is communicative.[14] The letter that Ovid expects would be written on a wax tablet. If the look of this "page" (or of these "pages") could be meaningful, so could the look of a papyrus scroll.

Some features, then, of the Gallus papyrus from Qasr Ibrim, perhaps two decades earlier than *Amores* 1.10,[15] are suggestive of a specifically textual form of communication. The archaizing spellings in the papyrus affect neither pronunciation nor meaning. The indentation of the second lines of the couplets could in no way be apparent in a recitation. These and perhaps other features of the papyrus are purely visual but not insignificant. The indentation, in particular, seems to communicate in material form the unepic "weakness" of the second line to which Ovid called much attention in *Amores* 1.1 (lines 1–4, 17–20, 27–30).

Acrostics are another example of how poems communicate materially and visually, in ways that would be completely opaque to an auditor. The acrostic signature of Vergil at *Georgics* 1.429, 431, and 433 is an example. The first two letters of the first words of these three lines are MA VE PU, that is, MAro VErgilius PUblius, the poet's name in reverse order. The existence of the acrostic is secured by comparison with Aratus, who, in the clearly corresponding passage, had used an acrostic.[16] Taken with the indications of *Amores* 1.10 and the Gallus fragment, acrostics strengthen the view that performance, whether public recitation or private reading by an *anagnostēs,* no matter how widespread these modes of reception might have been, should not be regarded as in every way primary.[17]

---

14. McGann 1985: 69–110; and the useful summary of his views in McGann 1991: 3–16.

15. Assuming a date in the late 20s B.C.E. for *Am.* 1.10 and Nisbet's dating of the Gallus papyrus to the 40s of the first century B.C.E. (Anderson, Parsons, and Nisbet 1979: 151–55).

16. Brown 1963: 96–105. For further bibliography on this and other acrostics, see Wills 1996: 23 n. 29. The existence of this acrostic is doubted by Cameron 1995: 327 n. 123. Another acrostic in Vergil, at *Aen.* 7.601–4 (*MARS*), was pointed out by Fowler 1983.

17. Cf. Dupont 1997: 48: "While the *recitatio* is a self-contained feature of the life of the City,

The private reading of their work expected by Roman poets corresponds, not surprisingly, to description of the reading of Greek and earlier Roman literature. For example, Cicero depicts Marcus Cato (95–46 B.C.E.) surrounded by Stoic texts in the library of Lucullus, the younger brother of the Lucullan Lucullus.

> Nam in Tusculano cum essem vellemque e bibliotheca pueri Luculli quibusdam libris uti, veni in eius villam ut eos ipse ut solebam depromerem. Quo cum venissem, M. Catonem quem ibi esse nescieram vidi in bibliotheca sedentem, multis circumfusum Stoicorum libris. Erat enim ut scis in eo aviditas legendi, nec satiari poterat; quippe qui ne reprensionem quidem vulgi inanem reformidans in ipsa curia soleret legere saepe dum senatus cogeretur, nihil operae rei publicae detrahens; quo magis tum in summo otio maximaque copia quasi helluari libris, si hoc verbo in tam clara re utendum est, videbatur. (*De fin.* 3.2.7)

> I was down at my place at Tusculum, and wanted to consult some books from the library of the young Lucullus; so I went to his country house, as I was in the habit of doing, to help myself to the volumes I needed. On my arrival, seated in the library I found Marcus Cato; I had not known he was there. He was surrounded by piles of books on Stoicism; for he possessed, as you are aware, a voracious appetite for reading, and could never have enough of it; indeed it was often his practice actually to brave the idle censure of the mob by reading in the senate-house itself, while waiting for the senate to assemble — he did not steal any attention from public business. So it may well be believed that when I found him taking a complete holiday [*in summo otio*], with a vast supply of books at command, he had the air of indulging in a literary debauch [*helluari libris*], if the term may be applied to so honourable an occupation.

Cato was an avid reader, who would read even in the senate, though Cicero is quick to note that he took nothing away from his civic duty (*operae rei publicae*). There is a hint of apology in Cicero's reference to the fact that Cato was, when seen in the library, *in summo otio*. It was therefore, Cicero implies, permissible to be in a library. Just as in the *Pro Archia* of 62 B.C.E., public life is primary. *Otium* is an interval in, and a preparation for, *negotium*.

---

in many cases it is nothing more than a prelude to the publication, in the form of a book, of the text being delivered."

   The beautiful scroll holders seen in Roman wall paintings might presuppose a private tactile and visual relation with the *libellus*. On these, see Knauer 1993. Consider also embellishment of the *libellus* itself (Ov. *Trist.* 1.1.3–10).

About four decades later,[18] *otium* can be presented as itself a worthy alternative to the traditional public career. This is a familiar Horatian theme.[19] Iccius is blamed in *Odes* 1.29.13–16 for abandoning the complete collection of the philosopher Panaetius that he had put together. Iccius goes off to campaign in the East, though he had "promised better things":

> cum tu coemptos undique nobilis
> libros Panaeti Socraticam et domum
>   mutare loricis Hiberis,
>   pollicitus meliora, tendis?

when you aim, though you had promised better things, to exchange for Spanish armor the noble books of Panaetius, collected from every source, and the house of Socrates.

A life devoted to private reading and study can now be opposed to the public career.[20]

Horace also describes himself as a reader. In *Epistles* 1.2.1–5, he says to a certain Lollius Maximus: "while you are practicing *declamatio* at Rome, I have reread Homer at Praeneste." In *Epistles* 1.7, Horace apologizes to Maecenas for his long absence. He has stayed away from Rome, the site of "busy concentration and legal jobs" (*officiosaque sedulitas et opella forensis*, 8) for the whole month of August, in the Alban hills. He proposes to stay on for the winter. If, he says, it snows, he will go down to the coast, and he "will read bundled up"[21] (*contractusque leget*, 12). He will return to Rome at the beginning of spring. In *Epistles* 1.18, in the prayer that he offers when he is on his Sabine estate, books and enough to live on for the year are the only goods that he asks for: *sit bona librorum et provisae frugis in annum / copia.*[22] In all of the

18. Hor. *Odes* 1–3, 23 B.C.E. Hor. *Ep.* 1, 20 B.C.E.
19. Esp. *C.* 2.16. *Otium* bibliography: Mauch 1986: 115 n. 2.
20. And with Christianity, the Bible, and new ascetic etc. forms of life comes a new sense of reading. Cf. Stock 1996: 41 on Augustine as a reader of Cicero in book 3 of the *Confessions:* "In the end, it is not the words that enlighten this reader, still less an official interpretation that is passed from one person to another. He 'enlightens' himself as he participates in a mind that is implanted in the literary work that is before him. Here, it is the mind of a human author; later, as he becomes acquainted with the Bible, it will be the mind of God."
21. *Oxford Latin Dictionary*, s.v. "contraho" (1.d); cf. Ov. *Met.* 14.345.
22. Cf. Mauch 1986: 56 n. 2 for Epicurean withdrawal.

places I have just cited, reading takes place outside of Rome, belongs to *otium*, and is the sign of an alternate life-style.[23]

The evidence for Romans as readers of earlier literature just set forth squares with the evidence for Roman poets' expectations concerning the reception of their own work by their contemporary readers. It was possible for Roman poets to conceive of their contemporaries reading them in the same way that these poets read earlier literature, both Latin (*Naevius in manibus non est . . .* ? Hor. *Epist.* 2.1.53) and Greek (as in the preceding paragraph). The person sitting alone reading (or sunk in thought) was indeed already a paradigm of sanctioned privacy.[24] Although Roman poets are likely to be at least as aware as we are of the performance contexts of Greek literature, these poets allude not to the performances of their Greek forebears but to their texts; and although Horace may refer to his lyre, no one will take him literally.[25] In this way, Roman poets have taken a step beyond their Alexandrian forebears, in whose work the references to poetry as song are still in a native tradition. For the Romans, song is a fiction, maintained more consistently, as by Vergil, by some than by others. But even Vergil once drops the fiction, referring in *Eclogue* 6.1–12 to reading and the written page in connection with praise of Varus. Michèle Lowrie observes: "The dependence of praise's longevity on poetic immortality necessitates grounding the evanescence of song in the physical reality of the page and an ever-replaceable sympathetic reader."[26]

Florence Dupont in *L'invention de la littérature* (1994) regards the disappearance of the performing "subject of enunciation" as a deficiency from which ancient literature never recovered. According to her, both Greek and Roman literatures are forever in mourning for orality. "L'écrit antique est un énoncé en quête d'énonciation."[27] This statement is unaware of the history of performance and reading that was traced in Chapters 2 and 4, even though much of that history could have been found in scholars on whom Dupont relies. In particular, as the Andrōn inscription showed, some readers could already be expected to take on the role of subject of enunciation. An important

---

23. Cf. Darnton 1990: 167 on the importance of the "where" of reading and its relation to the reading experience. Cf. note 16: *contractus* may imply a posture different from, for example, the one seen in the reliefs discussed by Knauer 1993.

24. Hor. *Sat.* 1.3.63–65.

25. See Lowrie 1997b: 55–70.

26. Lowrie 1997b: 64.

27. Dupont 1994: 17; 281.

phase that I do not discuss is Hellenistic poetry. Callimachus, for example, shows a high degree of sometimes humorous self-consciousness about the fact that his compositions are written and written to be read.[28] When the day of the Roman reader arrives, the conditions for silent reading, for the reader's perception and performance of the persona internal to the poetic text, are long since established, not to mention the custom of silent reading for practical purposes in everyday life, for example, in the reading of inscriptions.[29] (It is, of course, impossible to say what percentage of Roman readers were able to read in this fashion.)

Only one point needs to be added here to my history of reading, and it concerns reading aloud. A previously discussed article by Svenbro deals only with Greek evidence and presented silent reading as achieved in the fifth century, even if by only some small percentage of readers. Greeks had taken the decisive step from the archaic vocalization of the written text to the inner voice heard by the reader. This history is too simple or too short, however. The Roman reader, heir to a now long tradition of silent reading, may read aloud, as some examples cited here have suggested, *but with the attitude of the silent reader.* A Roman reader may read aloud because, one can imagine, of habits acquired in his primary education, or he may subvocalize as he reads to himself by moving his lips or by creating the sounds of the words in his mind without making them audible. But nothing prevents him, in so doing, from playing the role that was already required by the Andrōn inscription a half millennium earlier.

Indeed the Roman reader's experience of listening to a reader at a dinner party would have provided a model for that role. That reader's reading was itself a performance. The "strict attention to continuous flow in the ancient book" suggests the task that was set for the reader: a continuous rendition of the text. "Direction for pause and tone given by the author's metalinguistic markup in our texts (commas, quotes, italics, indentation, etc.) was left to the reader's interpretation." "Punctuation, if it existed, had no authorial force, and could be — and was — changed at will." The social reading here described is a performance because, beginning with its physical conditions, it must be an interpretation. The ancient bookroll gives the reader no straightforward way to convey the author's intent. The bookroll is tantamount to a script.[30]

28. Cf. Edmunds forthcoming.
29. Susini 1988.
30. In this paragraph, I have followed and quoted Johnson forthcoming.

The Act of Reading

Two poems are relevant to the discussion of the act of reading.[31] One is Horace *Epistles* 1.2, from which a passage was cited as an example of the private reading of Greek literature. To quote:

> Troiani belli scriptorem, Maxime Lolli,
> dum tu declamas Romae, Praeneste relegi;
> qui, quid sit pulchrum, quid turpe, quid utile, quid non,
> planius ac melius Chrysippo et Crantore dicit.

Lollius Maximus, while you are practicing *declamatio* in Rome, I have reread the writer of the Trojan War. He tells what is honorable [*pulchrum*], what is base, what is useful, what is not, more clearly and better than Chrysippus and Crantor.

Immediately there are two contrasts: One is between *declamatio* as preparation for a career and poetry as the source of moral lessons for life. The other contrast is between poetry and philosophy. Chrysippus and Crantor represent philosophy. It is the "old quarrel between poetry and philosophy" to which Plato refers in the *Republic* (607b5–6). Horace proceeds to give, in eleven lines, a moralizing interpretation of the *Iliad* as a whole and, in fifteen lines, a moralizing interpretation of the *Odyssey* as a whole. He summarizes his reading of the *Iliad* in two lines (15-16):

> seditione, dolis, scelere atque libidine et ira
> Iliacos intra muros et peccatur et extra

Inside the walls of Ilium and outside, wrongs are committed through sedition, treachery, injustice, lust, and rage.

The *Odyssey,* on the other hand, presents the good example of Ulysses, who is characterized by *virtus* and *sapientia.* Horace then, in the rest of the *Epistle,* delivers a protreptic to virtue, linked in various ways to what he has said about Homer. One of Horace's first recommendations is that Lollius call for a book and a lamp before daybreak and apply himself to serious study (34–37).

---

31. I am here excluding the reading of letters from lovers, for which two passages are relevant: Plaut. *Pseud.* 1–72; Ov. *A.A.* 3.469–72.

The discovery of moral lessons in Homer is not original with Horace. It goes back at least as far as Antisthenes in the fifth and fourth centuries B.C.E., and Horace could have found a recent example of the philosophic approach in Philodemus's essay *On the Good King According to Homer,* dedicated to Lucius Calpurnius Piso.[32] Like Philodemus, Horace takes Homer as the basis of protreptic. Unlike Philodemus, Horace can recommend the reading of Homer to his addressee. What is new in Horace's approach is the implicit claim that the moral lessons come concretely (note *planius*) in the experience of continuous reading. Horace's performance as a reader, as he describes himself in this *Epistle,* demonstrates this claim. He gives a reading of each of the two epics as a whole and an interpretation of each epic as a whole. He does not simply allegorize, relying on the philosophic traditions of this kind of exegesis, but reinterprets the texts that he is reading. What he does is truly to reread, to read again, *relegere.* For example, by calling Circe a *meretrix* (25), he Romanizes and makes specific — coarsens, says Heinze — the traditional interpretation of her as representing *hēdonē* or *truphē* — pleasure. Again, allegorizing the Phaeacians as us, ordinary mortals, in contrast to Ulysses, he describes them as

> in cute curanda plus aequo operata iuventus,
> cui pulchrum fuit in medios dormire dies et
> ad strepitum citharae cessatum ducere somnum.   (29–31)

young men immoderately occupied with looking after their physical well-being, in whose opinion it was noble to sleep until mid-day and to induce absent sleep to the sound of the lyre.[33]

Although the Phaeacians very early on became proverbial for soft living, there is nothing in the *Odyssey* about sleeping until midday. Horace's interpretation takes off from a single word (on the assumption that he had essentially the same text of Homer that I have), εὐναί, in book 8, lines 248–49, where Alcinous says:

32. It is not certain whether Horace had read this work. Asmis (1991: 20 n. 95) notes one precise point of comparison between it (col. 28.27–31) and Hor. *Ep.* 1.2.11–12 (on Nestor). For an overview of questions concerning Philodemus's *On the Good King,* see Gigante 1995: 63–78.

33. Some phrases in this translation come from Mayer 1994. See Mayer's comments on the readings *somnum* and *cessatum;* instead of the latter, he prefers *cessantem.*

αἰεὶ δ᾽ ἡμῖν δαίς τε φίλη κιθαρίς τε χοροί τε
εἵματά τ᾽ ἐξημοιβὰ λοετρά τε θερμὰ καὶ εὐναί

And always the banquet has been dear to us, and the cithara, and dancing, and changes of clothes, and warm baths, and bed.

Nor is there anything in the *Odyssey* about inducing sleep to the sound of the lyre. Demodocus does not sing his listeners to sleep at the court of Alcinous. But the fact that Demodocus sings three different songs in book 8 could have conveyed the impression that the Phaeacians never went to bed without a large dose of the cithara.[34] And it is this impression that Horace's reading records.

It is not the allegorizing as such but Horace's demonstration of his own reading that conveys the point made at the outset of the *Epistle,* that Homer teaches virtue more clearly than the philosophers. The concreteness of Horace's own reading conveys this point and leads on to the protreptic that follows the interpretation of Homer and occupies the second half of the *Epistle.* For Horace, the text that he reads answers an ethical question, in this case, the question, How should I live? The text can thus be an answer to a question that it did not ostensibly set out to answer, so that the text can replace or improve upon an answer that comes from somewhere else, in this case from philosophy. The answer emerges in a private reading — this is the relevance of the contrast between Praeneste and Rome. The answer emerges in the experience of reading — this is the implication of *planius.* The experience is concrete partly because of the reader's willingness to make it concrete, in fact to complete a possible meaning, as in the case of the Phaeacians just noted.

Horace's reading is a fuller one than the practice that Quintilian's *grammaticus* inculcates in boys in the first stage of their preparation for oratory (*Instit.* 1.8). While the boys must learn through practice to read aloud properly, and while they are taught metrics, diction, tropes, and arrangement (*oeconomia*), and also receive explanation of the stories (*enarratio historiarum*) that occur in poems, they are not expected to form any opinion about the meaning of a poem as a whole. Quintilian says that, in order to read aloud properly, the boys must understand what they read; but he does not say what constitutes understanding, except for the matters just noted. No hermeneutics

34. The three: (1) quarrel of Odysseus and Achilles; (2) Aphrodite, Ares, Hephaistos; (3) Trojan Horse and the fall of Troy.

is envisaged. What replaces the discovery of meaning is moral uplift, which for Quintilian is unproblematical: It is found, for example, in heroic verse and in some tragedies, but not in erotic elegy, which must not be read at an impressionable age. In Horace's reading of Homer, the moral concern has been retained, but the moral lessons that Horace finds emerge from reading in a fuller sense than the one found in Quintilian. Indeed, Horace, addressing the future orator Lollius Maximus, implicitly contrasts reading as Lollius Maximus would have learned it from a *grammaticus,* with reading as Horace practices it.

One might conclude that Horace has practiced that readerly completion of the text which, in the hermeneutic perspective, is always necessary. Compare Cicero as a reader of Homer. He says

> traditum est etiam Homerum caecum fuisse; at eius picturam, non poësin videmus: quae regio, quae ora, qui locus Graeciae, quae species formaque pugnae, quae acies, quod remigium, qui motus hominum, qui ferarum non ita expictus est, ut, quae ipse non viderit, nos ut videremus, effecerit?   (*Tusc.* 5.114–15)

> There is the tradition also that Homer was blind: but it is his painting not his poetry that we see; what district, what shore, what spot in Greece, what aspect or form of combat, what marshalling of battle, what tugging at the oar, what movements of men, of animals, has he not depicted so vividly that he has made us see, as we read, the things which he himself did not see?[35]

Against Cicero's examples of the pictorial aspect of Homer, one can set not only the observation that about half of the *Iliad* consists of speeches but also another consideration. The *Iliad* in fact provides the barest minimum of scene or setting. If it is necessary to describe a scene, usually one or two landmarks suffice, an altar, a spring, a tree. The Achaean camp outside Troy receives only a schematic description, in terms of the relative positions of some of the ships. If the narrative demands something more, the results are confusing (e.g., 14.27–40). Homer hardly indicates the look of the heroes' huts or tents. The city of Troy is a visual blank. If Cicero found pictures in Homer, it must have been his own imagination that provided them; that he filled in the blanks is suggested by his list of examples. Likewise, I have proposed, Horace (whose general formula *ut pictura poesis* [*Ars* 361] may have the same implications

35. King 1945.

for reading as Cicero's visualized reading of Homer) practiced a kind of reading that seems to presuppose Roman Ingarden's principle of incompleteness and need of supplementation.[36]

The second poem that describes an act of reading is *Satires* 1.10. Horace begins by replying to someone who has challenged his criticism of Lucilius, the inventor of satire, as Horace later calls him (48). Horace defends his criticism and moves obliquely to another subject, his own choice of satire. Others, he says, are better than he at other kinds of poetry, Fundanius at comedy, Pollio at tragedy, Varius at epic, and Vergil at bucolic. Horace then returns to his criticism of Lucilius and points out that Lucilius had criticized Ennius.[37]

> quid vetat et nosmet Lucili scripta legentis
> quaerere, num illius, num rerum dura negarit
> versiculos natura magis factos et euntis
> mollius ac siquis pedibus quid claudere senis,
> hoc tantum contentus, amet scripsisse ducentos
> ante cibum versus, totidem cenatus   (*S.* 1.10.56–61 Klingner)

What prohibits me, too, from asking, when I read the writings of Lucilius, whether his own nature, or whether the harsh nature of his content[38] denied him verses more finished and going more smoothly[39] than if someone, satisfied with only enclosing something in six feet, should take delight in having written two hundred verses before dinner and the same number afterward?

The two questions introduced by *num . . . num* are not alternatives but propose two different hypotheses. Logically, the field is open. Both hypotheses could prove true; both could prove false; or each could be partly true and partly false; and so forth. What are the two hypotheses? As for the *rerum dura . . . natura* (56–57), as my translation showed, I take *rerum* (57) to mean

36. And may already have been recognized in ancient theory of *phantasia*. I can do no more than cite Manieri 1998, of which I became aware, thanks to the review in *Scholia Reviews* (Basson 2000), only at the time of the final work on the manuscript of this book.

37. Cf. Ov. *Am.* 1.15.19: *Ennius arte carens.*

38. Lejay 1966 ad loc.: "Les sujets, les causes en dehors de lui," following Porphyrio: "Sensus est: Num illius natura, aut numquid magis rerum earum quas scripsit negarit ei versus molliores." Morris 1939 ad loc.: "in the most general meaning, *circumstances,* including his difficult subject-matter and the imperfection of his times in verse-writing." Kiessling and Heinze 1957 ad loc.: "vielleicht nicht er selbst, sondern die *res,* die außer liegenden Verhältnisse, als *durae* dafür verantwortlich zu machen seien, d.h. die geringe ästhetische Kultur seiner Zeit."

39. *Oxford Latin Dictionary*, s.v. "mollis" (8.b).

Lucilius's content, what he wrote about.[40] As for *natura* as applied to Lucilius (*illius . . . natura* 57–58), it refers to his *ingenium,* his inborn talent.[41] Like his content or subject matter, the talent of Lucilius is regarded as an aspect of his verse, and the common opposition between *natura* and *ars* is not the issue here.[42]

What is Horace's decision on the two hypotheses? He says:

> fuerit Lucilius, inquam,
> comis et urbanus, fuerit limatior idem
> quam rudis et Graecis intacti carminis auctor
> quamque poetarum seniorum turba; sed ille,
> si foret hoc nostrum fato delapsus in aevum,
> detereret sibi multa, recideret omne quod ultra
> perfectum traheretur, et in versu faciendo
> saepe caput scaberet vivos et roderet unguis.
>
> (*S.* 1.10.64–71 Klingner)

Lucilius may, I grant you, have been elegant and civilized, he may also have been more polished than a source of poetry rough and untouched by the Greeks[43] and more polished than the crowd of older poets.[44] But, if fate had brought him down to our times, he would rub out many things in his works [*sibi*], and he would cut back everything that dragged beyond perfection, and, in making his verses, he would often scratch his head and gnaw his nails to the quick.

40. Though perhaps *rerum* is more general, as some commentators have suggested, and refers also to the circumstances in which Lucilius wrote.

41. And, I hasten to add, his talent as an aspect of his verse and not as some quality that should be factored out of the verse and referred to the historical person Lucilius. I see no sign anywhere in Horace that he is ever talking about Lucilius as anything but a poet. Horace's opinion about Lucilius is extended by Quintilian to all of the older Latin poets: *plerique plus ingenio quam arte valent* (*Inst.* 1.8.8).

42. This opposition is the familiar, but here misleading, one on which much of the *Ars poetica* is built. In at least one passage in the *Ars poetica,* however, for example, 323–24, *ingenium* is regarded as an aspect of *ars,* as it is here. See Brink 1963–82: 2:327, 348 (comment on *ingenium . . . ore rotundo*).

43. Brown 1963: "The most convincing explanation of this much disputed line [66] is as an allusion to any writer in primitive, native Italian forms like Saturnian verse, whose metre was quite independent of Greek influence: such writers are contrasted, in *poetarum seniorum turba,* with the earliest Roman poets to adapt Greek metres, like Ennius, Accius, and Pacuvius." But Brink 1963–82: 1:165 n. 3: "Lucilius is an *inventor,* but what he achieved was to Romanize a (supposedly) Greek genre." Others have said that it could be Ennius: Horace distinguishes the inventor of satire from Lucilius: *illi* (48), referring to the inventor, cannot be the same as *hunc* (50), referring to Lucilius. As for *carmen* = "genre," see Lejay [1911] 1966 on 66.

44. For the hortatory or jussive subjunctive used to express a concession, see Woodcock 1959: 87 (§112).

In this passage, line 66 is problematical. In my opinion, this line is a round-about way of saying that the genre invented by Lucilius was polished because it *was* touched by the Greeks—which squares with what Horace says explicitly about Lucilius in relation to Old Comedy in *Satires* 1.4.1–8.

Which of the two hypotheses does Horace adopt? The phrase *comis et urbanus*—"elegant and civilized"—and the rest of the characterization in lines 65–67 must refer to the nature of Lucilius, to his *ingenium*, as expressed in his poetic art. The qualification beginning *sed ille* (67) also looks to the nature of Lucilius. That nature would have expressed itself differently if Lucilius had lived in Horace's times. In other words, the second hypothesis, that the roughness and prolixity of Lucilius are owing to the harsh nature of his content, is tacitly dropped.[45] Horace does not say, for example, that if Lucilius were alive today he would choose a different content. In sum, Lucilius was polished, more polished than his predecessors, but not polished enough. The aesthetic standard that Horace applies is a contemporary one, and by that standard not even Calvus and Catullus are good enough: Horace refers earlier in this *Satire* to a "monkey [identity uncertain] who only knows how to recite Calvus and Catullus" (18–19). So Lucilius is called to account in the court of the present. Although Horace is historical in approach—he can locate Lucilius, and also himself, in a history of Roman literature—he is not content to leave Lucilius within the perspective of Lucilius's own time. Lucilius is held to Horace's standards.

Immediately after the passages I have been discussing, Horace launches into instructions on style that must be applied if, he says, "you are going to write something worthy to be read a second time" (72–73)—that is, to be reread. These instructions do not concern me here. I only call attention to the expectation of rereading. To be read is to be reread. To read is to reread, as Horace represented himself rereading Homer.

The two acts of readings here discussed have this in common: They approach a text with a question that arises from a present concern—in the first case, philosophical; in the second, literary. As for the literary or aesthetic question, Horace presupposes that one ought to be able to read the poetry of the past with the same pleasure with which he reads his contemporaries Fundanius, Pollio, Varius, and Vergil, the same pleasure with which he hopes that elite readers among his contemporaries will read and reread him. The two acts

---

45. Oberhelm and Armstrong 1995: 253: "the choice of answers offered is an illusion. The answer to Horace's question is obvious: Nothing was wrong with the *res* Lucilius chose, but rather Lucilius lacked real *ingenium* and therefore *ars*."

also display an engagement with, one could even say participation in, the text that is being read. In *Satires* 1.10, much of this is implicit in Horace's intertextual relation with Lucilius.[46]

To return now to Dupont, Horace as reader already provides evidence against her thesis in *L'invention de la littérature* that there was no literary institution of reading in antiquity, neither for the Greeks nor for the Romans. But it is worth addressing directly her interpretation of Catullus 50 (*Hesterno, Licini, die*), one of her three cardinal texts,[47] in order to see more clearly the fatal consequences of her thesis. The framework for her approach to this poem is established in her introduction, where she gives a definition of reading (which, as will be seen, is fundamentally in accord with Jauss's method); and then asserts that, by this definition, neither the Greeks nor the Romans were readers. What she calls "literary reading" presupposes a literary text, a text intended to be read. Such a text is an "utterance [*énoncé*] in quest of an enunciation [*énonciation*],[48] in order that its semantic sense may be invested with a pragmatic sense in shifting into a relation between reader and writer that is socially defined in space and time. Only through this reading-enunciation is there textualization, i.e., application of a hermeneutic that permits the construction of a discursive sense eliminating ambiguities and dialogisms. The text is not produced by writing, which [only] proposes an utterance to readings that will make of it a text." She distinguishes this literary reading from the only kind of reading known to the Greeks and the Romans, which she calls "commemoration." "The reading of an utterance which is the trace of an event can only be the commemoration of this event, a citation; it cannot be a literary reading. Citation is only the oralization of the utterance; it actualizes the signifier without interest in the signified; it is an oral monument."[49]

The Greeks and Romans thus, she says, lacked the "institution of literature," which establishes "a social contract between absent writer and his reader, a contract that provides the only access to the text. . . . The text will

---

46. Brink 1963–82: 1:63–64, 168 with n. 7.

47. The others being Anacreon 2 Bergk and Diehl = 12 Page = 14 Gentili and *The Golden Ass* of Apuleius.

48. "Utterance" is the standard English translation of *énoncé;* "enunciation" of *énonciation.* The conceptual distinction, originating with Benveniste 1966, has had a large play in structuralist and poststructuralist theory. See Baldick 1990, s.v. "énoncé and énonciation"; Ducrot and Todorov 1979, s.v. "énonciation"; Greimas and Cortés 1982, s.v. "enunciation," with cross-references at the end of the article; Greimas and Cortés 1986, s.vv. "énonciation" and "énoncé."

49. Dupont 1994: 20.

persuade the reader that it belongs to literature, that it merits conservation once read, in order to be reread. . . . For the literary text presents itself as unfinished . . . an utterance without a subject of enunciation. But this absence is not a lack; the effacement of the subject of the utterance . . . allows the installation of another subject and another enunciation, the reading and the reader."[50] In short, the reader becomes the subject of enunciation in the institution of literature, or, to restate her point in Jauss's words, the reader becomes the performer of the text. (Dupont does not say when this institution came into existence, only that the Greeks and the Romans lacked it.)

How does Dupont discover the unreadability of Catullus 50? Her method is to reconstitute the enunciation of the poem in its historical context. "Historical reality" is her guide.[51] What, then, is the enunciation of Catullus 50? In order to answer this question, Dupont begins with the Roman custom of the *comissatio,* the drinking party, which preceded the *cena* — that is, with the *comissatio* in general, in order then to proceed to the particular case of the poem. Catullus's experience of a *comissatio* at which he and Licinius Calvus amused themselves by writing verses is the historical context of the poem. Catullus returns to this experience in the poem, which is a letter to Calvus.

The poem begins:

> Hesterno, Licini, die otiosi
> multum lusimus in meis tabellis,
> ut convenerat esse delicatos.
> Scribens versiculos uterque nostrum
> ludebat numero modo hoc modo illoc,
> reddens mutua per iocum atque vinum.   (1–6)

Yesterday, Licinius, having nothing to do, we amused ourselves with my tablets, as we had agreed to be risqué. Writing verses each of us was sporting now in this meter, now in that, replying to each other in wine-inspired jest.

The translation that I have given is necessarily a stopgap, because the code words of Catullus's circle (*otiosi, delicatos, ludere*) do not come easily into English.[52] Further, the translation does not bring out the implication that the

---

50. Dupont 1994: 15.
51. Dupont 1994: 18, 16.
52. For the translation, I have borrowed phrases from Fordyce 1961 and from Quinn 1973. On *ludere,* see Landolfi 1986: 78–81.

verses were amatory, an implication that it is reinforced by Calvus's identity as a love-poet (see Prop. 2.34.89–90 and context).[53]

For Dupont, it is of the utmost importance that the experience took place yesterday and the poem, the letter, was written today. The poem exists, she believes, only to recapture that ephemeral event, in which even the verses that the two friends composed on the wax tablets would have been erased as they went along in their exchanges. She imagines a strictly pragmatic, epistolary function of the poem (with other pragmatic aspects that I discuss). But Dupont overlooks the obvious. Whether or not the poem was ever in fact sent to Calvus, readers other than Calvus are presupposed by the opening lines, which cannot be addressed exclusively to Calvus. He already knew what he and Catullus had been doing yesterday.[54] The historical event, yesterday's encounter, is therefore not a reference point for the understanding of the poem as somehow pragmatic but a creation of the poem. The event is as good as fictional. Even if Catullus 50 was actually sent as a letter to Calvus, only for Calvus was it in any way a real letter. For every other reader, it demanded (and it still demands) to be read as a poem. It demanded what Dupont calls textualization.

As a poem, it will have been read as the artistic form of a certain kind of a letter. Cicero wrote to the jurist C. Trebatius Testa (*Ad fam.* 7.22; 44 B.C.E.?):

illuseras heri inter scyphos quod dixeram controversiam esse, possetne heres quod furtum antea factum esset recte furti agere. itaque, etsi domum bene potus seroque redieram, tamen id caput, ubi haec controversia est notavi, et descriptum tibi misi, ut scires id quod tu neminem sensisse dicebas, Sex. Aelium, M'. Manilium, M. Brutum sensisse. ego tamen Scaevolae et Testae assentior.

You made game of me yesterday over our cups for saying that it was a moot point whether an heir can properly take action for a theft in respect of a theft previously committed. So when I got home, though late and well in tipple, I noted the relevant section and sent you a transcript. You will find that the view, which, according to you, has never been held by anybody was in fact held by Sex. Aelius, Manius Manilius, and M. Brutus. However, for my part I agree with Scaevola and Testa.[55]

53. See Fordyce 1961 on line 3. For Calvus as love-poet, see also Chapter 2, note 4.
54. Fordyce 1961: 215: "The lines are 'To Calvus,' but Calvus did not need to be told what he had been doing the night [*sic*] before; Catullus is writing for other readers."
55. The translation is that of Bailey 1978: 499.

The similarities to the "letter" of Catullus are obvious: the playful (*illuseras ~ lusimus*) dispute on the day before (*heri ~ hesterno . . . die*) when the two were in their cups (*inter scyphos ~ vinum*). Cicero returns home, and, like Catullus, cannot sleep, but is still imbued with the spirit of the encounter with his friend.[56] This kind of letter, represented also by another one of Cicero (*Att.* 9.10.1), belongs to historical reality as much as the *comissatio* but is not mentioned by Dupont.[57] This is the reality of an epistolary social convention, the letter sent on the morning after. Catullus's poem takes this kind of a letter as a model, casting it in hendecasyllabics and proceeding to give it a humorous twist. He continues:

> Atque illinc abii tuo lepore
> incensus, Licini, facetiisque
> ut nec me miserum cibus iuvaret,
> nec somnus tegeret quiete ocellos,
> sed toto indomitus furore lecto
> versarer cupiens videre lucem,
> ut tecum loquerer simulque ut essem.   (7–13)

And then I departed thence so inflamed by your charm, Licinius, and your wit,
that neither did food help me in my misery nor did sleep cover my eyes with rest
but with uncontrolled passion twisting and turning on every square inch of my
bed I could not wait for daylight, so that I could talk with you and be with you.

Again, the translation for the most part fails to bring out a crucial ingredient of style, this time the topoi (cannot eat; cannot sleep; tosses and turns on his bed) and the diction of Roman love poetry (for which see the commentators). Catullus describes to Calvus his delirious affection for him in the same diction that, the reader assumes, they had been using in the verses that they wrote the day before. This erotic diction is a humorous sign of Catullus's delirium (especially because of the incongruity of this diction in hendecasyllabics) and also at the same time a serious sign of his affection. Dupont, for her part, takes Catullus literally and speaks of a "social seduction," in a cultural context in which "érotisme entre hommes," at least when limited to desire, was not censured. But this poem is no more erotic than the opening of the obviously

---

56. See Citroni 1995: 184–86.
57. The relevance of *Ad fam.* 7.22 to Cat. 50 was first pointed out by Fraenkel 1956: 282 = Fraenkel 1964: 107.

nonerotic poem 14: "If I did not love you more than my eyes, most delightful Calvus" (*Ni te plus oculis meis amarem, / iucundissime Calve*). What Catullus wants from Calvus is that the game continue; the poem that Catullus has written is, in addition to everything else, the final riposte in yesterday's contest, intended as a provocation to a new round.[58]

Dupont holds that Catullus "remains blocked in the preceding time of the *comissatio* and shows himself incapable of reintegrating the succession of social time-periods."[59] But the humor that has been noted shows that Catullus could take a detached, self-ironic view of his situation and that he knew how to execute the convention of the morning-after letter with perfect skill. Further, as an elegant gesture, or the representation in verse thereof, the letter fulfills the neoterics' ideal of a life-style that matches the aesthetic standards of their verse.[60]

But then, Dupont finds, Catullus does reintegrate himself in normal life, because of the letter, which, on her interpretation, appears as a letter only in the lines following those just discussed:

> At defessa labore membra postquam
> semimortua lectulo iacebant
> hoc, iucunde, tibi poema feci
> ex quo perspiceres meum dolorem.   (14–17)

But after my limbs, worn out with suffering were lying half dead on my couch, this poem I made for you, my delightful one, from which you might see my grief.

"The letter signifies the absent dialogue. . . . But the letter also heals, because the letter separates. . . . Catullus has reintegrated the space of ordinary life and the succession of days. The tablets that had served, in the *comissatio,* for fusional games, are reused differently to realize separation and return to normality."[61] Dupont speaks in this way because she believes that Catullus 50 is a real letter and that it has only now become such. (Up to this point, apparently, one did not know exactly what it was.) But then, because these lines also refer

58. See Burgess 1986: 585–86.
59. Dupont 1994: 139.
60. In the formulation of Landolfi 1986: 81: "la specularità degli atteggiamenti esistenziali con gli ideali artistici."
61. Dupont 1994: 141.

to the fact that Catullus has written a poem, Dupont adds that the form of the letter was only in passing.[62] The expression *poema feci* reminds Dupont of the *kalos* inscription found on Greek vases, and she now decides that the "letter-poem" is a vaselike trophy offered to Calvus.[63]

Further, in the concluding lines of the poem, she thinks that the poem becomes an epigram posted as a graffito:

> nunc audax cave sis, precesque nostras,
> oramus, cave despuas, ocelle,
> ne poenas Nemesis reposcat a te;
> est vemens dea: laedere hanc caveto.   (18–21)

Now do not be impudent and do not spurn my prayers I pray, apple of my eye, lest Nemesis claim retribution from you. She is a violent goddess. Beware of offending her.

"This epigram placed between them establishes a dissymmetry in the distance that the usage of the letter had already sketched. . . . The reader is no longer Licinius [Calvus] but the passersby. Licinius [Calvus], for his part, is the object of the discourse; he belongs to the utterance and is no longer the actor of the enunciation."[64] How the poem could have turned into a graffito, when Calvus continues to be addressed just as he was in the passage that identified the poem as a letter, and when the standard diction of Roman elegiac poetry continues,[65] Dupont does not say. She feels no obligation to provide explanations based on the text because she has already decided that the text is not, in her terms, textualized, but is an artifact surviving from some lost pragmatic function.[66]

Her conclusion was already determined by the extension of her premise concerning the Anacreon poem to the rest of antiquity, including Catullus and all of Roman literature. That premise was: "The song of Cleobulus is unread-

---

62. Ibid: "La forme de la lettre n'était qu'un passage . . ."
63. Dupont 1994: 142.
64. Ibid.
65. With *preces . . . nostras*, cf. Ov. *Am.* 1.3.4; with *audax*, cf. Prop. 1.15.27; with *caveto*, cf. Tib. 1.2.89; 6.17; 3.8.3. Warnings are common in erotic poetry. Nemesis as the goddess who humbles the haughty beloved appears already in Greek epigrams: *AP* 5.273; 6.283; 12.140.
66. "Reading-writing is always at the service of another social institution, whether it be the theater, correspondence, the education of children, political language [*la parole politique*] religious rituals, etc." (280).

able because the event, that is, the enunciation, has not been preserved in the utterance and the reader has access only to the utterance."[67] But this situation did not prevent what she calls the textualization of the poem, and, contrary to her suggestion, Dio Chrysostom, who preserves the poem, would hardly have been the first to receive it in the mode of reading. Horace's allusions to Anacreon presuppose an intensive and productive reading of this poet, for example, in *Odes* 1.23.1–3:

> vitas inuleo me similis, Chloe,
> quaerenti pavidam montibus aviis
> matrem . . .

> You avoid me, like a fawn, Chloe,
> seeking in pathless mountains its fearful
> mother . . .

Compare this fragment of Anacreon:

> ἀγανῶς οἷά τε νεβρὸν νεοθηλέα
> γαλαθηνόν, ὅστ᾽ ἐν ὕλῃ κεροέσσης
> ἀπολειφθεὶς ἀπὸ μητρὸς ἐπτοήθη.

> . . . her gently, like a tender unweaned fawn
> that's left alone in the forest by
> its antlered mother, trembling with fright.[68]

Horace was well able to read these words centuries after their first enunciation and to reshape in various ways the image of the fawn separated from its mother. It is unnecessary here to analyze the details, which include Horace's analysis of the finite verb in the Greek into two finite verbs in Latin (*inhorruit*, 5; *tremit*, 8) in the course of an expatiation on what seems to have been a local simile in Anacreon's poem.[69] Roman poets provide countless examples of this kind of close relation to a Greek poetry irreparably sundered from its performance context. To limit myself to the place in Horace just cited, it certainly meets Dupont's own criterion for intertextuality: It is not a mere citation that

---

67. Dupont 1994: 55.
68. Anacreon fr. 39 Diehl = 51 Bergk = 63 Page = 28 Gentili. Trans. by West 1993: 107. I refrain from discussing problems like the doe's antlers.
69. On the relation of this ode to Anacreon, see Cavarzere 1996: 178–81.

only affirms a technical imitation, but has a semantic effect internal to the text.[70] The kind of literary reading presupposed by Horace's allusion to Anacreon in *Odes* 1.23 must long since have typified Roman poets' relation to their predecessors: Consider the relation of the dream of Ennius recounted at the beginning of his *Annals* to the proems of Hesiod's *Theogony* and Callimachus's *Aetia*.

Dupont's procedure leads to complete indifference to the status of Catullus 50 as a poem, which is inferred from the opening lines, and which is corroborated by the reader's (ancient or modern) knowledge that the poem is part of a book of poems that the poet hopes will be read now and forever.[71] She does not understand that, with Catullus, if not earlier, the institution of literature has been achieved, and the reader is no longer merely the agent of the oralization of a nonliterary text but is called upon to play the role that she has well defined: The reader occupies the place of subject of enunciation,[72] which means that reading re-creates each time the subject position of the persona, the fictive speaker of the poem.

Methodological Epilogue

First, whenever I said *Horace, Catullus, Propertius,* and so forth, I was following the convention by which the name of the poet is a metonym for the text under discussion. In the case of Horace, my intent, therefore, was not to contribute something to his biography, but to establish views of reading that can be found in his poems. The reality to which these views correspond is the kinds of reading that Horace expected his readers to be able to grasp. If someone wants to refer these views to the activities of the historical person Horace, I have no objection, but he or she should remember that even in a satire there may be two distinct personae, as in *Satires* 1.10.[73]

Second, Horace as a reader emerged only from my reading of Horace, and my reading of Horace from this point of view comes under the provisions of my Chapter 3. It might be possible to reach a more historical description of

70. For her criterion, see Dupont 1994: 21.

71. Consider the final footnote of Dupont's chapter on Cat. 50: "Le livre aura des *lectores*, c'est-à-dire, comme l'a montré E. Valette-Cagnac, *La lecture à Rome*, thèse de l'EPHE (5ᵉ section), Paris, 1994, qu'il sera lu non pas dans des lectures publiques, mais par un lecteur pour lui-même comme seul destinataire."

72. Dupont 1994: 266.

73. See Brink 1963–82: 1:170–71.

how a Horace would have read, by studying Philodemus, the *Ars poetica,* fragments of Varro and the *grammatici,* and so forth. This historical reading of Horace as reader would not exactly replace my reading, for me anyway, but it might make my reading more self-conscious than it already is.

Third, in my critique of Dupont on Catullus, I did not distinguish the different readings enumerated in Chapter 3. Her interpretation is a failure from the perspective of any and all of the three readings.

EIGHT

Intertextuality
Terms and Theory

The theoreticians of intertextuality themselves represent a
model of intertextuality, inasmuch as the quoting, alluding,
dialogical intertwining of their theoretical products seems
to develop a new type of literary critical discourse.

— Renate Lachmann,
"Concepts of Intertextuality"

In order to avoid an enormous amount of repetition and periphrasis, this
chapter introduces several sigla. These are not my invention but are in use in
fields other than classics, and thus offer the possibility of comparisons.[1]

T_1:   Target text, the text to be explained
T_2:   Source text, the source of intertextual phenomena in T_1
Q_1:   Quotation (allusion, reference, echo) in T_1
Q_2:   Source of Q_1
C_1:   Context of Q_1
C_2:   Context of Q_2

Terms and Definitions

Because the terminology of intertextuality studies is far from standardized, this
discussion of intertextuality in Roman poetry first establishes some provisional
terms and definitions before considering the related theoretical problems.

---

1. Plett 1991b: 8 is my source for the sigla.

The study of intertextuality is the study of a certain kind of relation between texts: One text quotes another or others. *Quotation* is chosen here, in preference to the more common *reference, allusion, echo, reminiscence,* or *transformation*, as a general, inclusive way of describing the phenomenon. To quote means to repeat part of another text in such a way (which would sometimes entail sufficient quantity) that its status as a quotation and its source may be discernible. Quotation, of whatever length, may be either exact or inexact. At one extreme, the same word or words are repeated in the same case in the same metrical position. At the other extreme, scholars have discussed quotation through content, context, syntax, and also sound (i.e., even without repetition of any of the *same* words from one poem to another).[2] But none of these means of quotation is possible without the repetition of words (even if it is only the word shape, the word order, and the sound of the words that are perceived as repeated). Quotation can, of course, indicate a topos- or genre-affiliation, too, and even "weakly lexicalized" relations between texts and genres or topoi still have to be lexicalized. While *quotation* does not serve well to designate large-scale intertextual programs — for instance, Vergil's relation to Hesiod in the *Georgics* — the fact remains that such programs function only in virtue of small-scale, noncontinuous points of contact, and these one can call *quotations*.

Quotation and Citation

An especially perishable kind of quotation is citation, where a poet quotes not simply another poet's words but someone else's saying of those words. A good example is found in the third *Suasoria* of the Elder Seneca. After he gives examples of how various speakers handled the given theme (which is irrelevant to the present discussion), Seneca goes on to provide anecdotal material. He observes that one of the speakers, Arellius Fuscus (one of Ovid's professors of rhetoric, as it happens), was in the habit of introducing Vergilian quotation in order to curry favor with Maecenas. (This kind of quotation — for the purpose of currying favor with a friend of the quoted poet — is a good example of a lost intention, an intention that cannot be operative after the lifetime of Maecenas, except as a historical fact about an earlier function of the quotation.) One of Arellius Fuscus's Vergilian phrases, *plena deo* (not in extant

2. My list is hardly complete. See Wills 1996: 19–24 for a longer list, with examples.

Vergil), reminds Seneca of his friend Gallio, who habitually used the phrase as a way of describing heated declamation.[3] This mannerism became known to Messala and to Tiberius, both of whom found it amusing (*Suas.* 3.6–7). No doubt the feminine adjective *plena* applied to the male declaimer had something to do with the catchiness of the phrase. Then Seneca reports:

> Hoc autem dicebat Gallio Nasoni suo valde placuisse; itaque fecisse illum quod in multis aliis versibus Vergilii fecerat, non subripiendi causa, sed palam mutuandi, hoc animo ut vellet agnosci; esse autem in tragoedia eius: feror huc illuc, vae, plena deo.

> Gallio said that his friend Ovid had very much liked the phrase: and that as a result the poet did something he had done with many other lines of Vergil — with no thought of stealing it, but meaning that his piece of open borrowing should be noticed. And in his tragedy you may read: "I am carried hither and thither, alas, full of the god."[4]

When Ovid repeated the phrase, then, he was repeating not only Vergil but also Gallio, to whose idiolect the phrase was known to belong. If the relevant passage (in the case of Vergil) and text (in the case of Ovid) in which *plena deo* occurred had survived, then, at the beginning of the twenty-first century, the phrase would be a quotation (Ovid's of Vergil) that a scholar might study. In Ovid's time, it was not only a quotation of Vergil's poem but also a citation of Gallio, at least for Gallio's acquaintances. (To repeat, no reader can any longer hear it as such.) How could his acquaintances not have heard the phrase as one that Gallio liked to use? As a citation, it looks not to a source text but to a speaker. For this kind of repetition, it would be necessary to modify Antoine Compagnon's definition of citation: not "un énoncé répété et une énonciation

---

3. Ralph Hexter points out to me that the phrase must refer to the Sibyl and that Servius on *Aen.* 6.50 in fact uses the phrase (ADFLATA EST NUMINE nondum deo plena, sed adflata vicinitate numinis).

4. Winterbottom 1974: 545, with slight modification. As it happens, the phrase *plena deo* is not in extant Ovid, either. It is attributed to his *Medea*.

This passage of the Elder Seneca is often cited or quoted in discussions of Latin *imitatio* and intertextuality. But what does it mean? The opposition between stealth and concealment (*subripiendi*), on the one hand, and openness (*palam; agnosci*), on the other, is the basis of whatever Seneca is saying, I do not see how *subripiendi* can refer to copying or plagiarism (*pace* Silk 1996), because how could it go undetected? The theft of, the concealed use of another poet's work would be re-creation, appropriation (in the spirit of Hor. *AP* 131, *privati iuris*) and the open borrowing would be citation (in the sense in which I am using *citation*).

répétante" but "une énonciation répétée [Gallio's] et une énonciation répétante [presumably Medea's, in Ovid's *Medea*]."[5] But those who perceived the
citation also simultaneously perceived the quotation of Vergil. Neither kind of
perception has to be imagined as canceling out the other.

Another example of citation is Horace *Odes* 3.2.25–26: *est et fideli tuta
silentio / merces*. This sentence is a translation of Simonides (582 Page). Its
interpretation is in dispute. For present purposes, it is enough to observe that
Augustus is known to have quoted Simonides' line to the elderly philosopher
Athenodorus, apparently as a rebuke, when Augustus detained him in Rome,
against his wishes, for a whole year (Plut. *Mor.* 207C). In the context of the
second Roman Ode, the theme of which is service to the state, the line must be
a citation of Augustus as much as a quotation of Simonides. (Because the poem
of Simonides is not extant, it is impossible to interpret the quotation as such.)
So again "une énonciation répétée [Augustus's] et une énonciation répétante
[that of the speaker or persona of Hor. *C.* 3.2]."

Citation has a humorous effect when the source of, or authority for, the
citation is not someone in real life but a fictional character in another poem.
Thus, in Ovid's *Metamorphoses*, Mars reminds Juppiter of his promise to
deify Romulus:

> tu mihi concilio quondam praesente deorum
>
> . . . .
>
> "unus erit quem tu tolles in caerula caeli"
> dixisti.   (14.812–15)

You once said to me in the presence of the assembled gods, "There shall be one
whom you will raise up to the blue of heaven."

Mars cites the words of Juppiter in Ennius's *Annales* (54–55 Skutch):

> "unus erit quem tu tolles in caerula caeli
> templa"

In order to appreciate Ovid's humor one has to distinguish between Ovid's
citation of Ennius and Mars's citation of Juppiter. The latter citation presupposes — Mars is represented as presupposing — that his and Juppiter's and the

5. Compagnon 1979: 55–56. For these terms, see Chapter 7, note 48.

other gods' existence in Ovid is continuous with their existence in Ennius. But they are two separate poetic creations, they belong to two separate fictions. So it is nothing, Ovid suggests, but fiction. Ovid's citation of Ennius, far from confirming the deification of Romulus, reveals its fictionality. Ovid's ironic use of citation here is in keeping with his general skepticism toward Roman ideology.[6]

Ovid is not content, however, with a citation that deflates the authority of the source on which it pretends to rely. Ovid also uses Ennius's lines as a quotation in the intertextual sense here proposed. Ennius says *in caerula caeli / templa*—"into the blue spaces of heaven"—whereas Ovid says *in caerula caeli,* reducing the fuller Ennian phrase, perhaps with the suggestion that it was fulsome.[7] Whatever its effect, the quotation underlies the citation: "un énoncé répété [Ennius *Ann.* 54–55 Skutch] et une énonciation répétante [Ovid *Met.* 14.812–15]" and "une énonciation répétée [Juppiter's in Ennius] et une énonciation répétante [Mars's in Ovid]."[8] This overlapping of quotation by citation (or the other way around, if one prefers) is the same as in Vergil's quotation of Catullus at *Aeneid* 6.460, where Aeneas says to Dido, *invitus, regina, tuo de litore cessi.*

Terms and Definitions Continued; Sigla

The text—that is, for present purposes, a Roman poem—in which the quotation occurs is sometimes called the *target text*. A siglum for this text is T_1. The quoted text is sometimes called the *source text*. A siglum for this text is T_2. (It is usually assumed that T_2, a *pretext*, that is, an earlier [but sometimes still contemporary] text, is not affected by T_1, that intertextuality moves in only one direction. It is also assumed that T_2 is a poetic text. As is argued here, neither of these conditions is necessary.)

The quotation usually, in Roman poetry (and probably in all poetry), has one form in T_1 (Q_1) and another in T_2 (Q_2), though Q_1 and Q_2 may be identical. Classical philology has inventoried the types of relation between Q_1 and

6. With the interpretation here offered, cf. that of Conte (1986: 57–59), who holds that "The dominant function here is the 'authentication' of a new text by an old one." The passages in Ovid and Ennius are also discussed by Hinds 1998: 14–15. Conte's discussion of his other main example of citation (Ov. *Fast.* 3.469–75 in relation to Cat. 64.130–35, 143–44) recognizes Ovid's self-conscious display of the fictionality of his character (in this case, Ariadne).

7. For the extensive bibliography on this quotation of Ennius, see Bömer 1986: 240–41.

8. Cf. the analysis of Ovid *Met.* 14.812–16 in Hinds 1998: 14–16.

Q_2 and has analyzed the deviations between Q_1 and Q_2 in particular cases.[9] In this research, a central distinction is between "integrative" and "reflective" relations between Q_1 and Q_2.[10]

The relation between Q_1 and Q_2 necessarily goes beyond the word(s) of the quotation to the relation between the context of the one and the other (C_1 and C_2). How can one determine how much of C_2 has come into C_1? Here is a large theoretical problem. For now, I observe that, in a large-scale intertextual program like the one mentioned in the next section, the activation of the entire C_2 by C_1 means that C_1 can expose lacunae in C_2, things that, by C_1's inclusion of them, seem as if they ought to have been there in C_2.

Three terms have been rendered ineffective for discussion of intertextuality. One is *intertext*. It is used of T_2 and perhaps more often of Q_1.[11] It is used to characterize the dynamic intertextual relation between texts: "simultaneously pre-text and post-text."[12] It is also used of "a set of texts which are in a relation of intertextuality"[13] and of a "text between other texts."[14] Under these circumstances, it seems best either to avoid this word or to define it clearly and repeatedly for one's own purposes.

The second term is *subtext*. As used by Thomas Greene in his magisterial study of intertextuality in Renaissance poetry, *The Light in Troy,* this term was a synonym for *model*. He distinguished four different forms of a text's relation to its subtext.[15] As in the case of *hypertext,* however, a semantic broadening occurred, and *subtext* came to mean "any meaning or set of meanings which is implied rather than explicitly stated in a literary work, especially a play."[16]

The third term is *hypertext*. Theodor H. Nelson, who coined this word in the 1960s,[17] used it to refer to a kind of electronic writing, which was theorized by Jay David Bolter.[18] It is commonly used also to refer to the electronic

9. See the survey and bibliography in Edmunds 1995.

10. Conte 1986: 66–67.

11. Jenny 1976: 267.

12. Plett 1991b: 17.

13. Jenny 1976: 267 citing Michel Arrivé. Cf. Riffaterre 1980: 626: "The intertext proper is the corpus of texts the reader may legitimately connect with the one before his eyes, that is, the texts brought to mind by what he is reading." Again Riffaterre 1981: 4; 1990: 56.

14. Barthes 1977c: 160; Plett 1991b: 5.

15. Greene 1982: 36–48.

16. Baldick 1990, s.v. "subtext."

17. For the history and concept, see Landow 1992: 2–7.

18. Bolter 1991.

format and storage of texts originally written in a nonelectronic form;[19] in this sense, hypertext has more to do with electronic reading and research than with writing. In 1982, in *Palimpsestes: La littérature au second degré*, Gérard Genette reinvented the word to refer to every relation that unites a text (*hypertext* [T_1]) to an anterior text (*hypotext* [T_2]) on which it grafts itself in a manner which is not that of commentary.[20]

The success of the word *hypertext* in reference to electronic reading and writing has rendered it ineffective for discussion of intertextuality. But one senses that the double invention of the word in less than two decades was not a coincidence — that the two senses are somehow related. Electronic hypertext, whether as reading or writing, activates inter- and intrarelations of texts and produces effects analogous to those of a specifically literary or poetic intertextuality. In its predominant sense, then, *hypertext* seems to support the views of those literary scholars and theorists who regard intertextuality as a symptom of the modern or of the postmodern.[21]

Boundaries

How much of C_2 is comprehended in C_1? Hypothetically, the two extremes are (1) the situation in which Q_1 invokes nothing of C_2 and (2) the situation in which Q_1 invokes all of C_2. I doubt that a pure case of (1) can be found. Q_1 will always invoke something more than the mere words of Q_2. As for (2), there are various ways in which Q_1 can broadly invoke C_2.

(a) The indirect way is via C_1. Q_1's relation to Q_2 appears more fully in an

---

19. This sense of hypertext is assumed by Hodgkin 1991, an excellent short article. He gives this definition: "Current hypertext experiments tend to use two forms of 'non-linear' textual arrangement. Either, a collapsible 'hierarchical' model in which the reader may explore progressively deeper levels of a text by 'burrowing' from a headline or summary to fuller or earlier levels of the text — a hierarchical vehicle would be well suited to a hypertext critical edition of a classical author. Or, alternatively, a 'network' model in which nodes of text are linked by a multiplicity of routes. These two forms of non-linearity can be combined easily. But the 'network' method is used by systems which encourage user participation, and the 'hierarchy' will suit the editor or author who needs to maintain greater control and responsibility for the ways in which the text can be read."

20. Genette 1982: 11. Thus *hypertext* is distinct, supposedly, from *metatextuality*; cf. the top of 12, where he seems to acknowledge that the two could be subsumed in one category. The word *hypertext* caught on in discussion of intertextuality and is still heard, for example, Baldo 1995: 35, etc.

21. Pfister 1985: 10 n. 31, 22; 1994: 217.

enlarged C_1. Jeffrey Wills has shown how, in the course of a reading of book 4 of the *Aeneid*, an initial quotation (at lines 305–6) that links Dido to Catullus's Ariadne in poem 64 (lines 132–33) is reconfirmed and precisely elaborated, even to the point of showing the reader where reference to Ariadne ends.[22]

(b) Where an extensive intertextual program is at work, as in the *Aeneid*'s relation to Homer, a continuous C_2 must be assumed and registered for C_1. Joseph Farrell showed that the same is true of Vergil's *Georgics* in relation to Hesiod and Aratus (book 1), Lucretius (books 2–3), and Homer (book 4).[23] (This kind of extensive intertextual relation to a model or models should be distinguished both from the isolated Q_1-Q_2 relation and also from Conte's Model as Code, on which see the next section.) In such large-scale programs, the continuous relation between C_1 and C_2 is operative even in the absence of quotation. Something, for example, not in C_2 may appear in C_1 as an addition to C_2, and various other relations may emerge at the level of plot or structure. At the same time, the continuous relation between C_1 and C_2 provokes a heightened alertness for quotations and more intense scrutiny when they appear.

(c) The limit case of an extensive relation between C_1 and C_2 is obviously parody, in which T_1 repeats or closely follows a particular T_2 (as distinguished from the genre of T_2). Parody therefore ought to have something to contribute to a theory of intertextuality, and will be discussed at greater length than (a) or (b). (My procedure thus reverses the historical origin of the concept of intertextuality in Kristeva's 1969 essay, which was achieved by a downplaying of parody in the works of Bakhtin with which Kristeva began.)[24] The rival to parody for the status of limit case might seem to be translation, where T_1 in principle quotes all of T_2. But translation is not a matter of intertextuality except in the rare case in which the reader has a precise knowledge of the original (T_2) and reads the translation (T_1) *as such* and not *instead of* the original. Normally, T_2 is unknown to the reader of a translation, who is therefore unaware of any intertextual dynamic between T_1 and T_2. The reader takes it on faith that T_1 is an adequate approximation of T_2.

First, it might be argued, indeed has been argued, as by Bakhtin, that all repetition, thus all quotation, is parody. But then the term becomes useless for

22. Wills 1996: 26–28.
23. Farrell 1991.
24. Kristeva 1969a; Rose 1993: 178–80.

describing one side of intuitive distinctions, for example, the one between Vergil's *Aeneid* and Ovid's retelling thereof. Intuitively, very few would call Vergil's *Aeneid* a parody of Homer; but many would call Ovid's "Aeneid," the long stretch of the *Metamorphoses* modeled on Vergil's *Aeneid* (*Met.* 13.623–14.608), a parody of Vergil's. So parody might be kept as a term for a certain kind of intertextuality. Here I part company with Bakhtin's all-inclusive use of the term, but I would retain his broad distinction between stylized, unironic repetition, on the one hand, and ironic repetition, on the other.[25] The latter is properly parodic and is what is generally meant by parody. Often, as in dictionary definitions, parody is referred to as "ridicule," but this is going too far.

Sometimes in literary theory, the etymology of a term and the ancient concept of the thing that the term refers to are useful. In the case of parody, neither is useful. Aristotle uses the word *parody* in the *Poetics* but it remains a blank in his classification of genres.[26] The uncertainty of parody in Aristotle proves to have been ominous for its future. There is no continuity between ancient and modern views of the matter, and little clarity in the modern period. Gérard Genette has traced the history of the concept since the Renaissance — a record of confusion and disorder.[27] He provides an elaborate schematization, which, among other things, distinguishes between the functional and the structural or formal aspects of parody.[28] The latter are strikingly underdetermined. Parody may be of a style or of a whole work. Further, no particular genre is prescribed for parody, no matter what its object. A satyr play can parody an epic or part of an epic. Neither is parody determined as regards its extent within any particular work. One would have to describe parody, then, as a mode or a strategy.

As for function, it might seem, and has seemed, that all kinds of parody converge on humor. This opinion is simplistic, as appears when one looks at parody in a broader context. I would like to rely on two theories of parody that were developed on the basis of two vast, and vastly different, bodies of material. One is that of Bakhtin in the essays "From the Prehistory of Novelis-

25. Bakhtin 1981.
26. Lanza 1987: 25–26.
27. Genette 1982. Cf. Rose 1993: ch. 2.
28. A distinction not found in Genette: the distinction between literary parody, which is directed against a particular work or style, and instrumental parody, which is directed against some contemporary person or situation. *Catalepton* 10, a precise parody of Cat. 4, is not, or certainly not primarily, directed against Catullus. It makes fun of an upstart politician in the poet's milieu. Cf. Ax 1993.

tic Discourse" and "Discourse Typology in Prose."[29] The other is that of Linda Hutcheon in *A Theory of Parody* and in *A Poetics of Postmodernism*.[30]

Bakhtin, contemplating the relation between medieval Latin literature and its classical and ecclesiastical tradition, finds a key to a general process in *parodia sacra*, the parody of prayer, liturgy, and all ecclesiastical genres. He says, "it is often very difficult to know where reverence ends and ridicule begins." "The complex and contradictory process of accepting and then resisting the other's word, the process of reverently heeding it while at the same time ridiculing it, was accomplished on a grand scale throughout all the Western European world."[31] Hutcheon, taking postmodern architecture as a paradigm, but including every other form of art and literature in her survey, seeks to distinguish the postmodern from the modern. Parody is a criterion. She proposes a redefinition of parody as "repetition with critical distance that allows ironic signaling of difference at the very heart of similarity."[32] What she calls the "postmodern paradox" is this: "To parody is not to destroy the past; in fact to parody is both to enshrine the past and to question it."[33] The point that emerges for a theory of parody is the mixture of respect and critical distance. Parody is not, therefore, simply ridicule and will not even always be humorous.[34]

Although everything that has been said of parody up to this point might suggest that it is the clearest kind of intertextual relation between T_1 and T_2, the opposite is true. Consider first, Ovid's "Aeneid" again. Some take it seriously, as respectful to Vergil; others take it as parody.[35] Classical scholarship on the subject is divided. Also consider, the "Sokal hoax" of 1996. Alan Sokal, a physicist at New York University, published an article in *Social Text* that he had written as a parody of postmodern style and ideas. But the editors of the journal thought it was serious. Sokal published an explanation of the parody in *Lingua Franca*.[36] These two examples reveal a paradox in the nature of

29. Bakhtin 1981.
30. Hutcheon 1985, 1988.
31. Bakhtin 1981: 78–79.
32. Hutcheon 1988: 26.
33. Hutcheon 1988: 126.
34. Cf. Genette 1982: 38 for qualification of the dividing lines in his grids. There are works on the frontier between the ludic and the serious. Cf. also Rose 1993: 40, quoting Röhrich 1967, on the ambivalence of the parodist toward the parodied work.
35. Or even as travesty: Fowler and Fowler 1996. For a survey of opinions, see Brugnoli and Stok 1992: 17 n. 17; Baldo 1995: 29–37.
36. Sokal 1996a and 1996b. For these and related articles, see ⟨http://www.physics.nyu.edu/faculty/sokal/⟩.

parody: Where all of C_2 is invoked, apparently most clearly, the boundary between any Q_1 and C_2 may fail to be noticed,[37] or, if noticed (Ovid's "Aeneid") may be perceived in only one aspect (serious or humorous), to the exclusion of the other.

System Reference

The problem of boundaries becomes still more acute in the case of quotations that refer not to a particular text but to a system. The term *system* is used here to refer to verbal categories, literary and nonliterary, larger than single texts. The systems that I shall discuss are nonpoetic ones of various kinds, myth, and genre. The quotation of a system poses a problem different from the one posed by the quotation of another, identifiable text. When C_2 is a whole system, how much of the system does Q_1 invoke? When the exiled Alcmaeon, ill and destitute, fears the approach of death, he uses the phrase *cruciatum et necem* (Enn. *Scen.* fr. 14). It is closely modeled on contemporary Roman legal language and is thus an anachronism that will have caught the audience's attention.[38] But are the crime (i.e., his matricide) and the anticipated punishment thus to be understood within the framework of Roman law, or, contrariwise, does the very anachronism of the phrase limit its effect, so that it is tantamount to a metaphor (what Alcmaeon fears *is like* the punishment that a Roman criminal fears)? Of course, the loss of most of the tragedy makes this question all the more difficult to answer, but, in this example, as in the others to follow, I prefer to proceed on the hypothesis that the answer is not, or at least not always, a matter of choosing between mutually exclusive alternatives, either a dissolution of the target text into the system, so that the text appears nothing but Kristeva's "mosaic" of quotations, or a pinpointing, by means of Q_1, of some one element in the system.

Systems of Nonpoetic Discourse

One kind of system of discourse is the language specific to an institution, an organization, or a customary social practice. The scale may be large or small. An example of quotation of what might be called a small-scale, clearly delimi-

---

37. Cf. Rose 1993: 42 on conditions under which a reader may fail to perceive parody: "readers do not notice the signals of parody because their sympathy for a parodied text is so strong that their assumptions about it have not been affected by the parody."
38. Jocelyn 1967: 193–94.

table social custom has already been seen in Chapter 4: Horace *Odes* 1.36 (*Et ture et fidibus iuvat*). This ode as a whole clearly belongs to the custom of the *cena adventicia* and its preceding sacrifice, even if precise quotations or refusals to quote are difficult to assess. An example of quotation of a large-scale institution was seen in the passage of Ennius discussed at the beginning of this section.

Again on the small scale, Ovid quotes an institution of the Roman household when he describes Circe's supervision of her nymphs, whose task is not to card fleece and spin wool (i.e., not as in the Roman household), but to sort out the plants and flowers employed by their mistress in her magical arts.

> ipsa, quod hae faciunt, opus exegit, ipsa, quis usus
> quove sit in folio, quae sit concordia mixtis
> novit et advertens pensas examinat herbas.   (*Met.* 14.268–70)

She herself directs their work, she knows the efficacy of each leaf, and which can be mixed with which, and attentively checks the herbs that have been weighed out.

Pensas reminds of *pensum*, the daily quota of wool weighed out by the Roman matron to each of her slaves, to be spun into thread or woven into cloth. With this word, then, Ovid brings back the (anachronistic) model of the Roman household that he at first suggested only negatively (the nymphs' task is not to card fleece and spin wool). Anachronism raises the same question here as in the case of the Ennian example. Should one, at one extreme, see Circe's household as the Roman household mutatis mutandis? Or should one take *pensas* as an isolated, implied metaphor (the nymphs' tasks *are like* the Roman slaves' daily required spinning)?

As I have said, I doubt that an either-or answer is possible. In the case of these quotations of nonliterary systems (which, as just seen, may be institutions invoked by the language specific to them), the problem of the unfixed boundary between Q_1 and C_2 can be usefully stated in terms of Bakhtin's concept of the dialogized word, provided that one can get rid of the vague idea that intertextuality is a kind of dialogue. If by dialogue one means a compositional structure in which two or more participants speak back and forth among themselves, then dialogue is a poor model for intertextuality, in which Q_1 has the final word as soon as it has spoken and Q_2 can never regain its prequoted status (cf. the subsequent discussion of retroactive intertextuality). Which is not to say that a dialogue of texts cannot be an amusing poetic conceit, as it is in Ovid (*Trist.* 1.1.105–19). But if one only slightly reshapes Bakhtin's concept, which he thought did not apply to poetry, one has a useful way of thinking of the quotation of nonliterary systems.[39] For poetry, one can say that a word is dialogized when it is already someone else's (as in the case of system quotation, where the word is the system's — belongs to a particular anonymous group of users, which may extend to a whole social class as in the case of the *cena adventicia*), and at the same time is appropriated by the poet. So the word is, Bakhtin says, "internally dialogized." Two or more speakers are trying, as it were, to speak the word at the same time. This situation, Bakhtin thought, was a special instance of the ordinary, nonliterary social use of language, in which different languages are always competing in a dynamic, ever changing *heteroglossia*. Pursuing the implications of the image of dialogue in this concept of the *dialogized word*, one can say that in the quotation by a poem of a system, the dialogue remains open. Neither side has the last word.

Horace *Odes* 4.2 (*Pindarum quisquis studet aemulari*) can be read as an answer (or refusal to answer) the question, Whose word? The return of Augustus from Gaul is anticipated. A triumph is in preparation. Horace concedes to Iullus Antonius's superior ability the honor of the formal victory ode. His word, not Horace's. Horace's own role will be that of ordinary citizen (45–52). The only poetry that he will contribute will be popular verse:

> Tum meae, si quid loquar audiendum,
> vocis accedet bona pars et 'o sol
> pulcer, o laudande' canam recepto
> Caesare felix.   (45–48)

Then [i.e., on the occasion of the triumph], if I say anything worth hearing, there will be added [i.e., to your victory ode] a good share of my voice, and blessed I'll chant "O happy day, o praiseworthy one" at the return of Caesar.

My word ("my voice"), as distinguished from yours. But the sample of "his" prospective contribution, *o sol / pulcher, o laudande*, amounts to the first half of a trochaic septenarius, that is, of the meter of the songs traditionally sung at

39. Bakhtin 1981: 285: "In genres that are poetic in the narrow sense, the natural dialogization of the word is not put to artistic use, the word is sufficient unto itself and does not presume alien utterances beyond its own boundaries. Poetic style is by convention suspended from any mutual interaction with alien discourse, any allusion to alien discourse." One cannot imagine a more inaccurate description of, say, Horace's *Odes*.

triumphs. The diction of Horace's prospective song is undoubtedly traditional. So my word, not Iullus's, but not really mine, either, as the very contrast with the context (Sapphic stanza, Horatian style, complex recusatio, etc.) shows. The whole ode (n.b. *aemulari* in the first stanza [1] and *imitatus* in the last [58]) thematizes the problem of a poetic appropriation that would remove the word from its internally dialogized state and make it the poet's own.

Whenever Horace or another Roman poet uses an "unpoetic word," a word belonging to some system or other, this word will be internally dialogized. Another Horatian example is *officinas* in *Odes* 1.4.8 (*Solvitur acris hiems*), addressed to Sestius. David West observes that there is quotation in *officinas* of the stamp "OF" (for *officina*) found on the bricks and roof tiles produced in the factory of the Sestii at Cosa.[40] But the internal dialogue can have more than two participants. Horace *Odes* 3.21 (*O nata mecum consule Manlio*), which quotes the typical inscription on a wine jar,[41] is also hymnal, and may also recall Cicero's infamous *o fortunatam natam me consule Romam* (fr. 8 Courtney = 17M = 12B).

From a Marxist point of view, any kind of nonliterary quotation, as well as any kind of reference to contemporary reality that a poet may make, belongs to ideology. Every quotation, every reference is already ideologically informed and undergoes a transformation in poetry. Ideological analysis shows how this process, typically guided by "false consciousness" and complicity with social class and economic power, takes place. The term *ideologeme* is used for the unit of ideology that is identified in a text, which may appear in highly developed conceptual or narrative forms.[42] My disagreement with this Marxist approach to literature is expressed more fully in my subsequent remarks on Kristeva. My view is that, in order to discover that literature is a witting or unwitting tool of class struggle, Marxist analysis begins with an arbitrary cancellation of the ordinary conditions of reading, thus of the possibility of hermeneutic experience that might be liberating.[43]

40. And that there are other "personal" allusions as well. West 1995, referring to Will 1982.

41. Cf. *CIL* IV 2551 = Dessau 8584; *CIL* XV 4539 = Dessau 8580; *CIL* XV 4571 = Dessau 8581. Cf. Hor. *Ep.* 1.5.4–5.

42. Jameson 1981. For the history of the term, which begins with Bakhtin, see Angenot 1983: 124. Angenot observes that, despite the importance of the term in Kristeva (e.g., 1968: 312–13), her coinage *intertextuality* had a vastly greater success.

43. And, lest it be objected that I am talking about some outdated brand of Marxism, I observe that class struggle persists in Fredric Jameson. Cf. Dowling 1984: 128: "Jameson's system demands that we reconceive the social order at the cultural level in the form of a dialogue between antagonistic *class discourses,* which now become the categories within which a Marxist interpretation will rewrite individual texts" (his emphasis).

And yet, its Marxist baggage discarded, Kristeva's notion of the ideological function of the text should be retained. Just as T_1 has a retroactive effect on T_2 in a diachronic, literary perspective, T_1 has a contemporary effect on its social and political context, into which it "inserts itself" or "inscribes itself," to use Kristeva's expressions, and which it thus alters. She says: "Intertextuality is a notion that will be the index of the manner in which a text reads history and inserts itself in history."[44] An example is Horace's reference to Apollo at *Odes* 1.2.31–32, a poem in honor of Augustus. Here it is less useful to speak of an ideologeme entering the poem than it is to see the poem as entering the context of Augustus's association of himself with Apollo.[45] The poem becomes part of a larger "text" (for me, though not for Kristeva, it is a metaphor) or, better, a larger semiotic context. I offer an example of how it is happening even now. Paul Celan's "Todesfuge" (to say nothing of much of the rest of his oeuvre, which has the same effect) becomes part of the memory of a period in German history and contributes to making that memory permanent.[46]

Myth

Another kind of verbal system that poems quote, a myth is a set of narrative variants in poetry or prose or oral tradition or in two or in all three of these. (Of course, a myth may also be represented in pictorial or plastic arts, too.) To quote a myth is therefore usually to give a particular version of it. But this version cannot suppress the others. Indeed, it may evoke them — thus, the question of boundaries. What does this present version exclude? What does it evoke?

An example of mythical quotation is the story of the daughters of Anius in Ovid *Metamorphoses* 13.644–74. The first instinct of most readers is to read this story in relation to its primary model in Vergil's *Aeneid,* where the daughters are not, in fact, mentioned. But Ovid's version of the episode (the daughters trying to escape from their Achaean captors are saved by Bacchus, who transforms them into doves) inevitably evokes others.[47] Anius gave Aeneas his daughter Lavinia, who had the gift of prophecy, and Lavinium was named after her (i.e., not after the daughter of Latinus), who died during its construction and was buried on the spot (Dion. Hal. 1.59.3). Servius Danielis

44. Kristeva 1968: 311.

45. Nisbet and Hubbard 1970: 30 on line 32; Zanker 1988: 49–53.

46. And intertextuality is one of the ways in which it happens. Consider the title of Safranski 1994, a biography of Heidegger: *Ein Meister aus Deutschland.* It is a phrase from "Todesfuge." (As Barchiesi [1997: 221] said, "più la letteratura parla di se stessa, più parla del mondo.")

47. Before Ovid, the metamorphosis of the daughters is attested, if at all, only in Lycophron 580. For this and other sources, see the discussion in Irving 1990: 233–34.

knows a version in which a daughter (unnamed) of Anius was secretly debauched by Aeneas and bore a child (on *Aen.* 3.80). What might be called the
Trojan period (Trojan relations with the daughters after the Trojan War) bal-
ances the Achaean period (Achaean relations with the daughters before the
Trojan War). The latter is attested already in the *Cypria* (fr. 29 Bernabé).

Each period, in different versions, receives both a negative and a positive
slant. Aeneas's good and bad relations with the daughter have just been seen.
As for the Achaeans, they took the daughters by force (Ovid and perhaps
Simonides [fr. 537 Page = schol. Hom. *Od.* 6.164]). Or Anius graciously sent
them along with the Achaeans, and, with their magical powers to produce
wine, oil, and grain, the daughters supported the Achaeans at Troy (Phe-
recydes *FgrHist* 3 F 140). The story was so well established that Thucydides
was obliged to correct it: The Achaeans turned to plunder and to farming the
Chersonese (1.11.1). The usual number of daughters in the Achaean period is
three and their names are well known: Oino, Spermo, and Elaïs (Wine-girl,
Seed-girl, and Oil-girl). Ovid, however, tells of four daughters (and also a son,
who has no bearing on the point I am developing), without mentioning their
special powers (so the Achaeans were inspired by lust?). Why four?[48] The dis-
crepancy between Ovid's and the canonical number produces an extra daughter. The tradition also knew of an extra daughter, namely Lavinia, or the unnamed one debauched by Aeneas. Ovid's version seems, at this point, to open
onto that tradition. One does not know exactly where to draw the boundary.

Genre

If one assumes that every Roman poem belongs to some recognizable genre
or other, then every Q_1 points not only to Q_2 but also to the genre of Q_2. So
every quotation has a double function. Conte formulated this principle in
terms of "Exemplary Model" and "Model as Code,"[49] and said each quotation
"denotes a specific meaning" and "it also functions as the connotator of a
literary manner, a genre or a subgenre." Intertextuality, in short, "involves
a whole series of processes of generalization."[50] Someone who had never read
a Roman poem might think that it would be possible to trace these processes.
On the contrary, Roman poems tend to contest their generic affiliation(s) at
the same time that they (necessarily) affirm it or them. The question of genre

48. Bömer 1982: 372: "warum es bei Ovid vier sind . . . , dafür gibt es keine sichere Erklärung."
49. Conte 1986: 31. Cf. Conte and Barchiesi 1989: 93–95.
50. Conte 1994a: 135.

typically appears in the context of *recusatio*. So, for any Roman poem, its boundary with its genre or genres will be difficult to define.[51] Roman poems exemplify Jacques Derrida's "law of genre." Derrida focuses on the peculiarity of generic quotation that it does not itself belong to the genre that it quotes.

> What are we doing when, to practice a "genre," we quote a genre, represent it, stage it, expose its *generic law,* analyze it practically? Are we still practicing the genre? Does the "work" still belong to the genre it re-cites? But inversely, how could we make a genre work without refering to it [quasi-]quotationally, indicating at some point, "See, this is a work of such-and-such a genre?" Such an indication does not belong to the genre and makes the statement of belonging an ironical exercise. It interrupts the very belonging of which it is a necessary condition.[52]

In another of his essays on the subject, "The Law of Genre," he says that "the trait that marks the membership [in a set] inevitably divides, the boundary of the set comes to form . . . an internal pocket."[53]

Stephen Hinds has shown what one can expect to find in the pockets.[54] First, Roman poets tend to refashion particular traditions or genres for ad hoc purposes, for each new poem. So quotation is not of some "reified" or "essentialized" genre; rather, the genre is re-created. Hinds refers to "do-it-yourself literary tradition."[55] The tradition therefore appears in each poem not as such (it does not exist as such) but as the figure of the tradition. So one can speak of a troping of the tradition. In Hinds's main example, Statius has managed to write Catullus 64 into his *Achilleid* as the, or part of the, epic tradition for his epic, and he has done the same with Ovid's *Metamorphoses.* But the contents of pockets tend to be invisible and, as Hinds observes, it was not until lately, after the revival of scholarly interest in the *Metamorphoses,* that this side of Statius's code model could be perceived. (To anticipate my subsequent discussion, the uncertainty concerning the generic boundaries of the *Achilleid* is resolved, at any given time, within its readership's horizon of expectation.)

---

51. Conte 1991: 166 remarks: "Ogni nuovo testo giustifica in corso d'opera il proprio rapporto con il sistema dei generi letterari, che è *contemporaneamente preso a norma ed eluso*" (my emphasis).

52. Derrida 1979: 86.

53. Derrida 1992: 227–28. For a good, commonsense description of the phenomenon, see Lowrie 1997b: 37 (who, however, also cites Derrida).

54. Hinds 1998. And even, to continue the humor of the second section of his chapter 5 ("Local manipulation"), what Roman poets are handling.

55. This is the heading of the first section of his chapter 5.

Second, a generic marker may be overwritten by other markers. Hinds shows the difficulty of taking *me miserum* at Ovid *Amores* 1.1.25 as a quotation of, and thus a marker of generic affiliation to, Propertius 1.1.1. Hinds himself would like to take the phrase as such but shows the difficulty of hearing a specifically Propertian resonance above the hubbub of previous and contemporary reiterations in poetry and in life. This hubbub, Hinds says, is "composed of countless negotiations within and between the discourses of Roman culture."[56] How then does Ovid's use of the phrase in the first poem of the first book of the *Amores* align his poem with the genre that was in some sense announced in the first poem of Propertius's *monobiblos*?

Uncertainty

The two preceding sections have shown a difficulty that begins to appear specific to intertextuality, namely the problem of boundaries. Paradoxically, the intertextual gesture that ought, by contrast or even by opposition, as the case may be, to delimit the new text in fact simultaneously problematizes its self-delimiting. Parody, which presented itself as the limit case of intertextuality, points to this kind of uncertainty as a central feature of intertextuality, *even when its existence in a particular text is not in doubt* — uncertainty about tone or attitude in parody is just a clearer case of the uncertainty already encountered in the discussion of boundaries. The various kinds of system reference, for their part, all entail a blurring of boundaries.

In the rhetorical figure of syllepsis, the same word is used in two ways, one literal, the other figurative. (So another kind of *dialogization*.) Michael Riffaterre analyzed intertextuality on the model of this figure, which captures the principle of uncertainty that has emerged here.[57] In a poetic or literary text, a word has a contextual meaning and bears some referential relation to a nontextual realm; it also has an intertextual meaning, referring to another text or other texts or some other verbal system. The context, in its own best interest,

56. Hinds 1998: 33.

57. Riffaterre 1978: 81; 1979; 1980. With approval from Conte 1986: 30 n. 14 but repudiation by Conte and Barchiesi 1989: 98 n. 15. Cf. the more tentative assimilation of quotation to trope in Compagnon 1979: 69.

My use of Riffaterre's concept is a deliberate misappropriation, somewhat in the spirit of the phenomenon as described by him, that is, leaving a conflict between his use and my reuse. To take the most obvious example, whereas the individual word is the paradigm of intertextual syllepsis for him, I am applying syllepsis to phrases and longer sequences.

as it were, tries to repress the distracting intertextual meaning, but the re-
pressed returns and disseminates itself in the text.[58]

At this point, an example is in order.[59] In the first line of poem 101, Catullus
says: "borne through many lands and many seas" (*multas per gentes et multa
per aequora vectus*). This phrase has a certain sense, but demands, both gram-
matically and in other ways, to be completed. The following line provides the
completion: "I have come, brother, to make this sad offering" (*advenio has
miseras, frater, ad inferias*). So the sense is completed in an elegiac couplet; and
the reader sees the goal of the journey adumbrated in the first line: the performance of funeral rites for the speaker's brother. But the reader also hears
something else in the first line, the voyage of Odysseus, who saw the cities of
many men and suffered many sorrows on the sea (*Od.* 1.1–4). This "figurative" sense of Catullus's first line (the speaker is Odysseus) does not exactly
square with the contextual sense. Some degree of tension is created (already by
the reuse of Homeric epic in the opening of an elegiac epigram) and thus some
degree of uncertainty.[60]

Riffaterre thought that texts had, in general, two ways of working with this
uncertainty or undecidability. One was to leave an irreducible conflict between
the two meanings, contextual and intertextual (a conflict that, by the way,
is characteristic of parody). The other was to allow the figurative sense to
take over and determine the meaning (in the case of Catullus 101.1, the
reader would acquiesce [most improbably] in the meaning: I am Odysseus).[61]
Whereas Riffaterre takes an either-or approach to the matter, and also establishes a typology of intertextual syllepsis, I prefer to put undecidability on a
scale whereon most of intertexual research lies between an extreme in which
conflict seems irreducible and unmeaningful and an extreme in which T_2 becomes transparent in T_1 and may therefore go unnoticed (cf. the Sokal hoax).

A notorious example of irreducibility is *Aeneid* 6.460, where Aeneas says

58. Riffaterre 1979: 496 refers explicitly to the Freudian concept of repression. Riffaterre 1987
conceptualizes syllepsis in terms of psychoanalysis. "Intertextuality . . . is tantamount to a mimesis
of repression" (374).

59. This is the example with which the first chapter of Conte 1986 begins.

60. Conte (1986: 66–67) gives Cat. 101.1 as an example of "integrative allusion," which
"produces a condensation of two voices in a single image whose sense lies in an interdependence of
meanings that become subjectively equivalent." The counterpart of "integrative" is "reflective
allusion" (cf. the third section in this chapter). In the manner of Riffaterre, Conte establishes an all-
inclusive pair, obliging himself to put each example in one category or the other.

61. Riffaterre 1979: 497; 1980: 629.

to Dido, "Unwilling, queen, I departed from your shore" (*invitus, regina, tuo de litore cessi*). It is a quotation of Catullus 66.39, where the lock says to Berenice: "Unwilling, queen, I departed from your head" (*invita, o regina, tuo de vertice cessi*). For most readers, it is impossible to imagine that the Catullan source is nothing but a source and not a reference of some kind to the lock of Berenice. Any reference of C_1 (pathos, etc.) to C_2 (frivolity, etc.) seems, however, somehow wrong. Oliver Lyne has proposed to reduce the conflict between contextual and intertextual meanings by reading the citation in an expanded C_1. Recalling several other details in C_1 and also the fact that Dido, like Berenice, has a lock severed from her head (*Aen.* 4.693ff.), Lyne shows, in effect, that C_1 has to be expanded in order to accommodate Q_1.[62] From the expanded context in T_1, a tragic contrast between Dido and Berenice emerges that does not emerge from exclusive concentration on *invitus, regina, tuo de litore cessi* as an isolated quotation. In terms of the distinction that I have been employing, Vergil's quotation of Catullus is, like Aeneas's citation of the lock, a kind of tragic irony. The quotation *as a quotation,* however, as in the case of Ovid *Metamorphoses* 14.812–15, adds another layer of interpretation.[63]

The best example of transparency, though fictional, is a telling one. Jorge Luis Borges wrote about a French symbolist poet, Pierre Menard, who planned to compose another *Don Quixote* that would coincide word for word with the original.[64] He would not, however, transcribe or copy the original but rewrite it by his own efforts; and he succeeded in finishing two chapters and part of another before his death. T_2 is here perfectly transparent in T_1. But, says Borges (in the persona of a close friend of Menard writing in Nîmes in 1939): "The text of Cervantes and that of Menard are verbally identical, but the second is almost infinitely richer."[65] He proceeds to give examples, maintaining the humorous fiction that the two texts, while verbally identical, are quite different. Borges's reader knows that the difference lies not in the texts but in the reader's perspective, and, in the last paragraph of the essay, Borges

62. Lyne 1994. Cf. O'Sullivan 1993 for a formulation of the problem that Lyne is addressing: "So, unconscious or intended, the point about this particular passage [*Aen.* 6.460] is that Vergil cannot want us to think about the original context of the line he has adapted. . . . I conclude that the original context of Catullus' poem has nothing to do with the meaning of the line in Vergil." See Farrell 1993 for a reply to O'Sullivan.

63. Most recently Barchiesi 1997: 212–17.

64. Borges [1956] 1962. This passage is often quoted in discussion of intertextuality, but always without the last part, on reading.

65. Borges [1956] 1962: 52.

concedes the ploy: "Menard . . . has enriched, by means of a new technique, the . . . art of reading."[66] But Borges does so only for the sake of a new, climactic joke: It dawns on Menard's pretentious, excessively devoted, and somewhat dim-witted friend that reading is the mode in which the older text appears differently in the new text, even when the two are verbally identical.

Reader

Riffaterre's theory of intertextuality entails a theory of reading, for a critique of which this is not the place.[67] A central principle of his seems to me, however, indisputable: Intertextual reading is the opposite of linear reading.[68] For this reason, it always entails a retroactive movement[69] — consideration of at least one other text beside T_1; then rereading. In Chapter 3, following Jauss, I propose a series of rereadings. The reader's experience of intertextuality will be deployed, according to the nature of the text, the reader's initial competence, and the depth of his research, across these three readings. Given the peculiar nature of intertextuality, which has been described here as undecidability, the reader will have to make a decision or decisions, at least pro tempore, at least for the sake of his own reading, in the face of the text's undecidability. While the three, sequential readings impose a certain pattern, the fundamental procedure is not as far from common sense as it might seem to be at first.

Even in the case considered earlier, the *Aeneid*'s relation to Homer, where everything seems to be given, in reality only the general program of imitation is given. Everything remains to be decided, and the reader is the one who decides. Joseph Farrell has described the reader's relation to Vergil's *Aeneid* as follows:

My proposal is that in the presence of a great many phenomena (I think mainly of intertextual ones, such as allusions to Homer or self-quotations), we are encour-

66. Borges [1956] 1962: 54.
67. He maintains that it is not allusion or quotation but anomaly or obscurity that triggers the reader's perception of intertextuality (1980: 627–28). The perception, and the appropriate response, are obligatory. Cf. in my Chapter 4: "The test for allusion is that it is a phenomenon that some reader or readers may fail to observe" (Miner 1994). Riffaterre's invocation of a passage of La Fontaine in his interpretation of a passage of Laforgue seems to me an example of his perception of an allusion, though he insists that the "linguistic competence of the average Frenchman imposes" the perception on his reading (1979: 498).
68. Riffaterre 1981: 5–6.
69. Riffaterre 1980: 626.

aged to look for more of the same and in fact rewarded for doing so. That is to say, the more obvious, and obviously intended aspects of Vergil's allusive program encourage the reader to look further for less obvious, less obviously intended examples as well. This is especially so when a totalizing relationship is created, as for instance between the *Aeneid* and the two Homeric epics *toto caelo*. Here a situation arises in which, if a Homeric scene is not represented by an obvious Vergilian imitation, the reader is encouraged to hunt for it. And the fact that scenes can be represented by more than one imitation, as apparently happens in the case of Odysseus'/Aeneas'/Palinurus' voyage to Scheria/Libya/Italy, means that the search is in principle never really over. This is not to say that Vergil foresaw all the possible correspondences between the *Aeneid* and the Homeric poems. Rather he created a poem that encourages readers to think of it as a recapitulation of both the *Iliad* and the *Odyssey* in their entirety, one that is in theory exhaustive, but never complete in that it is not unlikely to return to the same Homeric scene several times. By writing in this way, I would suggest, Vergil sets in motion a process whereby he actively enlists the reader's cooperation in creating, or better, discovering intertextual relationships between the texts in question. He will not have foreseen them all himself, but he will have "deliberately" set in motion a process that extends his imitation of Homer well beyond his conscious design and will by implication have given his authorial approval to whatever the reader may perceive. The reader still has the burden of making sense out of whatever s/he notices, and this can be done well or badly, and other readers may accept or deny what s/he comes up with. But the apparent fact that Vergil's poetry encourages the perception of intertextual phenomena seems to me the factor that liberates the reader from concern with nothing but what s/he can feel the poet "intended" his allusions to accomplish, or even whether he intended all of them at all.[70]

Farrell has well described the position of the reader in relation to intertextual undecidability. Text-immanent approaches, including Conte's reader-addressee, cannot solve the problem of boundaries.

Signs and Markers

While Q_1 and Q_2 each have a material basis in writing or in sound, the relation between them does not. Karlheinz Stierle has formulated the matter as follows: "A relation in which what is present refers to what is absent is, in the most general respect, a semiotic one. In this sense, the intertextual relation is a com-

---

70. E-mail message to his Vergil course and external participants posted Oct. 26, 1995 (http://vergil.classics.upenn.edu).

plex semiotic relation insofar as therein a linguistically organized sign context refers to another linguistically organized sign context but in such a way that *this reference is not itself of a linguistic kind.*[71] If the reference is not linguistic, it is not semiotic either. Stierle has, in effect, presented a paradox: One context "refers" to another, but nonsemiotically. Lacking any linguistic or semiotic basis, reference can take place only in the mind of a reader,[72] and no amount of theorizing will ever be able to locate either the markers or the boundaries of intertextuality in texts. Pasquali's pronouncement takes on a new meaning: "Allusions do not produce their intended effect except on a reader who clearly recalls the text to which reference is made."[73]

So far as I know, no one has been able to provide a coherent semiotic theory of intertextual quotation. Antoine Compagnon attempted to interpret citation, in which he included what is here discussed as intertextuality, systematically in terms of C. S. Peirce's triadic structure of the sign (sign, object, interpretant), but, in so doing, he was (inevitably, I would say) led to violate Peirce's concept of the interpretant, speaking of it not as the mental concept that links sign and object but in terms of a reader, and even imagining what could be called a history of reception:

Le pouvoir de représenter l'objet est dévolu au signe par un interprétant, c'est-à-dire aussi par quelqu'un: auteur, lecteur, etc. L'objet lui-même n'est jamais saisi sans l'entremise de l'élément tiers qu'est l'interprétant. Or l'interprétant n'est jamais singulier, il est sériel: le *sens* d'une citation est infini, il est ouvert à la succession des interprétants.[74]

71. Stierle 1983: 13–14: "Eine Relation, bei der Gegebenes auf Abwesendes verweist, ist in allgemeiner Hinsicht eine semiotische Relation. In diesem Sinne ist die Intertextualitätsrelation eine komplexe semiotische Relation insofern, als in ihr ein sprachlich organisierter Zeichenzusammenhang auf einen anderen sprachlich organisierten Zeichenzusammenhang verweist, aber so daß diese Verweisung selbst nicht sprachlicher Art ist" (my emphasis in the translation). Cf. Iser 1978: 121 "something which is not stated by the linguistic signs."

72. This reader bears a superficial resemblance to Joseph Pucci's "full-knowing reader." As this term implies, Pucci's (1998: 43–44) reader is autonomous and makes the meaning of allusions. But the allusions themselves are also autonomous. They have their own existence and are there to "create" the reader: "My claim is that allusion demands, and in demanding creates, a powerful reader" (28). The apparent contradiction is resolved by the transitory nature of allusion in a poem: The reader is powerful when there is allusion, less powerful or not powerful when there is no allusion. The "non-allusive parts of the text are . . . more securely controlled interpretively by the intention of their author" (45).

73. 1968: 275: "[L]e allusioni non producono l'effetto voluto se non su un lettore che si ricordi chiaramente del testo cui si riferiscono."

74. Compagnon 1979: 61. For the reader, cf. also 359: "il revient à la lecture," etc. For Peirce's concept of the interpretant, cf. Ducrot and Todorov 1979: 85–86.

In fact, it is remarkable how the construal of a semiotics of citation on the basis of Peirce leads, via the interpretant, to something that looks more and more like hermeneutics. There is always something, Compagnon says, that escapes interpretation, and, in this way, interpretation differs from the totalizing and possessive act that comprehension is or aims to be. As the prepositional prefix of the word *interpretation* shows, the interpreter performs a different kind of act, occupying a place *between*, so that the thing to be interpreted is never absolutely and finally comprehended, *grasped* but remains open to the future, or, as suggested above, to a history of reception.[75]

Neither has German theory of the intertextual marker been able to ground marking in a semiotics of the intertextual sign. Ulrich Broich's "Formen der Markierung von Intertextualität" is illustrative. This essay assembles a dossier of internal and external markers, the latter in *Nebentexten* or what, thanks to Genette, English speakers now call paratexts. The examples are modern. The internal markers are not quoted words or phrases but things like the romances that Don Quixote reads, which indicate the generic affiliation of the novel *Don Quixote*. In fairness to Broich, it should be pointed out that he never pretended that markers, even those of the most explicit kind, had any autonomous status in texts. "In numerous respects," he said at the beginning of his essay, "the perceptibility of marking depends on the recipient."[76]

The negative position on the semiotics of quotation that I have taken is not at all contrary to recent thinking in the field of classics. Jeffrey Wills, in his magisterial study of intertextuality in Latin poetry, states early on that "although the technical methods I discuss pretend to independence of interpretation, I am well aware that detecting an allusion is a process of reading that depends on one's overall view of a given work or tradition."[77] Though Wills's use of the term *marker* will probably be seized on by some for positivist purposes, he has provided abundant elaboration of the point of view just cited. One kind of marker, however, is likely to retain a claim to independence, and this is the external marker to which David O. Ross gave the name "Alexandrian footnote" in 1975, when it already had a considerable history in scholarship.[78] It is often encountered in Roman poetry (e.g., *dicitur, fertur,*

---

75. Compagnon 1979: 74; and in this context he invokes Heidegger.
76. Broich 1985: 33.
77. Wills 1996: 16. In a footnote on this sentence, he cites Fish 1980.
78. Ross 1975: 77–78. For the history, see the bibliographies in Horsfall 1988: 32 n. 13 and 1990: 60 n. 3.

perhibent, ut fama est, ut aiunt, ut mihi narratur, recordor, repeto, refero, memini).[79] One can observe, first, that such markers primarily refer not to quotations in the contexts in which they occur but to other narrative traditions (and perhaps to other texts) that are invoked as authorities or rejected or otherwise signaled.[80] Second, quotations have to be perceived before such markers can be perceived as marking them. And the markers themselves are learned in the same process in which readers learn to recognize quotation.[81]

Reading

One has returned to reading. Intertextuality is only a particular case of the general condition of reading, which Iser has described as follows:

> We have outlined the reader's role as a textual structure, which, however, will be fully implemented only when it induces structured acts in the reader. The reason for this is that although the textual perspectives themselves are given, their gradual convergence and final meeting place *are not linguistically formulated and so have to be imagined.* This is the point where the textual structure of his role begins to affect the reader. The instructions provided stimulate mental images, which animate *what is linguistically implied, though not said.*[82]

What is true of the internal relations of the text is true a fortiori of its intertextual relations. The latter must be one of the things activated in the structuring activity of the reader, without which even a quotation set off by quotation marks fails to have meaning. I shall not pause here to pursue my misgivings about the apparently determining function of the text in this formulation.[83]

79. These examples are extracted from a longer list at Wills 1996: 31.

80. Cf. Stinton 1976.

81. Wills 1996: 32–33: "To state the circle fully: our interpretation of an allusion relies on a recognition of an allusion, which relies on a recognition of markings, which relies on an education about markings, which itself relies on our experience and interpretation of the tradition, including that allusion." In a footnote on this sentence, he cites Fish 1980.

82. Iser 1978: 36 (my emphasis).

83. Fish (1981) reacts to what I would call a tendency in Iser to suggest that the text is not only given but determinate and to some extent determining. In his reply to Fish, Iser (1981) emphasized a distinction between the given and the determinate (85) and said: "the reader . . . tries to make something determinate out of something indeterminate" (86). For a reflex of what I have called a tendency in Iser, cf. Pucci 1998: 29 n. 3: "Iser is concerned with the presence of a model reader, who is manipulated by the text." Pucci states, by the way, that his own concept of the reader, who is not a "general reader," is unrelated to the controversy between Fish and Iser (Pucci 1998: 43 n. 25).

This activity belies Kristeva's concept of the paragram in the tabular, non-linear model of the poem. At no level of reading, from the physiological-cognitive to the hermeneutic, does the reader build up a perception by aggregating discrete bits of information. Once he has learned to read, the reader does not read individual letters, then syllables, then words, and so forth; he reads phrases. Neither does the reader of a literary text read individual words; guided by memory and expectation, he builds up consistency from a selection of data, without ever perceiving all the data either discretely or as a sum.[84] The reader never has all the data in view, even in reading a short poem, and therefore never has the analytical, Kristevan perspective on the text. Kristeva's detached *sujet connaissant* is an artifical construct,[85] as is the text's material productivity, which is a highly abstract theory about the text, not the model of a text that anyone has ever perceived, or could perceive, in reading. The real conditions of the text, and, for that matter, of the institution of literature of which the text is a part, are left untouched by this theory.[86]

The activity of the reader is also the basis of a critique of Barbara Johnson's deconstructive application of Kristeva's paragram. Johnson argues that once intertextuality becomes a repeated, self-conscious gesture, it affects the relation of the text to itself as much as the relation of the text to other texts. In the case of Mallarmé, the poet was conscious, as some of his critical writings show, of creating "blanks," where echoes, in virtue of the intertextual program, might have been expected but were suppressed. Johnson says: "Through the breaks and the blanks in his texts, Mallarmé internalizes intertextual heterogeneity and puts it to work not as a relation *between* texts but as a play of intervals and interruptions *within* texts. Mallarmé's intertextuality then becomes an explicit version of the ways in which a text is never its own contemporary, cannot constitute a self-contained whole, conveys only its noncoincidence with itself."[87] As often happens, one feels that the deconstructive critic is beginning from the same observation as the hermeneuticist (in this case, blanks in the text) but, for reasons that lie far beyond the present discussion, reaching a conclusion 180 degrees distant. One of the things that the

---

84. Iser 1978: ch. 5. And the same is true of the ancient Roman reader. Cf. Susini 1988: 120, where he states that "the kind of reading familiar to Romans was a kind of global reading or reading in sets."

85. Kristeva 1968: 311, quoted in Chapter 1, note 53.

86. Critique of Kristeva's intertextuality from the phenomenological and aesthetic standpoint in Stierle 1983: 12–17.

87. Johnson 1985: 270 (her emphasis).

reader does is to fill in the blanks, which are not only the ones created by intertextuality but also the ones that are always, already there in every textual possible world. As for the intertextual ones, filling them may even, in an extreme case like *écriture automatique,* create a unity that would not otherwise appear.[88]

The reader is also the one who rescues the text from dissolution in the vastness of diachronic literary tradition — the "musée imaginaire" (Malraux), the "chambre d'échos" (Barthes), or the "Bibliothèque générale" (Grivel),[89] and even the "general text" (Derrida). "Literary works do have meaning for readers" (it is odd that one should have to be reminded; I use the words of Jonathan Culler),[90] and they have meaning because the reader in the course of reading keeps reestablishing the poem as a hermeneutic whole.[91] Different readers will be able to integrate different kinds and amounts of intertextuality into their readings. In this process, intertextuality, as said, discriminates among readers.[92] Further, differences between modern and ancient readers will appear: Some quotations will become known to some readers only in the third of the Jaussian readings, the historicizing one, and will go to answer the question, What did the text say? (past tense), which is not a useless question because the answer in turn goes to define the modern reader's relation to the text through the question, What does the text say? (present tense).

Retroactive Intertextuality

Once the reader becomes the locus of intertextuality, the paradox set forth by T. S. Eliot in "Tradition and the Individual Talent" (1917) becomes a matter of common sense. He conceived of the whole of European literature as a simultaneous order, readjusted, however, by each new work in such a way that the present alters the past.[93] His point is paradoxical if one thinks in terms of unchanging poets and texts but obvious (as finally even to Pierre Menard's

---

88. As Riffaterre (1990) shows in the case of a prose poem, the product of *écriture automatique,* by André Breton, in which the intertexts "make up for what automatic writing eliminates: the orderly teleological progress towards a conclusive and unified significance" (59).

89. Plett 1991b: 25.

90. Culler 1981: 38–39.

91. Lachmann 1989: 399, summing up the state of the question: "theoreticians of intertextuality have remained concerned with preserving the concept of the *one* ultimate meaning."

92. Cf. Farrell 1991: 24.

93. Eliot 1950.

friend) if one thinks in terms of readers, who inevitably read or reread earlier texts in the light of their reading of later ones. In the spirit of Eliot, Borges wrote in "Kafka and His Precursors" of how he had come to read several texts written before Kafka's lifetime as prefigurations of Kafka. In the concluding paragraph of his essay, he writes of one of these texts:

> The poem "Fears and Scruples" by Robert Browning is like a prophecy of Kafka's stories, but our reading of Kafka refines and changes our reading of the poem perceptibly. Browning did not read it as we read it now. The word precursor is indispensable in the vocabulary of criticism, but one should try to purify it from every connotation of polemic or rivalry. The fact is that each writer *creates* his precursors. His work modifies our conception of the past, as it will modify the future.[94]

This notion of precursor is rarely encountered in scholarship on Roman poetry, which keeps intertextuality in a one-way relation of later T_1 to earlier T_2 (T_1 quotes T_2). But this relation is reversible.[95] An obvious case is parody, discussed earlier as the limit case of intertextuality. A successful parody not only quotes an earlier work but changes every rereading of it. After Ovid's quotation of the scene in his "Aeneid," Cybele's transformation of the ships of Aeneas into sea nymphs (*Aen.* 9.77–122) came to seem too Ovidian, unworthy of Vergil.[96]

Parody can also be adopted as a transitory stylistic technique within a work that is not a parody as a whole. T_1 may quote T_2 with a limited parodistic effect.[97] An example is Aeneas's description of the blinded Cyclops: *monstrum horrendum, informe, ingens, cui lumen ademptum,* "a dreadful, misshapen, enormous monster, from whom the light of his eye had been taken" (*Aen.*

---

94. Borges [1951] 1964. Cf. Fowler 1994: 239: "the *Aeneid* of Vergilian scholars is very different from the *Aeneid* of Lucan specialists."

95. Cf. Bloom 1973: Browning, Dickinson, Yeats, and Stevens "achieve a style that captures and oddly retains priority over their precursors, so that the tyranny of time is almost overturned, and one can believe, for a startled moment, that they are being *imitated by their ancestors*" (his emphasis).

96. Cf. Fantham 1990: 102; Hinds 1998: 106 n. 12.

97. This is what Genette calls "minimal parody" or "parody in the strict sense," a citation turned from its original sense (1982: 24). I would call attention here to Genette's expression, "citation." The distinguishing characteristic of minimal parody is overt repetition that requires to be recognized as such and contrasts markedly with its former context.

3.658).[98] The phrase *lumen ademptum* quotes Catullus 68.93, where the same phrase is used to refer to the death of Catullus's brother: *ei misero fratri iucundum lumen ademptum*, "alas sweet light taken from a wretched brother." The Catullan association of the phrase in the Vergilian context is reinforced and made unmistakeable by similar locutions concerning his brother's death at Catullus 68.20 and 101.6 (and cf. *DRN* 3.1033, where *lumine adempto* occurs in line-initial position apropos of Xerxes in a series of exempla illustrating the topos: Death comes to all alike).[99] Vergil has transferred the phrase, with change of meaning from "light of life" to "light of the eye," from a pathetic to a grotesque object, with a subversive effect on the model, which no one can read again without thinking of the blinded Cyclops.[100] Only a strictly historicizing reading of Catullus 68.93 will suppress recollection of the Vergilian parody, and here, by the way, is an example of the need for the distinction between the third and the first or second reading.[101] Further, one cannot help but reflect that Catullus did not intend that *lumen ademptum* be quoted by Vergil, and here is another blow to the opinion that poems are to be explained with reference to the poet's intention.[102]

Vergil could have the same effect on an earlier Latin poet without parodying him. Otto Due wrote of the effect of the *Aeneid* on Ennius's *Annals:*

> Among many other works, the *Annals* of Ennius were a "model of reading" for the *Aeneid* — besides being, of course, one of Vergil's "models of writing." But once the *Aeneid* had come into existence, that poem became a "model of reading" for the *Annals.* After the *Aeneid* it was impossible to read the *Annals* in the

98. Another example may be *Aen.* 9.227 (*consilium summis regni de rebus habebant*) in relation to Lucilius fr. 4 Marx = 6 Krenkel (*consilium summis hominum de rebus habebant*).

99. Vergilian intertextual engagement with Cat. 104.2 and 4 is found at *Aen.* 5.80–81. Ovid, at *Her.* 12.159–60, was to correct Vergil and make the quotation more Catullan again. See Wills 1996: 96, 292.

100. Vergil had another go at Cat. 68.93 later in the *Aeneid* when he had a dead man, Palinurus, use the phrase *iucundum lumen*, again preserving the Catullan metrical position, again with change of meaning (this time, "daylight"), as he begs for proper burial (6.363). The effect of this second quotation of Cat. 68.93 may be different from that of the first.

101. Fowler (1993) stated, objecting to the Jaussian distinction, "There is ever only one reading," but I do not see what would be the single reading that would simultaneously hear and not hear parody of Catullus at Verg. *Aen.* 3.658.

102. And also a blow to Conte's notion that "Generating a text means activating a strategy that predicts the moves of others" (1986: 30). Catullus had no strategy to predict or prevent Vergil's move.

same way as before the *Aeneid,* and, eventually, the *Annals* were eclipsed as the national epos of Rome.[103]

Vergil thus turned Ennius into a (mere) precursor, in Borges's sense of the word.[104]

As T. S. Eliot said, the process never stops. Catullus's brother would have new precursorial roles to play long after Vergil's parody. No educated Italian reader of Catullus 101, discussed earlier in this chapter, can fail to have in mind Ugo Foscolo's sonnet "In morte del fratello Giovanni," which begins:

> Un dì, s'io non andrò sempre fuggendo
> di gente in gente, me vedrai seduto
> su la tua pietra, o fratel mio, gemendo
> il fior de' tuoi gentili anni caduto.

> Someday, if I shall not go always in exile from one people to another, you will see me seated on your tomb, bewailing the fallen flower of your gentle years.

Foscolo reverses Catullus's direction: not toward but away from the brother's tomb. This initial reversal signals a more profound revision of the Catullan model, which will culminate in a prayer that the poet's own remains be returned from a foreign land to his sorrowing mother. One of the possible effects of Foscolo's sonnet on the reading of Catullus 101 is to invoke the figure of the grieving mother, who is not mentioned or alluded to in Catullus, and who, it must be understood, has been denied the traditional role of the mother by the circumstances of the brother's death.[105] The mother has appeared already in the second quatrain of the sonnet, where she is imagined speaking of the poet to the mute (cf. Cat. 101.4) remains of his brother. In this case, one could say that Foscolo has enriched, not diminished, his model.

A retroactive effect is also caused by banalization. A commonsense example is *carpe diem.* Michèle Lowrie observes that it is Horace's "most successful cliché, as t-shirts, subway ads, and the name of a trendy line of leather and snakeskin goods (designed by Fabrizio) attest."[106] To this list one can add the

---

103. Due 1974: 18–19; cf. 41–42 on the effect of Ovid's *Met.* on Verg. *Aen.*

104. Whether one wants to understand Vergil's accomplishment with Bloom (1973) as driven by anxiety or with Borges ([1951] 1964) as nonpolemical depends upon one's knowledge of the psychology of Vergil.

105. Cf. the picture of mothers grieving at the funerals of their sons in Cat. 64.349–51.

106. Lowrie 1997a: 55.

use of *carpe diem* by the Alicia Silverstone character in the summer movie *Clueless* (1995). Can any reader of *Odes* 1.13 be indifferent to this banalization of the phrase? Again, a third, historicizing reading becomes necessary, a reading that would attempt to recapture the original reception of this phrase.

Conclusion

In sum, the reader of intertextuality in Roman poetry is the locus of a multiple referentiality. He or she integrates nonliterary quotation from the synchronic world of the poem into the aesthetic experience of the poem as furnishing, along with reference to things and persons of that world, the possible world of the poem. This possible world is also a poetic one, in the sense that, in virtue of poetic traditions, in the form, say, of genres, it is already there to be inhabited and re-created. Here the reader experiences a specifically poetic intertextuality. An especially self-conscious kind of quotation appears in so-called poetological or programmatic passages and poems. But any kind of intertextuality calls attention to itself, to its poetic status, so that, in addition to its reference to a possible world and to poetic traditions, it must be taken as metapoetic.[107]

107. An often noticed aspect of intertextuality: e.g., Pfister 1985: 26: "So treibt Intertextualität immer auch zu einem gewissen Grad Metatextualität hervor, eine Metatextualität, die den Prätext kommentiert, perspektiviert und interpretiert und damit die Anknüpfung an ihm bzw. die Distanznahme zu ihm thematisiert." And the intratextual kind of repetition called *mise en abyme* does the same: Dällenbach 1976: 285: "En tant que *second* signe en effet, la mise en abyme ne met pas seulement en relief les intentions signifiantes du *premier* (le récit qui la comporte): elle manifeste qu'il (n') est lui aussi (qu') un signe et proclame tel n'importe quel trope — mais avec une puissance décuplée par sa taille: *Je suis littérature, moi et le récit qui m'enchâsse*" (his emphasis).

Conclusion

The title of Stephen Hinds's recent book (1998) distinguishes between *allusion* and *intertext*.[1] The former is linked to the intention of the author and the latter to the freedom of the reader: "The intertextualist critic reacts to the *impasse* on the poet's intention by de-emphasizing the irretrievable moment of authorial production in favour of a more democratic stress upon plural moments of readerly consumption — on the grounds that, in practice, meaning is always constructed at the point of reception."[2] And Hinds distinguishes broadly between an intertextualist model of literature, in which all texts are always intertextual, and an allusionist one, which privileges conscious, artistic relations between texts.[3]

My discussion has led me to conclude that it is impossible to distinguish between an intertext and an allusion (not to mention the difficulties of the term *intertext*). But before I discuss this point, I pause to return to a matter of intellectual history that I discussed in Chapter 1. *Intertextuality*, the term and the concept, go back to Julia Kristeva, though she will not be found in Hinds's index. She, however, wanted to explain how texts were produced, and her concept of production was a materialist one. Her approach was anything but reader-based, and it was hardly democratic. On the contrary, only an elite *sujet connaissant*, possessed of Marxist insight, could understand the phenomenon, and literary-critical applications were not her concern. I quote Marc Angenot again. In Kristeva, "L'intertextualité se présente . . . dans une grande indétermination anhistorique, dans des passages quasi-allégoriques où Texte, Société, et Histoire entretiennent des rapports courtois mais imprécis. L'idée d'inter-

---

1. Hinds 1998.
2. Hinds 1998: 48.
3. Hinds 1997: 114–15.

textualité comme engendrement du texte sert au telquelien à proclamer la bonne nouvelle de la mort du Sujet."[4] The function of the reader in Hinds's intertextualist model is in no way a consequence, historically or logically, of Kristevan intertextuality, and it is unclear to what theory of intertextuality Hinds is linking "democratic stress upon plural moments of readerly consumption." Hinds cites a 1995 article of Duncan Kennedy that refers to a "Cold War . . . between those who study 'allusion' and those who study 'intertextuality,'" each term already "shorthand" for larger issues, but, again, the intellectual history of the opposing terms is opaque.[5]

Now to return to my point concerning the nondistinction between intertext and allusion, it is the necessary conclusion from the nonsemiotic relation of Q_1 to Q_2. There is no stronger semiotic relation between some Q_1 and some Q_2 that could be called *allusion*, by contrast with some weaker or less interesting semiotic relation between some other Q_1 and some other Q_2 that could be referred to as an *intertext*. The consequence of this collapsed distinction is not, however, the worst-case scenario that Hinds would imagine, one in which everything in every text is intertextual and the reader solipsistically construes arbitrary points of contact between texts. As I have said, intertextuality discriminates among readers. What Hinds calls an allusion is the result of a persuasive, successful reading of the relation between the Q_1 and the Q_2 in question.

Another conclusion to be drawn from the nonsemiotic relation of Q_1 to Q_2 is that intertextuality differs fundamentally from metaphor. Metaphor functions within a single text. It can be described semiotically in the same Peircean terms used in Chapter 8. The two parts of metaphor often called, in the terminology of I. A. Richards, *tenor* and *vehicle* can be called *object* and *sign*, and the concept that links them can be called the *interpretant*.[6] While metaphor is thus susceptible of a Peircean semiotic description, intertextuality is not. The intertextual relation between texts is nonsemiotic. Further, texts provide syntactic and other links between tenor and vehicle or object and sign,

---

4. Angenot 1983: 124–25. Cf. Chapter 1, note 34. (*Tel Quel* was the journal in which Kristeva and her circle published in the 1960s.)

5. Kennedy 1995: 86; cited by Hinds 1998: 17. I wrote to Kennedy in the summer of 1998 to ask him about the background of his comment and he replied: "My memory is that I had in mind those who would group themselves with or against Richard Thomas." He referred, I assume, to the position taken by Thomas 1986.

6. Richards 1965: 96–97. For the application of the Peircean triad to metaphor, see Kirby 1997: 534–35.

in such a way that the relation of the two is, or should be, hard to miss. (The *nature* of the relation, however, has been the subject of a vast amount of theory.) Indeed, one could say that the test of metaphor is that it is a phenomenon that may not go unobserved, whereas, to repeat, "The test for allusion is that it is a phenomenon that some reader or readers may fail to observe."[7] To miss a metaphor would always be a failing; to miss an instance of intertextuality is permissible and may even be inevitable, as I have said. So metaphor is not a good way to describe intertextuality.[8] At best, metaphor is a metaphor for intertextuality.

Lacking any semiotic basis, intertextuality is a matter of construction, thus of reading, and the appeal to the intention of the author has to be abandoned. The foundation of intertextual phenomena is not the author but the reader. Hinds has written that "we allusionists permit ourselves to look for authorial subject-positions, believing that the figure of the alluding author, however conjectural, is 'good to think with.' "[9] But if the author is only a "subject-position" or a figure, then how is the author different from one or another of the personae that I discussed in Chapter 4? Nothing in Hinds's account suggests that intention is anything more than a desiccated convention — the rhetorical add-on to which I referred in my Introduction. At the end of a discussion, the critic adds: And what I have shown you was the intention of the author.

What classics needs at the moment is more reflection on reading and less devotion to the admittedly powerful fiction that articulated itself in the Andrōn inscription. It may be that poets anticipate, calculate, create, and even thematize reader responses in their poems (Hexter), that poets fashion faces that entice readers to look for the real poet behind them (Oliensis), that "both Roman and modern readers construct the meaning of a poetic text by attempting to construct from (and for) it an intention-bearing authorial voice" (Hinds), but none of these manifestations of the poet can come to be except in reading.[10] Although none of the scholars just named is in any way engaged in a naive hypostatization of a real authorial presence in the poem, it is striking how the old fiction still casts its spell. Gregory Nagy has referred to "the

7. Miner 1994.
8. Cf. Conte 1986: 52–56.
9. Hinds 1997: 119.
10. Hexter 1990; 1992: 49; Oliensis 1998.

nostalgia of philology for the Muses of inspired performance."[11] In the field of Roman poetry, one might speak of nostalgia for the presence of the author.[12] What one would like to have from the talented readers just named is more reflection on their practices as readers — how they have discovered these representations (voices, faces, anticipated readers) in reading.

The conventions that hermeneutic reading can and should live with are the formal ones of scholarship in classics. All fields, as one now knows, have their discourses, are indeed constituted by their discourses: So to be a classicist is to use the discourse of classics, classical philology. To write about intertextuality in classical texts for an audience of classicists requires that one observe the norms of classical philology. Rare is the person who can get away with pronounced violations. Despite the differences between classics and hermeneutics with respect to reading, and despite my hermeneutical position on intertextuality, it does not follow from anything I have said that the conditions of discourse just mentioned are a constraint on reading. On the contrary, the traditional discourse of classical philology has proved to be the most suitable one for the study of intertextuality in Roman poetry, allowing room for a critique (though often muted) of its own presuppositions and certainly for fundamental reassessments of received opinions concerning various poets.

As far as my theory of intertextuality is concerned, it is not looking to replace disciplinary discourse with some higher-order one. As the epigraph to Chapter 8 already suggests, a theory of intertextuality will not culminate in some purportedly authoritative metadiscourse that speaks about classics from outside the usual practices of its discourse. Intertextuality thus abandons its Marxist origins in Kristeva, no matter how much of her thought it ultimately preserves, and it certainly abandons the imposture of a Marxism that "has typically represented its own relation to reality as one of pure transparency, thereby denying its own discursivity and textuality."[13]

Indeed, the discourse of classics has been able to accommodate not only intertextuality but other discourses, too, New Criticism in its day, then structuralism a generation ago, then feminism, and so forth. For this reason, classics and theory, classics and postmodernism or poststructuralism are not the

---

11. Nagy 1996: 4.

12. The two nostalgias are, of course, profoundly different. One is for something, performance, that once existed. The other is for something that never existed.

13. Bennett 1984: 5.

either-or challenge that is often assumed. As in the past, classics will enter into a dialectical relation with current trends, as it does, at least incipiently, in the case of reading. In the Introduction, I cited the New Latin's position on the reader. A consensus (difficult to quantify) is developing that intertextuality is not an object for positivistic research but an event, as Alessandro Barchiesi puts it, and the role of the scholar or critic is adjusting itself accordingly.[14]

What I have said about the discourse of classics is the beginning of an answer to the question that is always asked of theories of reading: What about the validity of a reading? How can one reading be better or worse than another? An interpretive community ultimately decides on validity, and classics is that community for the study of intertextuality in Roman poetry, perhaps not the only one but certainly the primary one, the one that the scholar or critic writing on this subject will have in mind as his or her audience. From this point of view, the conventions of discourse are a positive advantage: They provide a means of persuasion. And, as I have already said, persuasion has been effective. To return for a moment to authorial intention, a generation or two ago, it was a solid principle of interpretation. Now, after the New Criticism, structuralism, and deconstruction, few take it seriously, and Hinds, for example, has to use it with apology, conceding its epistemological vacuity.[15] Classicists' change of mind about intention did not come about because someone made a critique of classics from the point of view of one of the approaches just named. On the contrary, the change emerged within classical scholarship itself little by little, as classicists became persuaded of the inutility of the concept. (When a classicist explicitly invokes a particular body of theory for the sake of interpreting an ancient text, he or she invites suspicion and distrust.)[16]

But, for all of that, classics as a whole does not constitute an interpretive community in Stanley Fish's sense. Students of Roman poetry are already a subcommunity, and, among them, such are the differences that one must recognize at least a few sub-subcommunities, such as the New Latin. For some, reading as it has been argued for in this book is of no interest at all, and so any reading of any poem is already too long — a nuisance. Scholars ought to be doing something else, for example, producing new editions for other scholars. Indeed, one of the main differences between one Latin subcommunity and another lies in the degree to which it is able to conceive of its work as relevant

14. Barchiesi 1997: 210.
15. Hinds 1998: 50.
16. E.g., Clay 1996.

to a larger discussion in the humanities. To put the matter in terms of audience, Latinists differ a great deal in their sense of the comparability of their research with work in other fields of literature, or their sense of who might be interested in what they are saying.

Some will feel that what I have said about communities is still too optimistic. Communities are not just disciplinary and intellectual. They also have a professional basis, in teaching posts, editorships, and university departments. Under these circumstances, mild intellectual annoyances experienced on the borders between subcommunities may have terrible consequences for careers. Why should I offer a reading of a Roman poem if it is going to be judged by someone who is not a member of my subcommunity but has already ruled out this kind of activity? Raising the question of interpretive community in these terms causes me to restate more forcefully my point about the discourse of classics. A reading that presents itself securely within the conventions of this discourse has little to fear, in my opinion. Many of the works from the 1990s that I have cited have successfully followed this strategy. Hinds, I would say, is an excellent example. I refer to his readings, not to his theoretical discussion, which is mostly conservative. As with Conte a generation earlier, his reading is ahead of his theory.

So the discourse of classics need not inhibit the performance that, I have suggested, reading should be. Indeed, this discourse provides the stage, the costume, and the props. I use these metaphors to distinguish reading from the use of the "personal voice" in the sense of autobiography and personal anecdote.[17] The reader, like the philologist, is a construct. One of the advantages of the series of readings that I have proposed, following Jauss, is that it invites a maximum of self-consciousness about this construct.

17. Cf. Nisbet 1998: 50.

Works Cited

Abel, Walther. 1930. *Die Anredeformen bei den römischen Elegikern: Untersuchungen zur elegischen Form.* Charlottenburg: Gebrüder Hoffmann.

Anderson, R. D., P. J. Parsons, and R. G. M. Nisbet. 1979. "Elegiacs by Gallus from Qasr Ibrim." *JRS* 69:125–55.

Angenot, Marc. 1983. "L'intertextualité: Enquête sur l'émergence et la diffusion d'un champ notionnel." *Revue des sciences humaines* 60:121–35.

Asmis, Elizabeth. 1991. "Philodemus' Poetic Theory and *On the Good King according to Homer.*" *CA* 10:1–45.

Austin, J. L. [1962] 1975. *How to Do Things with Words.* 2d ed. Edited by J. O. Urmson and Marina Sbisà. Cambridge: Harvard University Press.

Ax, Wolfram. 1993. "Phaselus ille/Sabinus ille — Ein Beitrag zur neueren Diskussion um die Beziehungen zwischen Texten." In *Literaturparodie in Antike und Mittelalter,* edited by Wolfram Ax and R. F. Glei, 75–100. Trier: WVT.

Axelson, Bertil. 1945. *Unpoetische Wörter: Ein Beitrag zur Kenntnis der lateinischen Dichtersprache.* Lund: C. W. K. Gleerup.

Bailey, Cyril, ed. 1947. *Titi Lucreti Cari De Rerum Natura Libri Sex.* Vol. 1. Oxford: Oxford University Press.

Bailey, D. R. Shackleton. 1978. *Cicero's Letters to His Friends.* Atlanta, Ga.: Scholar's Press.

Bakhtin, M. M. 1981. *The Dialogic Imagination.* Translated by Michael Holquist. Austin: University of Texas Press.

Baldick, Chris. 1990. *The Concise Oxford Dictionary of Literary Terms.* Oxford: Oxford University Press.

Baldo, Gianluigi. 1995. *Dall'Eneide alle Metamorfosi: Il codice epico di Ovidio.* Studi testi documenti, 7. Padua: Università di Padova.

Barchiesi, Alessandro. 1989. "Voci e istanze narrative nelle Metamorfosi di Ovidio." *MD* 23:5-97.

———. 1997. "Otto punti di una mappa dei naufragi." *MD* 39:209–26.

Barsby, John. 1973. *Ovid: Amores I.* Oxford: Oxford University Press. Reprint, London: Bristol Classical Press, 1991.

Barthes, Roland. 1970. *S/Z.* Paris: Éditions du Seuil.

————. 1974. *S/Z.* Trans. Richard Miller. New York: Farrar, Straus, and Giroux.

————. 1977a. *Image, Music, Text.* Translated by Stephen Heath. New York: Hill and Wang.

————. 1977b. "The Death of the Author." In Barthes 1977a: 142–48.

————. 1977c. "From Work to Text." In Barthes 1977a: 155–64.

Basson, André. 2000. Review of Manieri 1998. *Scholia Reviews,* September 13, unpaginated. Electronic publication ⟨http://www.und.ac.za/und/classics/scholia/scholia.html⟩.

Beardsley, Monroe C. 1970. *The Possibility of Criticism.* Detroit: Wayne State University Press.

————. 1982. "Intentions and Interpretations: A Fallacy Revived." In *The Aesthetic Point of View: Selected Essays,* edited by Michael J. Wreen and Donald M. Callen, 188–207. Ithaca: Cornell University Press.

Bennett, Tony. 1984. "Texts in History: The Determinations of Readings and Their Texts." *Australian Journal of Communication* 5–6:3–12.

Ben-Porat, Ziva. 1976. "The Poetics of Literary Allusion." *PTL* 1:105–28.

Benveniste, Émile. 1966. *Problèmes de linguistique générale.* Paris: Gallimard.

Bloom, Harold. 1973. *The Anxiety of Influence: A Theory of Poetry.* New York: Oxford University Press.

Bolter, Jay David. 1991. *Writing Space: The Computer, Hypertext, and the History of Writing.* Hillsdale, N.J.: Lawrence Erlbaum.

Bömer, Franz. 1951. *Rom und Troia: Untersuchungen zur Frühgeschichte Roms.* Baden Baden: Verlag für Kunst and Wissenschaft.

————. 1982. *P. Ovidius Naso : Metamorphosen: Buch XII–XIII.* Heidelberg: Carl Winter.

————. 1986. *P. Ovidius Naso : Metamorphosen: Buch XIV–XV.* Heidelberg: Carl Winter.

Booth, Wayne C. [1961] 1983. *The Rhetoric of Fiction.* 2d ed. Chicago: University of Chicago Press.

Borges, Jorge Luis. [1951] 1964. "Kafka and His Precursors." In *Other Inquisitions: 1937–1952,* translated by Ruth L. C. Simms, 106–8. Austin: University of Texas Press.

————. [1956] 1962. "Pierre Menard, Author of Don Quixote." In *Ficciones,* edited by Anthony Kerrigan, 45–55. New York: Grove Press.

Braund, Susanna M. 1996. *The Roman Satirists and Their Masks.* Classical World Series. London: Bristol Classical Press.

Brink, C. O. 1963–82. *Horace on Poetry.* Vol. 1, *Prolegomena to the Literary Epistles*

(1963); vol. 2, *The "Ars Poetica"* (1971); vol. 3, *Epistles Book II: The Letters to Augustus and Florus* (1982). Cambridge: Cambridge University Press.

Broich, Ulrich. 1985. "Formen der Markierung von Intertextualität." In *Intertextualität: Formen, Funktionen, anglistische Fallstudien,* edited by Ulrich Broich and Manfred Pfister, 31–47. Tübingen: Max Niemeyer.

Brook, Peter. 1968. *The Empty Space.* New York: Atheneum.

Brooks, Cleanth. 1963. "Literary Criticism: Marvell's Horatian Ode." In *Explication as Criticism,* edited by W. K. Wimsatt Jr., 99–130. New York: Columbia University Press.

Brown, E. L. 1963. *Numeri Vergiliani: Studies in Eclogues and Georgics.* Collection Latomus 63. Brussels.

Brugnoli, Giorgio, and Fabio Stok. 1992. *Ovidius παρῳδήσας.* Testi e Studi di Cultura Classica, 10. Pisa: ETS.

Bücheler, F., and E. Lommatzsch, eds. 1895–1926. *Carmina Latina Epigraphica.* 3 vols. Leipzig: Teubner. [*CLE*]

Burgess, D. L. 1986. "Catullus c. 50: The Exchange of Poetry." *AJP* 107:576–86.

Burnyeat, Miles. 1991. Letter to the editor. *TLS,* April 19, 15.

———. 1997. "Postscript on Silent Reading." *CQ* 47:74–76.

Butler, H. E. 1921. *Quintilian: Institutio Oratoria Books IV–VI.* Loeb Classical Library. Cambridge: Harvard University Press.

Cairns, F. J. 1972. *Generic Composition in Greek and Roman Poetry.* Edinburgh: Edinburgh University Press.

Cameron, Alan. 1995. *Callimachus and His Critics.* Princeton: Princeton University Press.

Carroll, Lewis. 1946. *Alice's Adventures in Wonderland.* New York: Random House.

Carroll, Noël. 1992. "Art, Intention, and Conversation." In Iseminger 1992a: 97–131.

Casali, Sergio. 1995. "Altre voci nell'Eneide di Ovidio." *MD* 35:59–76.

Cavarzere, Alberto. 1996. *Sul limitare: Il "motto" e la poesia di Orazio.* Testi e Manuali per l'Insegnamento Universitario del Latino, 47. Bologna: Pàtron.

Citroni, Mario. 1995. *Poesia e lettori in Roma antica.* Bari: Laterza.

Clark, W. P. 1931. "Ancient Reading." *CJ* 26:698–700.

Clay, Diskin. 1998. "The Literary Persona in Antiquity." *MD* 40:9–40.

Clay, Jenny Strauss. 1996. "Literary Crockery." *Arion,* 3d ser., 3.2:274–91.

Compagnon, Antoine. 1979. *La seconde main ou le travail de la citation.* Paris: Éditions du Seuil.

Conte, Gian Biaggio. 1966. "Hypsos e diatriba nello stile di Lucrezio." *Maia* 18:338–68.

———. [1974] 1985. *Memoria dei poeti e sistema letterario.* 2d ed. Turin: Einaudi.

———. 1986. *The Rhetoric of Imitation: Genre and Poetic Memory in Virgil and Other Latin Poets.* Edited by Charles Segal. Ithaca: Cornell University Press.

————. 1991. *Generi e lettori: Lucrezio, l'elegia d'amore, l'enciclopedia di Plinio.* Milan: Mondadori.

————. 1994a. *Genres and Readers.* Translated by Glenn Most. Baltimore: Johns Hopkins University Press.

————. 1994b. *Latin Literature: A History.* Translated by J. B. Solodow. Revised by D. Fowler and G. W. Most. Baltimore: Johns Hopkins University Press.

Conte, Gian Biaggio, and Alessandro Barchiesi. 1989. "Imitazione e arte allusiva. Modi e funzioni dell'intertestualità." In *Lo spazio letterario di Roma antica,* vol. 1, *La produzione del testo,* edited by Guglielmo Cavallo, Paolo Fedeli, and Andrea Giardina, 81–114. Rome: Salerno.

Conte, Gian Biaggio, and Glenn W. Most. 1996. "Imitatio." In *OCD*³, 749.

Corcoran, Thomas H. 1971. *Seneca: Naturales Quaestiones.* Vol. 1. Loeb Classical Library. Cambridge: Harvard University Press.

Cornish, Francis W., J. P. Postgate, and J. W. Mackail, trans. 1988. *Catullus; Tibullus; Pervigilium Veneris.* 2d ed. Revised by G. P. Goold. Loeb Classical Library. Cambridge: Harvard University Press.

Culler, Jonathan. 1980. "Literary Competence." In *Reader-Response Criticism: From Formalism to Post-Structuralism,* edited by Jane P. Tompkins, 101–17. Baltimore: Johns Hopkins University Press.

————. 1981. *The Pursuit of Signs.* Ithaca: Cornell University Press.

Curran, L. C. 1966. "*Desultores Amoris*: Ovid *Amores* 1.3." *CP* 61:47–49.

Dällenbach, Lucien. 1976. "Intertexte et autotexte." *Poétique* 27:282–96.

Darnton, Robert. 1990. "First Steps toward a History of Reading." In *The Kiss of Lamourette: Reflections in Cultural History,* 154–87. New York: W. W. Norton. Originally published in *Australian Journal of French Studies* 23 (1986): 5–30.

DeJong, Irene J. F., and J. P. Sullivan, eds. 1994. *Modern Critical Theory and Classical Literature.* Leiden: Brill.

de Man, Paul. 1979. *Allegories of Reading: Figural Language in Rousseau, Nietzsche, Rilke, and Proust.* New Haven: Yale University Press.

————. 1981. "Hypogram and Inscription: Michael Riffaterre's Poetics of Reading." *diacritics* 11:17–35.

————. 1983. "Form and Intent in the American New Criticism." In *Blindness and Insight: Essays in the Rhetoric of Contemporary Criticism,* 20–35. 2d ed. Minneapolis: University of Minnesota Press.

de Marchis, Giorgio. 1994. *Il poeta, il ragazzo, la ragazza a Roma d'inverno 27 a.C.* Palermo: Sellerio.

Derrida, Jacques. 1978. *La vérité en peinture.* Paris: Flammarion.

————. 1979. "Living on/*Border Lines.*" Translated by James Hulbert. In *Deconstruction and Criticism,* by Harold Bloom et al., 75–176. New York: Seabury Press. Reprinted as "Survivre: Journal de bord," in *Parages,* by Jacques Derrida (Paris: Galilée, 1986).

———. 1982. *Margins of Philosophy.* Translated by Alan Bass. Chicago: University of Chicago Press. Originally published as *Marges de la philosophie* (Paris: Éditions de Minuit, 1972).

———. 1987. *The Truth in Painting.* Translated by Geoff Bennington and Ian McLeod. Chicago: University of Chicago Press.

———. 1988. *Limited Inc.* Evanston, Ill.: Northwestern University Press.

———. 1992. "The Law of Genre." Translated by Avital Ronell with revisions by Derek Attridge. In Jacques Derrida, *Acts of Literature,* edited by Derek Attridge, 221–52. New York: Routledge. Reprinted from *Glyph* 7 (1980): 176–232 (with French original, "La loi du genre"). French reprinted in *Parages* (Paris: Galilée, 1986), 249–87.

Doležel, Lubomír. 1980. "Truth and Authenticity in Narrative." *Poetics Today* 1.3:7–25.

———. 1989. "Possible Worlds and Literary Fictions." In *Possible Worlds in Humanities, Arts, and Sciences: Proceedings of Nobel Symposium 65,* edited by Sture Allén, 221–42. Berlin: de Gruyter.

Dopp, Jamie. 1993. "Materialist Criticism." In Makaryk 1993: 100–102.

Dover, K. J., ed. 1993. *Aristophanes: Frogs.* Oxford: Clarendon Press.

Dowling, William. 1984. *Jameson, Althusser, Marx: An Introduction to "The Political Unconscious."* Ithaca: Cornell University Press.

———. 1985. "Intentionless Meaning." In Mitchell 1985: 89–94. Originally published in *Critical Inquiry* 9 (1983): 748–89.

Ducrot, Oswald, and Tzvetan Todorov. 1979. *Encyclopedic Dictionary of the Sciences of Language.* Translated by Catherine Porter. Baltimore: Johns Hopkins University Press. Originally published as *Dictionnaire encyclopédique des sciences du langage* (Paris: Éditions du Seuil, 1972).

Due, Otto Steen. 1974. *Changing Forms: Studies in the "Metamorphoses" of Ovid.* Copenhagen: Glyndendal.

Dupont, Florence. 1994. *L'invention de la littérature.* Paris: Éditions la Découverte.

———. 1997. "Recitatio and the Space of Public Discourse." In *The Roman Cultural Revolution,* edited by Thomas Habinek and Alessandro Schiesaro, 44–59. Cambridge: Cambridge University Press.

Eco, Umberto. 1979. *The Role of the Reader: Explorations in the Semiotics of Texts.* Bloomington: Indiana University Press. Originally published as *Lector in Fabula* (Milan: Gruppo Editoriale Fabbri, 1979).

Eden, Kathy. 1997. *Hermeneutics and the Rhetorical Tradition: Chapters in the Ancient Legacy and Its Humanistic Reception.* Yale Studies in Hermeneutics. New Haven: Yale University Press.

Edmunds, Lowell. 1992. *From a Sabine Jar: Reading Horace, Odes 1.9.* Chapel Hill: University of North Carolina Press.

———. 1995. "Intertextuality Today." *Lexis* 13:3–22.

———. 1998. "Verschränkung in Horace, *Odes* 1.9.9–13: A Reply to E. J. Kenney." *EMC/CV,* n.s., 17:57–65.

———. Forthcoming. "Callimachus, *Iamb* 4: From Performance to Reading." In *Iambic Ideas,* edited by Antonio Aloni, Alessandro Barchiesi, and Alberto Cavarzere. Lanham, Md.: Rowman and Littlefield.

Edwards, Catharine. 1996. *Writing Rome: Textual Approaches to the City.* Cambridge: Cambridge University Press.

Eliot, T. S. 1950. "Tradition and the Individual Talent" (1970). In *Selected Essays,* 3–11. San Diego: Harcourt Brace Jovanovich.

Else, Gerald F. 1967. *Aristotle's Poetics.* Cambridge: Harvard University Press.

Engler, Rudolf. 1968. *Lexique de la terminologie Saussurienne.* Utrecht/Anvers: Spectrum.

Esterhammer, Angela. 1994. *Creating States: Studies in the Performative Language of John Milton and William Blake.* Toronto: University of Toronto Press.

Fabre, J. 1986. "La narration illustrée: Étude de quelques digressions dans l'Enéide ovidienne." *REL* 64:172–84.

Fantham, Elaine. 1990. "*Nymphas . . . e navibus esse:* Decorum and Poetic Fiction in *Aeneid* 9.77–122 and 10.215–59." *CP* 85:102–19.

———. 1996. *Roman Literary Culture from Cicero to Apuleius.* Baltimore: Johns Hopkins University Press.

Farrell, Joseph. 1991. *Vergil's Georgics and the Traditions of Ancient Epic: The Art of Allusion in Literary History.* New York: Oxford University Press.

———. 1993. "Allusions, Delusions and Confusions: A Reply." *Electronic Antiquity,* January 6, unpaginated. Electronic publication ⟨http://scholar.lib.vt.edu/ejournals/ElAnt/⟩.

Fedeli, Paolo. 1989. "Le intersezioni dei generi e dei modelli." In *Lo spazio letterario di Roma antica,* vol. 1, *La produzione del testo,* edited by Guglielmo Cavallo, Paolo Fedeli, and Andrea Giardina, 375–97. Rome: Salerno.

Feeney, Denis. 1995. "Criticism, Ancient and Modern." In *Ethics and Rhetoric: Classical Essays for Donald Russell on His Seventy-Fifth Birthday,* edited by Doreen Innes, Harry Hine, and Christopher Pelling, 301–12. Oxford: Clarendon Press.

Fish, Stanley. 1980. *Is There a Text in This Class? The Authority of Interpretive Communities.* Cambridge: Harvard University Press.

———. 1981. "Why No One's Afraid of Wolfgang Iser." *diacritics* 11:2–13.

Fordyce, C. J. 1961. *Catullus: A Commentary.* Oxford: Oxford University Press.

Foucault, Michel. 1984. "What Is an Author?" In *The Foucault Reader,* edited by Paul Rabinow, 101–20. New York: Pantheon Books.

Fowler, Don. 1983. "An Acrostic in Vergil (Aeneid 7.601–4)?" *CQ* 33:298.

———. 1993. "Subject Reviews (Roman Literature)." *G&R,* 2d ser., 11:85–97.

———. 1994. "Postmodernism, Romantic Irony, Closure." In DeJong and Sullivan 1994: 231–55.

———. 1995. "Modern Literary Theory and Latin Poetry." *Arachnion* 1.2 (September): unpaginated. Electronic publication ⟨http://gaia.cisi.unito.it/arachne/arachne.html⟩.

———. 1997a. "Second Thoughts on Closure." In *Classical Closure: Reading the End in Greek and Latin Literature,* edited by D. H. Roberts, F. M. Dunn, and Don Fowler, 3–22. Princeton: Princeton University Press.

———. 1997b. "Intertextuality and Classical Studies." *MD* 39:13–34.

Fowler, Peta G., and Don P. Fowler. 1996. "Parody, Latin." In *OCD*³, 1115.

Fraenkel, Eduard. 1956. "Catulls Trostgedicht für Calvus." *WS* 69:278–88. Reprinted in *Kleine Beiträge,* vol. 2 (Rome: Edizioni di Storia e Letteratura, 1964), 103–13.

———. 1957. *Horace.* Oxford: Oxford University Press.

———. 1961. "Two Poems of Catullus." *JRS* 51:46–53.

Füger, Wilhelm. 1989. "Intertextualia Orwelliana: Untersuchungen zur Theorie und Praxis der Markierung von Intertextualität." *Poetica* 21:179–200.

Galinsky, Karl. 1975. *Ovid's Metamorphoses: An Introduction to the Basic Aspects.* Berkeley: University of California Press.

———, ed. 1992. *The Interpretation of Roman Poetry: Empiricism or Hermeneutics?* Studien zur klassischen Philologie 67. Frankfurt am Main: Peter Lang.

Gavrilov, A. K. 1997. "Techniques of Reading in Classical Antiquity." *CQ* 47:56–73.

Genette, Gérard. 1980. *Narrative Discourse: An Essay in Method.* Translated by Jane E. Lewin. Ithaca: Cornell University Press. Originally published as *Discours du récit* (Paris: Éditions du Seuil, 1972).

———. 1982. *Palimpsestes: La littérature au second degré.* Paris: Éditions du Seuil.

———. 1988. *Narrative Discourse Revisited.* Translated by Jane E. Lewin. Ithaca: Cornell University Press. Originally published as *Nouveau discours du récit* (Paris: Éditions du Seuil, 1983).

———. 1990. "Fictional Narrative, Factual Narrative." *Poetics Today* 11:755–74.

Gentili, Bruno. 1999. "Ecdotica e critica dei testi classici." In *I nuovi orizzonti della filogia; Ecdotica, critica testuale, editoria scientifica, e mezzi informatici elettronici,* 19–27. Atti dei Convegi Lincei, 151. Rome: Accademia Nazionale dei Lincei.

Gigante, Marcello. 1995. *Philodemus in Italy: The Books from Herculaneum.* Translated by Dirk Obbink. Ann Arbor: University of Michigan Press.

Gilliard, Frank D. 1993. "More Silent Reading in Antiquity: *Non Omne Verbum Sonat.*" *JBL* 112:689–94.

———. 1997. Letter to the editor. *TLS,* August 8, 19.

Goodman, Nelson. 1978. *Ways of Worldmaking.* Indianapolis: Hackett.

Greene, Thomas. 1982. *The Light in Troy: Imitation and Discovery in Renaissance Poetry.* New Haven: Yale University Press.

Greetham, D. C. 1999. *Theories of the Text.* Oxford: Oxford University Press.

Greimas, A.-J., and J. Cortés. 1982. *Semiotics and Language: An Analytical Dictionary.* Translated by Larry Crist et al. Bloomington: Indiana University Press.

――――. 1986. *Sémiotique: Dictionnaire raisonné de la théorie du langage.* Vol. 2. Paris: Hachette.

Griffin, Jasper. 1985. *Latin Poets and Roman Life.* London: Duckworth.

Habib, M. A. R., and Gary Wihl. 1994. "Marxist Theory and Criticism." In *The Johns Hopkins Guide to Literary Theory and Criticism,* edited by Michael Groden and Martin Kreiswirth, 490–500. Baltimore: Johns Hopkins University Press.

Habinek, Thomas. 1998. *The Politics of Latin Literature: Writing, Identity, and Empire in Ancient Rome.* Princeton: Princeton University Press.

Hansen, P. A. 1983–89. *Carmina Epigraphica Graeca.* 2 vols. Berlin: de Gruyter. [*CEG*]

Heinze, Richard. [1923] 1938. "Die Horazische Ode." In *Vom Geist des Römertums,* edited by Erich Burck, 185–212. Leipzig: Teubner.

Henkel, Jacqueline. 1996. *The Language of Criticism: Linguistics Models and Literary Theory.* Ithaca: Cornell University Press.

Heseltine, Michael, and W. H. D. Rouse, trans. 1987. *Petronius; Seneca: Apocolocyntosis.* Revised by E. H. Warmington. Loeb Classical Library. Cambridge: Harvard University Press.

Hexter, Ralph. 1990. "What Was the Trojan Horse Made Of?: Interpreting Vergil's Aeneid." *Yale Journal of Criticism* 3.2:109–31.

――――. 1992. "Sidonian Dido." In Hexter and Selden 1992: 332–84.

Hexter, Ralph, and Daniel Selden, eds. 1992. *Innovations of Antiquity.* New York: Routledge, Chapman and Hall.

Hinds, Stephen. 1997. "'Proemio al mezzo': Allusion and the Limits of Interpretability." *MD* 39:113–22.

――――. 1998. *Allusion and Intertext: Dynamics of Appropriation in Roman Poetry.* Cambridge: Cambridge University Press.

Hirsch, E. D., Jr. 1967. *Validity in Interpretation.* New Haven: Yale University Press.

Hodgkin, Adam. 1991. "Ur-text or Er-text." *TLS,* February 22, 23.

Holoka, James P. 1991. "Homer, Oral Poetry, and Comparative Literature." In *Zweihundert Jahre Homer-Forschung: Rückblick und Ausblick,* edited by Joachim Latacz, 456–81. Colloquium Rauricum, 2. Stuttgart: Teubner.

Hornblower, Simon, and Antony Spawforth, eds. 1996. *The Oxford Classical Dictionary.* Oxford: Oxford University Press. [*OCD*³]

Horowitz, Rosalind. 1991. "A Reexamination of Oral versus Silent Reading." *Text* 11: 133–66.

Horsfall, Nicholas. 1979. "Stesichorus at Bovillae?" *JHS* 99:26–48.

――――. 1988. "Camilla, o i limiti dell' invenzione." *Athenaeum* 66:31–51.

――――. 1990. "Virgil and the Illusory Footnote." In *Papers of the Leeds Latin Seminar,* edited by Francis Cairns and Malcolm Heath, 6:49–63. Leeds: Francis Cairns.

Hunter, Richard. 1995. *Theocritus and the Archaeology of Greek Poetry.* Cambridge: Cambridge University Press.

Hutcheon, Linda. 1985. *A Theory of Parody.* London: Routledge.

———. 1988. *A Poetics of Postmodernism: History, Theory, Fiction.* London: Routledge.

Ingarden, Roman. 1973. *The Literary Work of Art: An Investigation on the Borderlines of Ontology, Logic, and Theory of Literature.* Evanston, Ill.: Northwestern University Press.

Innes, Doreen C. 1989. "Augustan Critics." In *The Cambridge History of Literary Criticism,* vol. 1, *Classical Criticism,* edited by George A. Kennedy, 245–73. Cambridge: Cambridge University Press.

Irving, P. M. C. Forbes. 1990. *Metamorphosis in Greek Myths.* Oxford: Clarendon Press.

Iseminger, Gary, ed. 1992a. *Intention and Interpretation.* Philadelphia: Temple University Press.

———. 1992b. "An Intentional Demonstration?" In Iseminger 1992a: 76–96.

Iser, Wolfgang. 1978. *The Act of Reading: A Theory of Aesthetic Response.* Baltimore: Johns Hopkins University Press.

———. 1981. "Talk Like Whales: A Reply to Stanley Fish." *diacritics* 11:82–87.

Jameson, Frederic. 1981. *The Political Unconscious: Narrative as a Socially Symbolic Act.* Ithaca: Cornell University Press.

Jauss, Hans Robert. 1982a. "The Poetic Text within the Change of Horizons of Reading: The Example of Baudelaire's 'Spleen II.' " In *Toward an Aesthetic of Reception,* 139–85. Translated by Timothy Bahti. Minneapolis: University of Minnesota Press.

———. 1982b. *Aesthetic Experience and Literary Hermeneutics.* Translated by Michael Shaw. Minneapolis: University of Minnesota Press.

Jenny, Laurent. 1976. "Stratégie de la forme." *Poétique* 27:257–81. Translated by R. Carter as "The Strategy of Form," in *French Literary Theory Today: A Reader,* edited by Tzvetan Todorov (Cambridge: Cambridge University Press, 1982), 34–63.

Jocelyn, H. D. 1967. *The Tragedies of Ennius: The Fragments.* Cambridge: Cambridge University Press.

Johnson, Barbara. 1980. "Poetry and Performative Language: Mallarmé and Austin." In *The Critical Difference: Essays in the Contemporary Rhetoric of Reading,* 52–66. Baltimore: Johns Hopkins University Press. Originally published in *Yale French Studies* 54 (1977): 140–58.

———. 1985. "*Les fleurs du mal armé*: Some Reflections on Intertextuality." In *Lyric Poetry: Beyond New Criticism,* edited by Chaviva Hošek and Patricia Parker, 264–80. Ithaca: Cornell University Press.

Johnson, Ralph. 1992. "The Death of Pleasure." In Galinsky 1992: 200–214.

Johnson, William. Forthcoming. "Towards a Sociology of Reading in Classical Antiquity." *AJP.*

Jouve, Vincent. 1993. *La lecture.* Paris: Hachette.

Kellner, Douglas. 1993. "Marxist criticism." In Makaryk 1993: 95–100.

Kennedy, Duncan F. 1993. *The Arts of Love: Five Studies on the Discourse of Roman Love Elegy.* Cambridge: Cambridge University Press.

———. 1995. "Subject Review of Roman Literature." *G&R* 42:83–88.

Kenney, E. J. 1994. "Review Article: Nempe Ergo Aperte Vis Quae Restant Me Loqui?" *Echos du monde classique / Classical Views,* n.s., 13:365–71.

Kiessling, Adolf, and Richard Heinze, eds. 1957. *Q. Horatius Flaccus: Satiren.* 6th ed. Berlin: Weidmann.

King, J. E. 1945. *Cicero: Tusculan Disputations.* Loeb Classical Library. Cambridge: Harvard University Press.

Kirby, John T. 1997. "Aristotle on Metaphor." *AJP* 118:517–54.

Kirkpatrick, Ross S. 1969. "Two Horatian Proems: *Carm.* 1.26 and 1.32." *YCS* 21:215–39.

Knapp, Steven, and Walter Benn Michaels. 1985. "Against Theory." In Mitchell 1985: 11–30. Originally published in *Critical Inquiry* 8 (1982): 723–42. Partially reprinted in *Twentieth-Century Literary Theory: A Reader,* edited by K. M. Newton, 2d ed. (New York: St. Martin's Press), 254–59.

Knauer, Elfriede. 1993. "Roman Wall Paintings from Boscotrecase: Three Studies in the Relationship between Writing and Painting." *Metropolitan Museum Journal* 28:13–46.

Knauer, Georg Nicolaus. 1979. *Die Aeneis und Homer: Studien zur poetischen Technik Vergils mit Listen der Homerzitate in der Aeneis.* 2d ed. Hypomnemata 7. Göttingen: Vandenhoeck and Ruprecht.

Knox, Bernard M. W. 1957. *Oedipus at Thebes: Sophocles' Tragic Hero and His Time.* New Haven: Yale University Press.

———. 1968. "Silent Reading in Antiquity." *GRBS* 9:421–35.

———. 1998. "Horace, Our Contemporary." *New York Review of Books,* June 11, 46–49.

Kripke, Saul A. 1963. "Semantical Considerations on Modal Logic." *Acta Philosophica Fennica* 16:83–94. Reprinted in *Readings in Semantics,* edited by Farhang Zabeeh, E. D. Klemke, and Arthur Jacobson (Urbana: University of Illinois Press, 1974), 803–14.

———. 1980. *Naming and Necessity.* Rev. ed. Oxford: Basil Blackwell.

Kristeva, Julia. 1968. "Problèmes de la structuration du texte." In *Théorie d'ensemble,* 297–316. Paris: Éditions du Seuil.

———. 1969a. "Le mot, le dialogue et le roman." Reprinted with slight changes in Σημειωτικὴ: *Recherches pour une sémanalyse,* 143–73. Paris: Éditions du Seuil. Originally published in *Critique* 23 (1967):438–65.

———. 1969b. "Pour une sémiologie des paragrammes" (1966). In Σημειωτικὴ: *Recherches pour une sémanalyse,* 174–207. Paris: Éditions du Seuil.

———. 1969c. "Le texte clos" (1966–67). In Σημειωτικὴ: *Recherches pour une sémanalyse,* 113–42. Paris: Éditions du Seuil.

————. 1974. *La révolution du langage poétique.* Paris: Éditions du Seuil.

————. 1980. "Word, Dialogue, and Novel." In *Desire in Language: A Semiotic Approach to Literature and Art,* edited by Leon S. Roudiez, 64–91. Translated by Thomas Gora et al. Columbia University Press: New York.

————. [1985] 1996. "Intertextuality and Literary Interpretation." Interview by Margaret Walker (1985). In *Julia Kristeva Interviews,* edited by Ross M. Guberman, 188–203. New York: Columbia University Press. Originally published in *Intertextuality and Contemporary American Fiction,* edited by P. O'Donnell and R. C. Davis (Baltimore: Johns Hopkins University Press, 1989), 280–93.

Kroll, Wilhelm. 1989. *G. Valerius Catullus.* 7th ed. Stuttgart: Teubner.

Lachmann, Renate. 1989. "Concepts of Intertextuality." In *Issues in Slavic Literary and Cultural Theory,* edited by Karl Eiermacher, Peter Grybek, and Georg Witte, 391–99. BPX, 21. Bochum: Universitätsverlag Dr. Nobert Brockmeyer. Originally published as "Ebenen des Intertextualitätsbegriff," in *Das Gespräch,* edited by Karlheinz Stierle and Rainer Warning (Munich: Wilhelm Fink, 1984), 133–38.

Laird, Andrew J. W. 1996. "Speech Presentation." In *OCD*[3], 1434.

————. 1999. *Powers of Expression, Expressions of Power: Speech Presentation in Latin Literature.* Oxford: Oxford University Press.

Lamarque, Peter, and Stein H. Olsen. 1994. *Truth, Fiction, and Literature: A Philosophical Perspective.* Oxford: Clarendon Press.

Landolfi, Luciano. 1986. "Il *lusus* simposiale di Catullo e Calvo o dell' improvvisazione conviviale neoterica." *QUCC* 53 = n.s. 24:77–89.

Landow, George P. 1992. *Hypertext: The Convergence of Contemporary Critical Theory and Technology.* Baltimore: Johns Hopkins University Press.

Lanza, Diego, ed. 1987. *Aristotele: Poetica.* Milan: Rizzoli.

Lejay, Paul. [1911] 1966. *Horaces: Satires.* Hildesheim: Georg Olms.

Levin, Samuel R. 1976. "Concerning What Kind of Speech Act a Poem Is." In *Pragmatics of Language and Literature,* edited by T. A. van Dijk, 141–60. Amsterdam: North-Holland.

————. 1977. *The Semantics of Metaphor.* Baltimore: Johns Hopkins University Press.

Lowrie, Michèle. 1997a. " 'Spleen' and the 'Monumentum': Memory in Horace and Baudelaire." *Comparative Literature* 49:42–58.

————. 1997b. *Horace's Narrative Odes.* Oxford: Clarendon Press.

Lyas, Colin. 1992. "Wittgensteinian Intentions." In Iseminger 1992a: 132–51.

Lyne, R. O. A. M. 1994. "Vergil's *Aeneid:* Subversion by Intertextuality: Catullus 66.39–40 and Other Examples." *G&R* 41.1:187–204.

Magnusson, A. Lynne. 1993. "Speech Act Theory." In Makaryk 1993: 193–99.

Mai, H.-P. 1991. "Bypassing Intertextuality: Hermeneutics, Textual Practice, Hypertext." In Plett 1991a: 30–59.

Makaryk, Irena A., ed. 1993. *Encyclopedia of Contemporary Literary Theory: Approaches, Terms, Scholars.* Toronto: University of Toronto Press.

Manguel, Alberto. 1997. "How Those Plastic Stones Speak: The Renewed Struggle between the Codex and the Scroll." *TLS,* July 4, 8–9.

Manieri, Alessandra. 1998. *L'immagine poetica nella teoria degli antichi: Phantasia ed enargeia.* Pisa: Istituti editoriali e poligrafici internazionali.

Mao, Douglas. 1996. "The New Critics and the Text-Object." *ELH* 63:227–54.

Martin, Richard. 1989. *The Language of Heroes: Speech and Performance in the* Iliad. Ithaca: Cornell University Press.

Martindale, Charles. 1994. Review of Conte 1994b. *LCM* 19:153–58.

Mauch, Helmut. 1986. *O laborum dulce lenimen: Funktionsgeschichtliche Unter-suchungen zur römischen Dichtung zwischen Republik und Prinzipat am Beispiel der ersten Odensammlung des Horaz.* Frankfurt am Main: Peter Lang.

Mayer, Roland. 1994. *Horace: Epistles, Book 1.* Cambridge: Cambridge University Press.

McGann, Jerome J. 1983. *A Critique of Modern Textual Criticism.* Chicago: University of Chicago Press.

———. 1985. *The Beauty of Inflections: Literary Investigations in Historical Method and Theory.* Oxford: Clarendon Press.

———. 1991. *The Textual Condition.* Princeton: Princeton University Press.

Miner, Earl. 1994. "Allusion." In Preminger and Brogan 1994: 14–15.

Mitchell, W. J. T., ed. 1985. *Against Theory: Literary Studies and the New Pragmatism.* Chicago: University of Chicago Press.

Mitsis, Phillip. 1994. "Committing Philosophy on the Reader: Didactic Coercion and Reader Autonomy in *De Rerum Natura.*" In Schiesaro, Mitsis, and Clay 1994: 111–28.

Mörland, Henning. 1968a. "Die Carmina des Horaz in der Aeneis." *Symb. Os.* 42:102–12.

———. 1968b. "Horaz, Vergil, und andere Gestalten in der Aeneis." *Symb. Os.* 43:57–67.

Morris, Edward P. 1939. *Horace: Satires and Epistles.* New York: American Book Company. Reprint, Norman: University of Oklahoma Press, 1968.

Murgatroyd, Paul. 1980. *Tibullus I: A Commentary on the First Book of the Elegies of Albius Tibullus.* London: Bristol Classical Press.

Nagy, Gregory. 1990. *Pindar's Homer: The Lyric Possession of an Epic Past.* Baltimore: Johns Hopkins University Press.

———. 1996. *Homeric Questions.* Austin: University of Texas Press.

Nauta, Ruurd R. 1994. "Historicizing Reading: The Aesthetics of Reception and Horace's 'Soracte Ode.' " In DeJong and Sullivan 1994: 207–30.

Nehemas, Alexander. 1981. "The Postulated Author: Critical Monism as a Regulative Ideal." *Critical Inquiry* 8:133–49.

Newman, J. K. 1967. *The Concept of Vates in Augustan Poetry.* Collection Latomus 89. Brussels.

Nisbet, Gideon. 1998. Review of *Compromising Traditions: The Personal Voice in Classical Scholarship,* edited by Judith P. Hallett and Thomas Van Nortwick. *BMCR* 9:49–58. Electronic publication ⟨http://ccat.sas.upenn.edu/bmcr/⟩.

Nisbet, R. G. M., and Margaret Hubbard. 1970. *A Commentary on Horace Odes, Book I.* Oxford: Oxford University Press.

Nussbaum, Martha. 1994. *The Therapy of Desire: Theory and Practice in Hellenistic Ethics.* Princeton: Princeton University Press.

Oberhelm, Steven, and David Armstrong. 1995. "Satire as Poetry and the Impossibility of Metathesis in Horace's *Satires.*" In *Philodemus and Poetry: Poetic Theory and Practice in Lucretius, Philodemus, and Horace,* edited by Dirk Obbink, 210–54. Oxford: Oxford University Press.

O'Hara, James J. 1990. *Death and the Optimistic Prophecy in Vergil's Aeneid.* Princeton: Princeton University Press.

Ohmann, Richard. 1971. "Speech Acts and the Definition of Literature." *Philosophy and Rhetoric* 4:1–19.

Oliensis, Ellen. 1998. *Horace and the Rhetoric of Authority.* New Haven: Yale University Press.

O'Sullivan, Neil. 1993. "Allusions of Grandeur? Thoughts on Allusion-Hunting in Latin Poetry." *Electronic Antiquity,* January 5, unpaginated. Electronic publication ⟨http://scholar.lib.vt.edu/ejournals/ElAnt/⟩.

Parry, Milman. 1971. *The Making of Homeric Verse.* Oxford: Oxford University Press.

Pasquali, Giorgio. 1962. *Storia della tradizione e critica del testo.* 2d ed. Florence: Le Monnier.

———. 1968. "Arte allusiva." In *Pagine stravaganti* (Florence: Sansoni), 2:275–82. Originally published in *L'Italia che scrive: Rassegna per il mondo che legge* 25 (1942):185–87. Reprinted in *Stravaganze quarte e supreme* (Venice: Nerri Pozza, 1951), 111–20.

Patterson, Annabel. 1995. "Intention." In *Critical Terms for Literary Study,* edited by Frank Lentricchia and Thomas McLaughlin, 135–46. 2d ed. Chicago: University of Chicago Press.

Pavel, Thomas G. 1986. *Fictional Worlds.* Cambridge: Harvard University Press.

Pavese, C. O. 1996. "La iscrizione sulla kotyle di Nestor da Pithekoussai." *ZPE* 114:1–23.

Pearcy, Lee T. 1998. Review of Edwards 1996. *BMCR,* January 18, unpaginated. Electronic publication ⟨http://ccat.sas.upenn.edu/bmcr⟩.

Perkell, Christine. 1996. "The 'Dying Gallus' and the Design of *Eclogue* 10." *CP* 91:128–40.

Perri, Carmela. 1978. "On Alluding." *Poetics* 7:289–307.

Perry, John O. 1965. *Approaches to the Poem.* San Francisco: Chandler.

Petrey, Sandy 1990. *Speech Acts and Literary Theory.* New York: Routledge.

Pfister, Manfred. 1985. "Konzepte der Intertextualität." In *Intertextualität: Formen, Funktionen, anglistische Fallstudien,* edited by Ulrich Broich and Manfred Pfister, 1–30. Tübingen: Max Niemeyer.

———. 1991. "How Postmodern Is Intertextuality?" In Plett 1991a: 207–24.

———. 1994. "Intertextualität." In *Moderne Literatur in Grundbegriffen,* edited by Dieter Borchmeyer and Viktor Žegač, 215–18. 2d ed. Tübingen: Max Niemeyer.

Plett, Heinrich F., ed. 1991a. *Intertextuality.* Research in Text Theory, vol. 15. Berlin: de Gruyter.

———. 1991b. "Intertextualities." In Plett 1991a: 3–29.

Powell, Barry. 1991. *Homer and the Origin of the Greek Alphabet.* Cambridge: Cambridge University Press.

Preminger, Alex, ed. 1965. *Princeton Encyclopedia of Poetry and Poetics.* Princeton: Princeton University Press.

Preminger, Alex, and T. V. F. Brogan, eds. 1994. *The New Princeton Handbook of Poetic Terms.* Princeton: Princeton University Press.

Pucci, Joseph. 1998. *The Full-Knowing Reader: Allusion and the Power of the Reader in the Western Literary Tradition.* New Haven: Yale University Press.

Quinn, Kenneth, ed. 1973. *Catullus: The Poems.* 2d ed. London: Macmillan.

———, ed. 1980. *Horace: The Odes.* London: Macmillan.

———. 1982. "The Poet and His Audience in the Augustan Age." *ANRW* 2.30.1:75–180.

Rabinowitz, Peter J. 1995. "Speech Act Theory and Literary Studies." In *The Cambridge History of Literary Criticism,* vol. 8, edited by Raman Selden, 347–74. Cambridge: Cambridge University Press.

Raval, Suresh. 1993. "Intention." In Preminger and Brogan 1994: 611–13.

Reitzenstein, Richard. 1924. "Eine neue Auffassung der horazischen Ode." *Neue Jahrbücher für das klassische Altertum* 53:232–41. Reprinted in *Aufsätze zu Horaz: Abhandlungen und Vorträge aus den Jahren 1908–1925* (Darmstadt: Wissenschaftliche Buchgesellschaft, 1963).

Richards, I. A. 1965. *The Philosophy of Rhetoric.* New York: Oxford University Press.

Ricoeur, Paul. 1981. "What Is a Text? Explanation and Understanding" (1970). In *Hermeneutics and the Human Sciences: Essays on Language, Action and Interpretation,* edited by John B. Thompson, 145–64. Cambridge: Cambridge University Press.

Riffaterre, Michael. 1978. *The Semiotics of Poetry.* Bloomington: Indiana University Press.

———. 1979. "La syllepse intertextuelle." *Poétique* 10:496–501.

———. 1980. "Syllepsis." *Critical Inquiry* 6:625–38.

———. 1981. "L'intertexte inconnu." *Littérature* 41:4–7.

———. 1983. *Text Production*. Translated by Terese Lyons. New York: Columbia University Press. Originally published as *La production du texte* (Paris: Éditions du Seuil, 1979).

———. 1987. "The Intertextual Unconscious." *Critical Inquiry* 13:371–85. Reprinted in *The Trial(s) of Psychoanalysis*, edited by Françoise Meltzer (Chicago: University of Chicago Press, 1988), 211–26.

———. 1990. "Compulsory Reader Response." In *Intertextuality: Theories and Practices*, edited by Michael Worton and Judith Still, 56–78. Manchester: Manchester University Press.

Roberts, Deborah H. 1997. "Afterword: Ending and Aftermath, Ancient and Modern." In *Classical Closure: Reading the End in Greek and Latin Literature*, edited by D. H. Roberts, F. M. Dunn, and Don Fowler, 251–73. Princeton: Princeton University Press.

Röhrich, Lutz. 1967. *Gebärde — Metapher — Parodie: Studien zur Sprache und Volksdichtung*. Wirkendes Wort, 4. Düsseldorf: Schwann.

Ronen, Ruth 1990. "Paradigm Shifts in Plot Models: An Outline of the History of Narratology." *Poetics Today* 11.4:817–42.

———. 1994. *Possible Worlds in Literary Theory*. Cambridge: Cambridge University Press.

Rose, M. A. 1993. *Parody: Ancient, Modern, and Post-Modern*. Cambridge: Cambridge University Press.

Ross, David O., Jr. 1975. *Backgrounds to Augustan Poetry: Gallus, Elegy and Rome*. Cambridge: Cambridge University Press.

Rudd, Niall. 1989. *Horace: Epistles Book II and Epistle to the Pisones ("Ars Poetica")*. Cambridge: Cambridge University Press.

Ryan, Marie-Laure. 1992. "Possible Worlds in Recent Literary Theory." *Style* 26.4: 528–53.

Safranski, Rudiger. 1994. *Ein Meister aus Deutschland: Heidegger und seine Zeit*. Munich: C. Hanser Verlag. Translated by Ewald Osers as *Martin Heidegger: Between Good and Evil* (Cambridge: Harvard University Press, 1998).

Schiesaro, Alessandro. 1994. "Il destinatario discreto: Funzionzi didascaliche e progetto culturale nelle Georgiche." In Schiesaro, Mitsis, and Clay 1994: 129–47.

Schiesaro, Alessandro, Phillip Mitsis, and J. Strauss Clay, eds. 1994. *Mega nepios: Il destinatario nell'epos didascalico. The Addressee in Didactic Epic*. Materiali e discussioni per l'analisi dei testi classici 31. Pisa: Giardini.

Schmid, Wolf, and Wolf-Dieter Stempel, eds. 1983. *Dialog der Texte: Hamburger Kolloquium zur Intertextualität*. Wiener Slawistischer Almanach Sonderband 11. Institut für Slawistik. Vienna: University of Vienna.

Scott, Robert Ian. 1995. "The *Waste Land* Eliot Didn't Write." *TLS*, December 8, 14.

Searle, John. 1969. *Speech Acts*. Cambridge: Cambridge University Press.

———. 1974. "The Logical Status of Fictional Discourse." *New Literary History* 6:319–32. Reprinted in *Expression and Meaning: Studies in the Theory of Speech Acts* (Cambridge: Cambridge University Press, 1979), 58–75.

———. 1977. "Reiterating the Differences: A Reply to Derrida." *Glyph* 1:198–208.

Selden, Daniel L. 1987. "Textual Criticism." *Helios* 14:33–50.

———. 1990. "Classics and Contemporary Criticism." *Arion*, 3d ser., 1:155–78.

———. 1992. "*Ceveat lector:* Catullus and the Rhetoric of Performance." In Hexter and Selden 1992: 461–512.

Sharrock, Alison. 1994. *Seduction and Repetition in Ovid's Ars Amatoria II.* Oxford: Oxford University Press.

Shklovsky, Victor. [1917] 1965. "Art as Technique." In *Russian Formalist Criticism,* edited and translated by Lee T. Lemon and Marion J. Reis, 3–24. Lincoln: University of Nebraska Press.

Showerman, Grant, trans. 1986. *Ovid (Heroides* and *Amores).* Vol. 1. 2d ed. Revised by G. P. Goold. Cambridge: Harvard University Press.

Shusterman, Richard. 1988. "Interpretation, Intention, and Truth." *Journal of Aesthetics and Art Criticism* 46:399–411.

———. 1989. "Organic Unity: Analysis and Deconstruction." In *Redrawing the Lines: Analytic Philosophy, Deconstruction, and Literary Theory,* edited by Reed Way Dasenbrock, 92–115. Minneapolis: University of Minnesota Press.

Sidney, Philip. [1595] 1970. *Sir Philip Sidney's Defence of Poesy.* Edited by Lewis Soens. Lincoln: University of Nebraska Press.

Silk, Michael S. 1996. "Plagiarism." In *OCD³,* 1188.

Skinner, Marilyn. 1971. "Catullus 8: The Comic *Amator* as *Eiron.*" *CJ* 66:298–305.

Smart, C. 1855. *The Works of Horace.* New York: Harper and Brothers.

Smith, Barbara Herrnstein. 1974. "Poetry as Fiction." In *New Directions in Literary History,* edited by Ralph Cohen, 165–87. Baltimore: Johns Hopkins University Press.

Smith, R. Alden. 1997. *Poetic Allusion and Poetic Embrace in Ovid and Virgil.* Ann Arbor: University of Michigan Press.

Sokal, Alan. 1996a. "Transgressing the Boundaries: Toward a Transformational Hermeneutics of Quantum Gravity." *Social Text* 46–47:217–52.

———. 1996b. "A Physicist Experiments with Cultural Studies." *Lingua Franca* (May-June):62–64.

Solodow, Joseph. 1988. *The World of Ovid's Metamorphoses.* Chapel Hill: University of North Carolina Press.

Stallman, R. W. 1994. "Intentions." In Preminger and Brogan 1994: 398–400.

Starobinski, Jean. 1964. "Les anagrammes de Ferdinand de Saussure." *Mercure de France* (February):243–62.

———. 1971. *Les mots sous les mots.* Paris: Gallimard.

————. 1979. *Words upon Words.* Translated by Olivia Emmet. New Haven: Yale University Press.

Starr, Raymond J. 1990–91. "Lectores and Book Reading." *CJ* 86:337–43.

Stempel, Wolf-Dieter. 1983. "Intertextualität und Rezeption." In Schmid and Stempel 1983: 86–109.

Stierle, Karlheinz. 1983. "Werk und Intertextualität." In Schmid and Stempel 1983: 7–26. Also in *Das Gespräch,* edited by Karlheinz Stierle and Rainer Warning (Munich: Wilhelm Fink, 1984), 139–50.

Stinton, S. T. W. 1976. " 'Si credere dignum est.' " *PCPhS* 22:60–89.

Stock, Brian. 1996. *Augustine the Reader: Meditation, Self-Knowledge and the Ethics of Interpretation.* Cambridge: Belknap Press at Harvard University Press.

Susini, Giancarlo. 1988. "Compitare per via: Antropologia del lettore antico: meglio, del lettore romano." *Alma Mater Studiorum* 1:105–24.

Svenbro, Jesper 1988. *Phrasikleia: Anthropologie de la lecture en Grèce ancienne.* Paris: Éditions la Découverte.

————. 1990. "The 'Interior Voice': On the Invention of Silent Reading." In *Nothing to Do with Dionysus? Athenian Drama in Its Social Context,* edited by John J. Winkler and Froma Zeitlin, 366–84. Princeton: Princeton University Press.

Syme, Ronald. 1939. *The Roman Revolution.* Oxford: Oxford University Press.

————. 1978. *History in Ovid.* Oxford: Oxford University Press.

Syndikus, H. P. 1993. Review of Edmunds 1992. *JRS* 83:216–17.

Tarrant, Richard J. 1995a. "On Classics and Graduate Education." *Harvard Graduate School Alumni Association Newsletter* (Fall):1.

————. 1995b. "Classical Latin Literature." In *Scholarly Editing: A Guide to Research,* edited by D. C. Greetham, 95–148. New York: Modern Library of America.

Thomas, Richard. 1986. "Virgil's *Georgics* and the Art of Reference." *HSCP* 90:171–98.

————. 1988. *Virgil: Georgics.* Vol. 1, *Books I–II.* Cambridge: Cambridge University Press.

Tissol, Garth. 1993. "Ovid's Little *Aeneid* and the Thematic Integrity of the *Metamorphoses.*" *Helios* 20:69–79.

Tynianov, Jurii. [1927] 1965. "La notion de construction." In *Théorie de littérature,* edited by Roman Tzvetan Todorov, 114–37. Paris: Éditions du Seuil.

Usener, Hermann. 1900. "Italische Volksjustiz." *RM* 61:1–28. Reprinted in *Kleine Schriften,* vol. 4, *Arbeiten zur Religionsgeschichte* (Leipzig: Teubner, 1913), 356–82.

van Oort, Richard. 1995. "The Anthology of Speech-Act Literary Criticism: A Review Article." *Anthropoetics: The Journal of Generative Anthropology* 1.2 (December): unpaginated. Electronic publication ⟨http://www.humnet.ucla.edu/humnet/anthropoetics⟩.

Veyne, Paul. 1988. *Roman Erotic Elegy: Love, Poetry, and the West.* Translated by David Pellauer. Chicago: University of Chicago Press.

———. 1991. *La société romaine.* Paris: Éditions du Seuil.

von Albrecht, Michael. 1992. "Ovidian Scholarship: Some Trends and Perspectives." In Galinsky 1992: 176–90.

Watkins, Calvert. 1976. "Syntax and Metrics in the Dipylon Vase Inscription." In *Studies in Greek, Indic and Indo-European Linguistics, offered to L. R. Palmer,* edited by A. Morpurgo Davies and W. Meid, 431–41. Innsbruck: Institut für Sprachwissenschaft der Universität Innsbruck.

Wellek, René, and Austin Warren. 1956. *Theory of Literature.* New York: Harcourt, Brace.

West, David. 1995. "Cast Out Theory: Horace *Odes* 1.4 and 4.7." *Proceedings of the Classics Association* 92:12–23.

West, Martin L. 1973. *Textual Criticism and Editorial Technique.* Stuttgart: Teubner.

———. 1993. *Greek Lyric Poetry.* Oxford: Clarendon Press.

Wheeler, Arthur L. 1934. *Catullus and the Traditions of Ancient Poetry.* Berkeley: University of California Press.

Will, E. L. 1982. "Ambiguity in Horace's *Odes* 1.4." *CP* 77:240–45.

Williams, Gordon. 1968. *Tradition and Originality in Roman Poetry.* Oxford: Clarendon Press.

———. 1992. "Poet and Audience in Senecan Tragedy: *Phaedra* 358–430." In *Author and Audience in Latin Literature,* edited by T. Woodman and J. Powell, 138–49. Cambridge: Cambridge University Press.

Williams, R. D., ed. 1973. *The Aeneid of Virgil: Books 7–12.* Basingstoke: Macmillan.

Wills, Jeffrey. 1996. *Repetition in Latin Poetry: Figures of Allusion.* Oxford: Clarendon Press.

Wimsatt, W. K., Jr., and M. C. Beardsley. 1946. "The Intentional Fallacy." *SR* 54:468–88. Reprinted in Wimsatt and Beardsley, *The Verbal Icon: Studies in the Meaning of Poetry* (Lexington: University of Kentucky Press, 1954), 3–18.

Winterbottom, M. 1974. *The Elder Seneca: Declamationes.* Vol. 2, *Controversiae 7–10; Suasoriae.* Loeb Classical Library. Cambridge: Harvard University Press.

Woodcock, E. C. 1959. *A New Latin Syntax.* London: Methuen.

Zanker, Paul. 1988. *The Power of Images in the Age of Augustus.* Translated by Alan Shapiro. Ann Arbor: University of Michigan Press.

Zetzel, James E. G. 1993. "Religion, Rhetoric, and Editorial Technique: Reconstructing the Classics." In *Palimpsest: Editorial Theory in the Humanities,* edited by George Bornstein and Ralph G. Williams, 99–120. Ann Arbor: University of Michigan Press.

Index of Ancient Citations

General Index

Abel, Walter, 92–93
Accius, 122n43
Achilleid (Statius), 74, 149
Actium, Battle of, 88–89
The Act of Reading (Iser), 100
addressee, xiv, 27, 31, 83–94; and implied
    reader, 64; internal, 92–93; as real per-
    son, 28, 31n49, 85–87, 90–92; and
    rigid designators, 85. *See also* reader-
    addressee
adynata, 57
"Aeneid" (Ovid), 58–59, 75–76, 160; as par-
    ody, 141–42
Aeneid (Vergil), xxn16, 30, 37, 151–52; and
    Aeneas as model reader, 79–81; and
    Homer, 140–41, 153–54; and Ovid, 53,
    57, 59, 75–79, 137, 147
Aetia (Callimachus), 131
aition, 78
Alcaeus, 10, 48, 84, 88, 101, 338
Alexandrian footnote, 78, 156
Allegories of Reading (de Man), 25
allusion: and Catullus, 13, 20, 74; and Conte,
    13–14, 151n60; in Eliot, 21–22, 43n15;
    in Horace, 73, 130–31; and intertext, vii,
    xi, xvii–xviii, 76, 164–66; and irony,
    72–74, 79; and Kristeva, 12–14; and
    New Criticism, 13, 21n9; and Pasquali,
    xii, 2–3; and reading, xvii, xviii, 43, 46,
    57, 76, 81, 155–56; in Vergil, xviii, 53,
    59, 77–79, 137, 147, 152–54
"Allusion" (Preminger), 3

Althusser, Louis, 15
Ambrose, Saint, 66n10
American Philological Association, 46n30,
    103n33
Amores (Ovid), 58, 150; and addressee, 91–
    94; persona in, 64, 66, 69; as written
    communication, 111–12
Anacreon, 46n30, 47, 84, 129–31
anagnostēs, 112
anaphora, allusive, 81n43
Andrōn inscription, 66, 115–16, 166
Angenot, Marc, 164
Annals (Ennius), 131, 136, 161–62
Antisthenes, 118
The Anxiety of Influence (Bloom), 38
aoidos, 64
Apocolocyntosis (Seneca), 57–58
apostrophe, 92
Arachnion, xviii
Aratus, 112, 140
Archilochus, 29, 105
Aristophanes, 102n30
Aristotle, 75, 141
Ars amatoria (Ovid), 19, 53–54, 58
Ars poetica (Horace), 108–9, 122n42, 132
"Arte allusiva" (Pasquali), xii, 2, 43
Athenodorus, 13, 136
Athens, 59
Atticus, 92
Auden, W. H., 3, 4
audience: internal, 63, 79; original, 39, 84–
    85, 89n17